Consciousness and Being

Consciousness and Being

From Being to Truth in the Thomistic Tradition

Robert C. Trundle

Foreword by
Peter A. Redpath

☙PICKWICK *Publications* • Eugene, Oregon

CONSCIOUSNESS AND BEING
From Being to Truth in the Thomistic Tradition

Copyright © 2019 Robert C. Trundle. All rights reserved. Except for brief quotations in critical publications or reviews, no part of this book may be reproduced in any manner without prior written permission from the publisher. Write: Permissions, Wipf and Stock Publishers, 199 W. 8th Ave., Suite 3, Eugene, OR 97401.

Pickwick Publications
An Imprint of Wipf and Stock Publishers
199 W. 8th Ave., Suite 3
Eugene, OR 97401

www.wipfandstock.com

PAPERBACK ISBN: 978-1-5326-4968-4
HARDCOVER ISBN: 978-1-5326-4969-1
EBOOK ISBN: 978-1-5326-4970-7

Cataloguing-in-Publication data:

Names: Trundle, Robert C., 1943–, author. | Redpath, Peter A., foreword.

Title: Consciousness and being : from being to truth in the Thomistic tradition / Robert C. Trundle, with a foreword by Peter A. Redpath.

Description: Eugene, OR: Pickwick Publications, 2019 | Includes bibliographical references and index.

Identifiers: ISBN 978-1-5326-4968-4 (paperback) | ISBN 978-1-5326-4969-1 (hardcover) | ISBN 978-1-5326-4970-7 (ebook)

Subjects: LCSH: Realism | Anti-realism | Science—Philosophy | Philosophy and science | Ontology | Truth | Ethics | Thomas—Aquinas, Saint,—1225?–1274—Philosophy | Sartre, Jean Paul,—1905–1980.

Classification: Q175.32 T78 2019 (print) | Q175.32 (ebook)

Manufactured in the U.S.A.   JANUARY 2, 2019

For Janeanne

But modern man, brought up on Kantian idealism, regards nature as being no more than an outcome of the laws of the mind. Losing all their independence as divine works, things gravitate henceforth round human thought, whence their laws are derived.

~ ÉTIENNE GILSON

Missed also by modern man is that Kant's idealism, by his own criteria, is a truth-less metaphysical judgment. In judging that our mind has a priori categories wherein the "categories" and "mind" are different *synthesized* concepts, the judgment is not logically true. And it is not true empirically in being assumed *a priori* to explain reality's appearances. Appearances that afford inexact truths about reality are rooted in our observational consciousness of things *in themselves* of which we are also at once incontrovertibly and phenomenologically conscious.

~ ROBERT TRUNDLE

Contents

Foreword by Peter A. Redpath ix
Preface xvii

1. Phenomenology Prior to Truth: Truth and Realism 1
2. Realism Rooted in Our Observational Consciousness 18
3. Consciousness and a Robust Realism in Science 60
4. Science and Observation Infused by Theory 80
5. Theory-Dependence: A Relativism Founded by a Famous "Realist" 107
6. A Robust Realism for Increasing Scientific Truth 134
7. From Scientific Truth to Truths of Theology, Ethics, Art, and Politics 165

Bibliography 213
Name and Subject Index 233

Foreword

In chapter five of his extraordinary monograph, Robert C. Trundle makes an observation that few scholars who know anything about present-day philosophy would passionately disagree: That an existential phenomenology, based upon Jean-Paul Sartre's analysis of consciousness, could bolster "some basic elements of Thomism" (although this "would seem outlandish to the vast majority of philosophers"). Beyond outlandish, these philosophers would judge it to be what, in several places related to egregious mistakes about physics, Trundle calls a "howler." More than this howler, a near apoplectic fit would likely be the reaction generated by a further assertion: The synthesis of a Sartrean existential phenomenology and teachings of St. Thomas Aquinas serve as a sounder approach for grasping the actual nature of science than that of even eminent scholars such as Sir Karl Popper, Thomas Kuhn, Paul Feyerabend, Larry Laudan, Hilary Putnam, William H. Newton-Smith, Frederick Suppe, and others who are eruditely discussed. Despite realizing the kind of negative psychological reactions he would tend to elicit from these scholars, Trundle with no little courage makes such singular claims. And I concur with him.

In support of his observation about the unlikely intellectual teaming of Sartre and Aquinas to throw light on the realist nature of science in general and mathematical physics in particular, Trundle refers to a 2009 publication by Stephan Wang (*Aquinas and Sartre*). Wang notes "some profound similarities" and even "an almost identical approach" in the teachings of these two men, especially as they related to both the nature of human free will and "what happens when we face a choice." In connection to the like approach of these two men toward understanding the psychology involved in making a choice, Trundle quotes Wang:

> When there are different options before me, and I have to make a decision, a number of factors will usually influence that decision. Three of the most important factors are undoubtedly who I am, where I am, and what I am seeking. In other words, my personal identity, the objective circumstances in which I find myself, and the goals I am seeking will all have some kind of influence on the choice I eventually make. They make up what we could call the "total situation" that informs my choice. In philosophical theories about human action, it is common to assume that this total situation . . . is something stable and accessible. So when I have a choice to make, I think about what kind of person I am (what would suit me, what I am interested in, what I am capable of, etc.); I think about the objective circumstances confronting me (what is going on here, what needs to be done, what the practical options available are, what the consequences of any action will be, etc.).

Crucial to note about Wang's observation is that human choice always occurs in a real-life individual situation, including personal interests and capabilities. As Trundle well understands, making the move to become a philosopher, scientist, involves an initial life-changing choice constituted by the psycho-biological ability of persons to experience, on the sense and intellectual levels, *an induction* of their personal capability to change: to execute a change *as a doable deed* for him or her in the here and now.

While Wang is praised by Trundle for (1) recognizing that we cannot make choices without being conscious of ourselves and (2) our free choice enables us to change the way we look at ourselves and the goals we seek, Trundle focuses on a necessary condition in the psychology of a person who would first set about becoming a philosopher, scientist: The reality of free choice of will is related inextricably to a unique awareness of ourselves that Trundle maintains confronts us "without concepts" in what he calls a "phenomenological awareness of ourselves." This is to say, not just anyone can become a philosopher, scientist. To even seek to become one, a person must have the proper psycho-biological constitution. People who have no interest in science are as psychologically unfit to become scientists as are seven-foot persons from becoming racehorse jockeys or people who hate sports becoming Olympic gold-medalists, and they are *aware* of this. Trundle notes:

> To behave in given ways, for example, is ordinarily to be implicitly aware of our freedom to behave or not behave in those

ways. When Kant held that free will was a mere possible reality (*noumenon*), for example, was he not aware of his freedom to think or not to think that thought? Thought, though, is less basic than our consciousness since there can be a consciousness of [something] without thought but there can be no thought without consciousness. Consciousness *per se* reveals and does not conceal reality by any mode of thought. This supports as such a strong realism. And in appealing to our phenomenological experience of ourselves, there is support for a Thomistic realism, à la Étienne Gilson, and for Thomas himself, who appeals to our "introspection" of being "*aware* that in particular situations . . . we might not have acted as we in fact did or that we might not have acted at all." This is one of the reasons Thomas holds "that people have free choice (*Summa Theologiae*, I, q. 83, a. 1,)." So the essay herein bolsters Thomas' defense of free will. And our irrefutable consciousness of reality as it is *in itself*, of which we are aware, both conflicts with iconic modern anti-realists and upholds a realism of Aristotle and Thomas.

Trundle's language, such as "non-conceptually observed" and "direct non-conceptual observational consciousness of which we are indirectly consciousness," may sound at times to be singularly un-Thomistic. But his language does not merely augment that about our perceptual awareness by the iconic analytic philosopher Fred I. Dretske to whom he refers. Also his appeal to our incontrovertible phenomenological experience strongly supports a Thomist realism. And appeal to this realist experience does so à la Redpath and that of my esteemed colleague John N. Deely (*requiescat in pace*). I am certain that Deely, if not Charles S. Peirce and others, would concur with me on all the immediately-preceding claims.

In regard to the claims, let us recall that Aquinas held that our rationality is essentially an animal rationality. Considered as such, rational or intelligible content that exceeds the grasp of some human faculties, say the external senses, is grasped by the internal sense faculties (sensing danger, or personal strength, being something that transcends the power of the sense of sight). So some real activities such as the act of existence transcend, except reflexively, the power of conceptualization. And hence in a way, even though images and concepts always attend human judgments, the aforesaid activities are nonetheless known "without concepts." In summary, far more exists in our intelligible experience of sense reality than is conveyed by human concepts. Our concept-less experience includes co-natural knowledge, knowledge through habituation, and knowledge through actual intellectual presence in the execution of sense act—together with immediate sense and intellectual awareness. By this awareness *inter alia* we possess faculties of a human soul that enable us to generate, cause, human action. Philosophy, science, in short, depend essentially on an existing subject who is capable of causing the philosophical or scientific; a knowing subject, that is, possessed of a knowing principle which can be habituated by human relations, and in which human habits can exist: a human soul.

Regarding the soul and the complexity of our rationality, we do well to recall that although St. Thomas considers our reason to be a faculty of an immortal soul, he holds that the specific difference of a human being resides in the genus "animal," not in the genus "spirit." Strictly, for St. Thomas, *human beings are not incarnate, Cartesian, or Hegelian, spirits.* Human beings do not belong to the genus "spirit." We are not differentiated in our genus by being on the lowest degree of intellectual spirit. Essentially, we belong to the highest rank within the genus animal, which is specifically divided into the rational and irrational. So St. Thomas locates our specific difference in a "difference in the sensitive soul"!

So true is what I say about the teaching of St. Thomas, and the novel support Trundle lends to it, that there is this startling passage from the same "Treatise on Man" of the *Summa Theologiae* cited by Trundle above (in English and Latin):

> [LATIN:] Respondeo dicendum quod potentia, secundum illud quod est potentia, ordinatur ad actum. Unde oportet rationem potentiae accipi ex actu ad quem ordinatur, et per consequens oportet quod ratio potentiae diversificetur, ut diversificatur ratio actus. Ratio autem actus diversificatur secundum diversam rationem obiecti. Omnis enim actio vel est potentiae activae, vel passivae. Obiectum autem comparatur ad actum potentiae passivae, sicut principium et causa movens, color enim inquantum movet visum, est principium visionis. Ad actum autem potentiae activae comparatur obiectum ut terminus et finis, sicut augmentativae virtutis obiectum est quantum perfectum, quod est finis augmenti. Ex his autem duobus actio speciem recipit, scilicet ex principio, vel ex fine seu termino, differt enim calefactio ab infrigidatione, secundum quod haec quidem a calido, scilicet activo, ad calidum; illa autem a frigido ad frigidum procedit. Unde necesse est quod potentiae diversificentur secundum actus et obiecta.

Sed tamen considerandum est quod ea quae sunt per accidens, non diversificant speciem. Quia enim coloratum accidit animali, non diversificantur species animalis per differentiam coloris, sed per differentiam eius quod per se accidit animali, per differentiam scilicet animae sensitivae, quae quandoque invenitur cum ratione, quandoque sine ratione. Unde rationale et irrationale sunt differentiae divisivae animalis, diversas eius species constituentes. Sic igitur non quaecumque diversitas obiectorum diversificat potentias animae; sed differentia eius ad quod per se potentia respicit. Sicut sensus per se respicit passibilem qualitatem, quae per se dividitur in colorem, sonum et huiusmodi, et ideo alia potentia sensitiva est coloris, scilicet visus, et alia soni, scilicet auditus. Sed passibili qualitati, ut colorato accidit esse musicum vel grammaticum, vel magnum et parvum, aut hominem vel lapidem. Et ideo penes huiusmodi differentias potentiae animae non distinguuntur.

[ENGLISH:] *I answer that,* A power as such is directed to an act. Wherefore we seek to know the nature of a power from the act to which it is directed, and consequently the nature of a power is diversified, as the nature of the act is diversified. Now the nature of an act is diversified according to the various natures of the objects. For every act is either of an active power or of a passive power. Now, the object is to the act of a passive power, as the principle and moving cause: for color is the principle of vision, inasmuch as it moves the sight. On the other hand, to the act of an active power the object is a term and end; as the object of the power of growth is perfect quantity, which is the end of growth. Now, from these two things an act receives its species, namely, from its principle, or from its end or term; for the act of heating differs from the act of cooling, in this, that the former proceeds from something hot, which is the active principle, to heat; the latter from something cold, which is the active principle, to cold. Therefore the powers are of necessity distinguished by their acts and objects.

Nevertheless, we must observe that things which are accidental do not change the species. For since to be colored is accidental to an animal, its species is not changed by a difference of color, but by a difference in that which belongs to the nature of an animal, that is to say, by a difference in the sensitive soul, which is sometimes rational, and sometimes otherwise. Hence "rational" and "irrational" are differences dividing animal, constituting its various species. In like manner therefore, not any variety of objects diversifies the powers of the soul, but a difference in that to which the power of its very nature is directed. Thus the senses of their very nature are directed to the passive quality which of itself is divided into color, sound, and the like, and therefore there is one sensitive power with regard to color, namely, the sight, and another with regard to sound, namely, hearing. But it is accidental to a passive quality, for instance, to something colored, to be a musician or a grammarian, great or small, a man or a stone. Therefore by reason of such differences the powers of the soul are not distinct (*S.T.* 77, a. 3, respondeo; Benzinger Brothers ed. (http://dhspriory.org/thomas/summa/index.html).

St. Thomas does not locate our specific difference in spirit. For he is conceiving of the difference as a proximate generator (cause) of action; the action directly ordered to causing a specific kind of generic animal wholeness that enables a rational animal to act so as perfectly to fulfill the generic aim of the animal genus—here, in relation to an animal body. This essentially relates the intellectual soul to generating action through sensitive faculties of the soul (*especially particular reason*) so that it can only execute through essential connection to organic activities of an animal body. This enables the animal genus to be perfectly itself. The "sensitive soul," the generic part of the human nature, generates animal rationality. This rationality refers to universal reason flowing into particular reason as a specific difference. So the resulting composite, an animal that senses with its intellect and intellectualizes with its senses (as Gilson said), is able to execute the highest form of *animal* activity and not the lowest generic form of *angelic* activity! Without generating the faculty of the particular or cogitative reason—that corresponds to "instinct" in brute animals, *which enables universal reason to overflow into the human body*, the animal or sensitive soul cannot achieve its generic perfection as a sensitive soul in being a deliberative (free) animal! (See, *S.T.* I, q. 78, a. 4, ad 5).

According to St. Thomas moreover, science, philosophy, is the act of a habit of the human soul: an intellectual virtue, essentially involving a cooperative act of universal and particular reason, and dependent upon the existence of a moral culture (virtues of justice and prudence) that allows for the existence of human teamwork to exist. St. Thomas holds that the habit of human science starts with an initial intellectual/sensory induction. Some organizational whole is generically sensed and its intrinsic first principles implicitly grasped as a conflated "this something." For example, he famously says that a baby first senses this something before perceiving it to be mother. Mother aside, St. Thomas maintains that the main aim of science is to wonder about this initial induction so that the first principles (causes), which generate this initial primitive generic awareness, transform this awareness into an explicit explanatory understanding of the specific principles that are first generically sensed.

Thus the phenomenological picture that Trundle provides of how scientific theory and observation historically relate, to spawn more precise understandings of a previously less well-known truth, appears to me to be in perfect agreement with: (1) the teaching of St. Thomas regarding the way the perfection of the habit of human science is achieved and (2) the way all intellectual progress proceeds from more primordial to more perfected states. And Trundle's Sartrean phenomenological account of human self-consciousness, as involving a complexity that transcends the grasp of concepts, is also entirely consistent with the teachings of St. Thomas.

More, Trundle is refreshingly unlike many current Thomists as well as most philosophers and scientists falsely-so-called. Trundle recognizes the evident truth, which he repeatedly celebrates as being induced from the first act of philosophical scientific consciousness, that science is not epitomized by either an impersonal systematic syllogistic or truth-functional logic. Instead, the logic involves the personal (intentional) act of scientists and a qualitatively different kind of reasoning for grasping how science progresses. The progress is both based on what it makes sense to say in a Wittgenstein-like way, in concert with continental phenomenology, and rooted finally in a concept-less sheer awareness of reality.

Regarding this revealed reality, Trundle makes further saliently sound inferences: Intrinsic to this reality is a temporal *continuity* or evolving change, which exists as a continuum whole constituted by essential parts, of which scientists are aware. The awareness led to a causal relation principle that, as a novel conditional proposition to which truth is ascribable, gives expression to the *continuity* that essentially involves a future, not-yet-existing, relational end term (numerically-one last act). And this last-act end term essentially influences and *orders, constitutes, as parts* all the many acts of one, temporal, continuum whole. Even though the end term does not exist as an actual reality at the start of the change, that term exerts from the change's start a relational influence on the motion and the order, organization, of all its many acts; as do many (but finite number) of external causes to which a moving body must essentially relate, react, and proportionately adjust its movement to maintain its many acts as essential parts of numerically-one organizational whole. Modern science presupposes change as thus described.

But how to explain that change? How can a non-existing relational term exert causal influence so as to constitute individual acts to be essential parts of a temporal continuum, temporal orderly whole? How can intermediate acts generated from a start term self-adjust, and proportionately modify their behavior mid-course, in reaction to changing material conditions so as to remain parts of a continuum, whole, numerically-one motion? How to explain that this self-adjusting motion exists within a finite number of external causal relations that enable it so proportionately to self-adjust? Were the external causes infinite in number, no such motion could occur. How, rationally, may we explain their numerical finitude?

Modern science presupposes all the preceding inferences that Trundle makes. Only an inferable supreme norm, an extra-temporal first principle, capable of creating the existing universe(s) with the ordering principles of motion that it essentially contains (as natural theology shows in detail), can render intelligible the existence and nature of modern science. And only this theology begets an inferable supreme norm that has created our psycho-biological nature as it ought to be, thereby affording inferences from modern scientific truth about our nature to a naturalistic ethics that fulfills it without any naturalistic fallacy. So apart from this alleged fallacy, which resulted from senseless restrictions of modern truth-functional logic, an alternative modal logic allows for truths of science and ethics to inform a politics that is an institutionalization of ethics. Trundle's insights are a breadth of fresh air. If appreciated, his astuteness will liberate present-day philosophy, science in general, ethics, art, and politics from the shackles of both skepticism and sophistry that have chained them for so many centuries. I applaud Robert C Trundle for authoring this ground-breaking and redemptive work.

—Peter A. Redpath
Rector, Adler-Aquinas Institute; Chair, Holy Apostles College and Seminary—St. John Paul II Graduate Concentration in Christian Wisdom; and Senior Fellow Center for the Study of The Great Ideas

Preface

This essay reflects evolving developments of my thought, some of the more recent thoughts vented in my last two works. The most recent work is *Integrated Truth and Existential Phenomenology: A Thomistic Response to Iconic Anti-Realists in Science* (Leiden: Brill-Rodopi Publishers, Value Inquiry Book Series of Philosophy and Religion, Book 283, 2015). And the work before that is "A Thomistic Integration of Truth vs. a Truthlessness of Today's Science, Ethics and Politics" in *Sztuka i realism* (*Art and Realism*): *Commemorative Book, Jubilee Birthday and Scientific Work of Professor Henry Kieresia at KUL*, edited by Fr. Tomasz Duma, Andrzej Maryniarczyk SDB, and Paulina Sulenta, 721–38 (Lublin: Polish Society of St. Thomas Aquinas and Faculty of Philosophy, Catholic University of Lublin, 2014). Virtually all of my points in these works are updated, modified, or strengthened in this essay. And by several newly added key references to Étienne Gilson, this essay ensures that its critiques of modern philosophy will agree with at least one well-regarded species of Thomistic realism.

The realism herein is further fortified by an updated existential phenomenology: We are observationally conscious of how existing things are *in themselves*. These things are not Kant's *things-in-themselves* (*noumena*) but are that of which we are directly but non-conceptually conscious. This consciousness, of which we are also indirectly aware, is infused into our conceptual consciousness. So our "self-consciousness" reveals and does not conceal how reality really *is* from certain perspectives, averting knotty epistemological problems. There are many problems, but consider three. One averted problem is Kant's allied notions of both an *a priori* structure of mind that imposes *categorial* interpretations on reality and an unknowable "good," God, and self (*noumena*). These *noumena*, notwithstanding Kant's avowed practical reason, lead to moral skepticism.

And a skepticism about our knowing physical reality follows from his idealism. A second avoided problem is an anti-realist pragmatism that ensued inter alia in order to elude his truth-valueless *synthetic-a priori* judgments. For a novel point herein is that these judgments are presupposed by, but undercut, the purported "truths" of science and ethics *alike*; leading to the thorny epistemological problem of a K-K Thesis of "how we Know we Know"? Thus in effect, for the pragmatism in question, there is no objective truth. Rather, "truth" is that which truly works, not the truth of a truth-claim because it reflects what reality is really like, at any rate inexactly or approximately.

A third precluded problem is the thesis that our observation is either theory-laden or theory-dependent. The dependence, à la Sir Karl Popper, Thomas Kuhn, Paul Feyerabend, and later post-modern philosophies, results in a trivial if not incoherent relativism. And while relativism may not burden theory-laden observation, no one including well-regarded mainstream scientific realists such as W. H. Newton-Smith and Frederick Suppe, for example, have even tried to show how observation can be concept-neutral where reality is not obscured. The obscuration renders problematic a certifiable success of observational predictions by which theories may be corroborated, much more the notion, per this essay, that the predictions actually strictly imply approximately true theories in given domains.

Besides eluding these snags, the phenomenology posits a pre-conceptual consciousness of really existing things *in themselves*; providing a primal ontological soundness for truths that are strictly implied by virtue of an elemental modal logic. This logic, which is rooted in what it makes sense to say (in a Wittgenstein-like way), affords strict implications that bear on the following: inferring a causal principle's truth; truths of scientific theories being inferred from their observed success via an epistemic necessity; and the strict implication of a first cause by the causal principle, the principle being presupposed by science so that science and natural theology are related logically. This modal logic nicely captures the meanings of the words used in St. Thomas' proof of a first cause. And as an inferred supreme norm, this cause created our psycho-biological nature as it *ought* to be. A collapse of the *is-ought* divide allows for a naturalistic ethics that is inferred from scientific descriptions of our nature without any *naturalistic fallacy*. This fallacy aside, historically increasing scientific truths about our nature proceed *pari passu* with an ever truer naturalistic ethics: The ethics has a verisimilitude that parallels the famed verisimilitude of approximate scientific truth. And we can infer from these increasing truths ever truer facts about the goodness of art and politics. Politics is largely the *institutionalization of ethics* even if this ethics is enriched by supernatural virtues that even more fulfill our nature. In sum, natural theology, which overlaps with supernatural theology, is interrelated logically with science, ethics, art, and politics.

Robert C. Trundle
Ph.D. University of Colorado at Boulder, Fellow—Adler-Aquinas Institute and former faculty member at Regis College, the University of Colorado (CS), and Northern Kentucky University.

1

Phenomenology Prior to Truth
Truth and Realism

The following chapter summarizes how existential phenomenology affords true observational predictions, which strictly imply true scientific theories, by being ultimately grounded in a pre-conceptual observational consciousness of things *in themselves*. Our being conscious of these things is certifiable by our indirect consciousness *of* that direct observational consciousness. This self-consciousness, while a version of Sartre's basic phenomenological analysis, does not imply his atheism, ethics, or any other position that he contends follows from his analysis.[1] The analysis herein establishes also that the thesis is false that observation reports presuppose theories that undercut objective descriptions of reality. A robust realism is so litigious, nonetheless, that even scholars sympathetic to it tend at best to defend only a weak realism. This realism, however, is shown to *presuppose* the strong realism. Consider briefly how this realism roots truths of theology, ethics, art, and politics in scientific truth after a longer examination of several knotty epistemic problems in the philosophy of science that threaten any form of realism.

---

1. The existential phenomenology herein evolved from my Ph.D. dissertation. My dissertation advisor Dr. Hazel Barnes, who supported me and was the leading Sartre scholar in the world, insisted I note that my phenomenological analyses *for* the philosophy of science are uniquely my own. So I refer to the analyses as a *Sartrean* existential phenomenology; less many of Sartre's existentialist inferences, such as his atheism, which do not follow necessarily.

Realism's Knotty Problems in the Philosophy of Science

Problems of epistemology that challenge a strong scientific realism do so because the realism holds that theories can be true or false in virtue of what reality is really like apart from what we will, wish, or think. To express this thought about realism as such, in the Kantian-positivist-analytic tradition, is to utter an unverifiable metaphysical judgment and not a statement to which "truth" is ascribable: a judgment, that is, that is *synthetic a priori* and thus not true or false either *a posteriori* or analytically (Kant); meaningless because the expressed realism cannot be shown to be true or false either empirically or logically (logical positivism); or senseless because no empirical evidence would count against it (analytic philosophy). Consequently, since most philosophers whose expertise includes the philosophy of science are Anglo-American philosophers, most of these philosophers would reject this realism out-of-hand were it not for this fact: The positivist notion of "meaningless" holds also for their "conservative verification principle" since the principle is not itself true or false either empirically or logically. And the analytic philosophers' notion of "senseless" extends also to their own "liberal verification principle" since this principle, a revision due ironically to the aforesaid self-refutation, is itself self-refuting because it has no evidence counting against it, either! Accordingly, the utter dogmatic scope of the conservative principle, which resulted in its self-refutation, proceeded *pari passu* as well with the self-refuting nature of the unqualified liberal principle.

Oddly, the liberal principle was not included by Hilary Putnam when he appropriately stated: "Strangely enough, this criticism [of self-refutation] had very little impact on the logical positivists . . . ," adding that this "philosophical gambit was a great mistake . . . [because] the forms of 'verification'" were "*institutionalized* by modern society."[2] In this society, even many ordinary persons as well as philosophers misused the principles to simplistically dismiss as meaningless virtually any extra-scientific discourse, much more the discourse of realism. That realism would be undercut along with other unverifiable sentences (including the verificationism itself) is stressed by David Ingram. Ingram notes that the "Logical positivists were strongly motivated by a quest for logical clarity and epistemic certainty" via the "so-called 'verificationist' theory of meaning that had been advanced by Wittgenstein in his *Tractatus* (1921)."[3]

---

2. Putnam, "Philosophers & Human Understanding," 99–100, emphasis.
3. Ingram, *The History of Continental Philosophy*, 281–99.

Impacts of the *Tractatus* in this respect, continues Ingram, "were deeply disturbing and paradoxical: not only were the evaluative and expressive statements of ethics, religion, metaphysics, and aesthetics . . . consigned to practical irrelevance but (as Wittgenstein ironically noted) so were the [purported] propositions of philosophy that asserted the verificationist theory of meaning."[4]

Given a meaninglessness of the verificationist theory itself, the impediment of seeking to dismiss realism by this self-refuting theory was cynically disregarded in favor of questioning things that include predicating "truth" of theories and theoretical sentences for reasons of roughly two sorts. One sort was historical and the other epistemological as well as logical.[5] Concerns of the latter include both observation's theory-dependence and an arcane "Under-determination-of-Theory-by-Data (or UTD) Thesis."[6] This thesis and theory-dependent observation result in knotty epistemological predicaments. Thus for example, if observation presupposes theory, then how can theory be evidenced by observation? And if observed data (phenomena) so underdetermine scientific theories that these theories can be contradictory but empirically equivalent in their predictions, then how are theories that to which "truth" is allegedly ascribable? The schema below illustrates the dilemma:

FIGURE 1

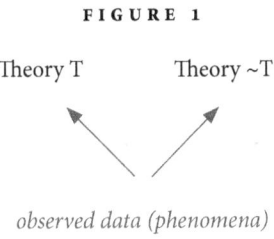

observed data (phenomena)

Underdetermination-of-Theory-by-Data (UTD) Thesis

"The main argument of the *anti-realist* viewpoint," observes Pawel Kawalec, tellingly, "is from *under-determination* of theory by empirical

---

4. Ibid.

5. Niiniluoto considers these problems in "Scientific Progress as Increasing Verisimilitude," 73–77.

6. This schema was first shown in Trundle, *A Theology of Science*, 2.

evidence."⁷ As enlarged upon later, however, the UTD Thesis is in fact a pseudo-problem, a problem that is irrelevant for even a robust scientific realism. The realism is not contravened precisely because empirically equivalent contradictory theories may actually both be approximately true in terms of having *evidence-based* inferences *a posteriori* from the data (phenomena) to the theories. The theories may make steadily successful predictions whose truths, which strictly imply inexact truths of the theories, can be confirmed by way of observations. While these observations are conceptual, they include a concept-free consciousness of predicted phenomena as they really are *in themselves*. These things *in themselves* avoid the theory-dependent and theory-laden problems that are addressed later. In short, the reasoning is *a posteriori*, not an *a priori* one that results in an epistemic relativism.⁸

Even so, many philosophers are concerned that conundrums of ascribing "truth" to theories may nonetheless be problematic by theories that involve certain historical hindrances. Hindrances in the history of science purportedly include foundational changes where "truth" is relative to conceptual revolutions, or to paradigm shifts that cause new vertiginous worldviews (the Ptolemaic versus the Copernican), or to non-converging theories wherein we are left with an epistemic anarchy of "anything goes." If anything goes, then conflicting scientific truth-claims and claims of theology, which are influenced by scientific changes, may be incoherently both true and false either at the same or different historical periods.

On the one hand, this epistemological dilemma bears on a claim by the eminent astronomer Fr. George Coyne, S.J., former Director of the Vatican Observatory, for whom "results of modern science" make it very "difficult to believe that God is omnipotent and omniscient in the sense of many of the scholastic philosophers."⁹ Neither these philosophers nor Coyne could be correct about God, however, if claims about God depend on scientific theories whose truths are relative to events such as historical periods.

On the other hand, these periods with their seeming epistemic difficulty relate in a different way to St. Augustine's claims. His claims suppose a theological and scientific realism rather than an historical

---

7. Kawalec, "Understanding Science of the New Millennium," 3, emphasis.
8. Cf. Trundle's "Aristotle *Versus* Van Til and Łukasiewicz," 323–44.
9. Coyne, "God's Chance Creation," 6–7.

relativism, when he says that Scripture is a "history of past things, an announcement of future things, and an explanation of present things" (*On Christian Doctrine*). He brings to mind an idea of verisimilitude (historically increasing truth or truth-likeness of theories in science) in which scientific findings inconsistent with Scripture may yield consistent future findings. And this point relates to Augustine's critique of the idea, at odds with the Scripture, that there could be no creation of the world because there would have to be a time before the world. But there could be no time before it, per the influence of Aristotle, because time *inter alia* is a measure of the motion of phenomena and phenomena being absent would imply an absence of time. Notwithstanding Augustine's astute retort that time may have been created *with* the world, a notable physicist once noting wryly that relating the world's beginning to religion in this way resulted in some scientists having to be dragged kicking and screaming to accept the Big Bang Theory because it implied an absence of time before the beginning in a tiny singularity.

Challenges to a reality of the singularity, *if* scientific realism is untenable since "truth" is relative to incommensurable historical paradigms, among other things, implies *a fortiori* that truths in theology as well as in ethics, aesthetics, and politics face fatal *epistemological* objections. There would not only be no objective truth about phenomena but also none about God, the "good," good art, and good government. And the trouble with truth-claims about them would be related inextricably, as well, to the *history of science*. Consequently, the history of science and epistemology cannot be viably examined in an entirely separate way. Having noted in this way some central historical and epistemological problems for scientific realism, problems with this realism are now examined in greater detail. Some largely historical dilemmas will be considered after those that are principally epistemological.

One of the most vexing epistemological problems for objective scientific truth and realism arose ironically in England and America because of the domination of the twentieth-century's science-exalting logical positivists. More than any other movement, these positivists proselytized that formalized theories of physics were the epitome of pristine knowledge: the paradigm knowledge-yielding enterprise. This enterprise, however, relied surreptitiously upon the assumption that even esoteric scientific theories, which were competing with each other, could be rationally decided between by virtue of objective observation reports rooted in the reliability of sense experience. The alleged knowledge-yielding nature of this experience came to be undermined by the notion that theories and their terms are *presupposed* covertly by observational truth-claims: The claims, in presupposing either theories or their terms, were *theory dependent*. This dependence on theory by virtually all of the language of science turned upside down a positivist notion of theories where an observation term O_x had meaning *inter alia* by virtue of corresponding to a theoretical term T_x ($T_x \equiv O_x$).[10] The theory dependence conflicted as well with the later pragmatic or instrumentalist approaches that relied on observational evidence to evaluate, not a theory's truth, but its adequacy (success).

While the success of theories is held herein to be related logically to their truth and thus to a robust realism, consider now why this realism is incompatible with the positivists—despite their accepting that sense experience could issue in objectively true observation reports for theories. Though theories that change led to changing meanings of theoretical terms such as "mass" and "H_2O," according to the positivists, the latter argued that the meanings of the corresponding observation terms "weight" and "water" were invariant. The invariance was assumed naively by the positivists to signify that observation terms and sentences were theory-neutral, there being no need for an articulation of a theory-neutral element in observation.[11] Hence an observational objectivity, held by the positivists but not established by them, led them to nonetheless hold that the theories of Newton and Einstein were comparable at the observational level. At this level, rational theory choices could be made because if Einstein's theory implied observation sentence O and Newton's not-O, then the theories would be in conflict.[12] Hence one theory might not be as good as the other theory if, for instance, its observational consequences tended to be false while those of the other theory tended to be true. Since ascriptions of "true" and "false" were rejected for theoretical sentences that changed but accepted for unchanging observation sentences, the

---

10. Cf. Sal's *Scientific Progress on the Semantic View*, 17.

11. Cf. Newton-Smith, *The Rationality of Science*, 132. I am indebted here to Newton-Smith's analysis. For a superb follow-up on perception, see Smith's *The Problem of Perception*. Having studied under Strawson, Smith's phenomenological approach to perception includes analysis also in the analytic tradition. This tradition is included by me by way of the analytic philosopher Fred I. Dretske who, rooting non-epistemic seeing in ordinary language, brings to mind the phenomenology herein of a non-conceptual observational consciousness.

12. Ibid., 11–12.

logical positivists espoused an ignoble so-called observation-theoretical distinction.

The distinction, besides ignoring terms that are neither purely observational nor theoretical, such as "galaxy" or more classically as "electric charge," drew the attention of iconic anti-realists such as Sir Karl Popper, Thomas Kuhn, and Paul Feyerabend, who held variously that theoretical conjectures, or empirically ungrounded theories, or theoretical paradigms were presupposed by any so-called observational language. The idea that any language for observations is underlain by theories or theoretical frameworks meant that possibly contradictory theories would ultimately define possibly contradictory meanings of observation terms. Given that the terms have different meanings determined by conceivably contradictory theories, for instance, Newton and Einstein could not even communicate about the observational results of their own theories. In terms of their theories, these scientists would mean something different by the common theoretical term "mass" as well as by the customary observation term "red." And since the meaning of "red" and any other term would change with changing theories, theories would not be either comparable or responsive to rational theory choice.[13] This lack in choice of theories, while related to epistemology, strengthens a specter of the history of science being typified by incommensurable theories and theoretical paradigms such that there could be no intelligible talk of scientific progress from the paradigm theories of Aristotle to Newton to Einstein.

Einstein's theory not establishing any scientific progress from Newton's theory and this theory Aristotle's, if different historical interpretations of theoretical terms render the terms and theories incomparable, brings to mind theories being empirically equivalent but logically inconsistent if not contradictory. While contradictory theories T and $\sim T$ may equally explicate, predict, and manipulate phenomena, they can be so systematically underdetermined by data (phenomena) that observation reports could not decide which theory was truer. And since either "truth" ascribable to theories—because they reflect what reality is roughly like—or at least theoretical entities being possibly real is essential to scientific realism, any realism would be untenable. And an untenable realism of physics might be exacerbated by implications for various anti-realisms that afflict the social and political sciences, much more ethics and theology, *if* a formalized physics is the ideal knowledge-yielding enterprise

13. Ibid., 12.

whereby when physics "sneezes" epistemologically, all of the other disciplines "catch pneumonia."[14]

"Pneumonia," a metaphor for the collapse of all objective truth, is a serious epistemological threat insofar as a straightforward translation process could obtain between pairs of contradictory theories wherein theory T's account of a given phenomenon could be a phenomenon accounted for in the same exact way by $\sim T$. And the translatability between $\sim T$ and T might guarantee their empirical equivalence for all possible results. Thus, although these results would strictly be the only realist criteria for gauging the theories and the theories would have truth-values, at least hypothetically, the rejection of the contradictory theories and truths by realists would proceed prima facie with realism being untenable *a fortiori* in other areas of study that are far less rigorous than physics. In addition to physics, would not ethics, psychology, and the social and political sciences be suspect in regard to theories providing objective truth? The aforesaid under-determinations would precipitate problems not only for epistemology but also for contradictory ontologies. These ontologies include discordant empirical predicates, having to be endorsed by realists regardless of what reality is really like.

Problems with Even a Weak Realism?

The pursuit of what reality is really like via scientific theories is, unsurprisingly, not pursued by many philosophers who even so are not necessarily anti-realists. Avoiding realist pitfalls is an aim of Ian Hacking, Nancy Cartwright, and Bas C. Van Fraassen, who do not predicate truth of theories. While theories being true implies empirical adequacy, says Van Fraassen, the adequacy does not imply any truth in a truth-functional propositional logic.[15] To ascribe truth to a theory T is to know *inter alia* that T is true. And its truth being known excludes error since we would

---

14. Physics "sneezing" epistemologically, causing epistemic "pneumonia" elsewhere is illustrated by John Worrall. He brought the Under-determination-of-Theory-by-Data (UTD) Thesis to broad notice in "Scientific Realism and Scientific Change," 201–31. While a strong UTD Thesis was devised earlier by Henri Poincaré, a weak inductive version was proposed in Stanford's "Refusing the Devil's Bargain," S1–S12. See also Stanford's "Scientific Realism, the Atomic Theory," 253–69. These approaches wrongly view the UTD Thesis as being fatal for realism.

15. Compare this paradigmatic banal "middle ground" between realism and anti-realism in, among other literature, Van Fraassen's *The Scientific Image*, 21, and Hanna's "The Scope and Limits of Scientific Objectivity," 339–61.

not ordinarily say that someone knew that T is true if T turned out to be false. Its turning out false, however, agrees with believing in T's adequacy since we can express without senselessness that our belief that T was adequate even if it turned out to be false. Permitting for the possible falsity reflects a liberal epistemic status of "belief" in the history of science and may seem to resolve underdetermined theories. Though these theories trouble realists because no evidence can evidently count for the truth of two theories if they are contradictory, the low benchmark of empirical adequacy appears to apply nicely to empirically equal theories even when those theories are contradictory.

Contradictory theories cannot both be true for a strong realism, according to received views on the contradiction, but Cartwright and Hacking note (wrongly) that a weak or restrained realist can deny ascriptions of truth to theories and still affirm that theoretical entities are real. Their reality is related to, among other things, a philosophy of science called "experimentalism." While experimentalists do not believe in electrons because they "save the phenomenon" but rather because they can be employed to *create* new phenomena, according to Hacking, his position is augmented by Cartwright who defends this weak realism against underdetermined theories (UTD Thesis) by arguing that talk about these theories tends to conflate causal and theoretical explanations.[16] So although explanations of phenomena by theories involve truth as an *external* characteristic, accounts that are causal invariably involve truth as an ingredient that is *internal* as well as *existential*. The existence of a cause such as that of an electron must be accepted for accepting a given causal account. This account has an epistemic import since underdetermined theories do not undermine a weak realism. While this realism does not speak of true theories, it posits really existing theoretical entities. In addition to this epistemic import, a practical import is a use of the entities to predict, manipulate and even create new phenomena.

Phenomena reacting as such to theoretical entities by continual testing not only fortifies a case for the entities being real but also, per my article "Physics and Phenomenology" (1992), supposes the systematic law-like behavior of the phenomena. This phenomena, which led to the inference of a *weak realism*, however, presupposes a *strong realism* of inexactly true theories by which the entities must be understood! And

---

16. See Fuller's "Discussion Notes," 565–72, and a weak realism of Hacking and Cartwright in both "Experimentalism and Scientific Realism," 84, and "When Explanation Leads to Inference," 111–21.

this understanding means that "to accept the causal account together with the reality of the cause is to accept the [inexact] truth of the laws or theory in terms of which the cause and account are understood."[17] How could a theory be entirely false when it has theoretical entities that make steadily true predictions, manipulations, explications and even creations of new phenomena? Thus, the *internal* ingredient of a causal account's truth implies the *external* truth of a theory. And the theory's truth implies the reality *certeris paribus* of at least some entities. So the UTD dilemma is not eluded by a weak realism when it presupposes one that is strong. But the strong realism herein shows that the issue is a pseudo-problem because the data (D) afford *a posterior*, not *a priori*, inferences to the truth of a supposed underdetermined theory (UT).

Having noted the UTD Thesis and problems of truth that seem to threaten any realism, consider in more depth how realism may supposedly be problematic because of historical quandaries. These are said to be so daunting that philosophers such as Paul Feyerabend and physicists who include Thomas Kuhn, known less for research in physics than for the philosophy of science—his later joining the philosophy department at MIT, urge us "to *set aside our rational reconstruction of... theories*" and to view their history in order to learn.[18] Since the learning proposed by Kuhn and Feyerabend holds that observations occur in the context of either changing historical theories or theoretical paradigms to which truth is relative, one is not surprised by their advice. The advice bears on distinguishing equally successful rival theories with conflicting ontologies, in a given historical period, from periods when the conflicts come from successive theories. While the former sorts of theories in given historical periods are underdetermined, the latter theories are tackled in terms of Larry Laudan's non-relativistic anti-realism.

This anti-realism specifies that some of the successive theories were empirically adequate (*pace* Van Fraassen) but that the theories were not thereby held to be true by the scientific community.[19] This community, although often assuming a history of successively truer theories (verisimilitude), must contend with the following examples according to Laudan: chemical theories of the 1920s that assumed a structurally ho-

---

17. Trundle, "Physics and Phenomenology," 66–86.

18. Cf. Newton-Smith, *The Rationality of Science*, 195, emphasis.

19. See Laudan's "Two Dogmas of Methodology," 585–97 and "A Confutation of Convergent Realism," 19–45. See also how success is related logically to truth by, among other essays, Trundle's "A Thomistic Integration of Truth," 721–38.

mogeneous atomic nucleus, chemical and physical theories which held that matter was neither created nor destroyed, Copernican astronomy that did not preserve all of the mechanisms of Ptolemaic astronomy, evidently incompatible ontologies of the wave theories and corpuscular theories of light, and so on.

Realism Inferred from Mature Theories?

The foregoing history of allegedly adequate but not necessarily true theories is countered by others philosophers and scientists. For example, physicist Fritz Rohrlich and philosopher of science Larry Hardin argue that within validity limits both the atomic nucleus is described suitably as structurally homogeneous and the possibility of creating or annihilating matter may be justifiably ignored.[20] They argue that succeeding theories *do* in fact preserve the mechanisms and laws of earlier theories, with a reasonable disclaimer that the preserved laws and mechanisms are applicable to *mature* theories. These theories are mathematically formulated, conceptually and predictively powerful, make predictions beyond the data base on which they were founded, support one another when they bear on the same problem and, finally, when one mature theory supersedes another, the previous theory is not eliminated but rather restricted to a domain of validity.[21] Valid domains to which "truth" is restricted bears, as enlarged on latter, on a principle of pessimistic induction that mistakenly specifies that theories are only falsified.

The falsification notwithstanding, this sort of validity is not applicable to *immature* theories whose historical retentions, at best, will often be checkered. So while Rohrlich and Hardin acknowledge that Copernican astronomy did not retain all of the mechanisms of Ptolemaic astronomy and agree with a proviso about what Laudan says about Newton, Descartes, and Franklin's electrical theory, they maintain that the both the relatively mature wave and corpuscular theories retained geometrical optics within its validity limits when diffraction effects are small. And in bringing to mind Cartwright's weak realism of inferring *existing* causes from causal accounts, they remark that the relationship of ether to relativity theory warrants maintaining that "Electromagnetic theory is . . . a

---

20. See Hardin's "Perceptual Transparency," 341–45, Rohrlich's "Realism Despite Cognitive Antireductionism," 73–88, Rohrlich's "Cognitive Scientific Realism," 185–202, and Hardin and Rohrlich's "Established Theories," 603–16.

21. Hardin and Rohrlich, "Established Theories," 604–8.

[mature] theory, one which correctly represents its appropriate domain. And so to be a *realist* about this theory is to accept the *existence* of the electro-magnetic field and its associated variables of state":[22]

> What we must ask about is the relationship between the ontology of electromagnetic theory and the ontology [supposed realities] of ether theory[;] . . . it is appropriate, in light of the total history of ether theories from Fresnel to Lorentz, to regard the subject of these theories to be the electromagnetic field. . . . What Einstein threw out was not the field, but Lorentz's ether and absolute space with which it was identified.[23]

In terms of the identification, Rohrlich and Hardin expound on how the mechanical underpinnings of ether and absolute space were not retained because there was no evidence for a mechanical ether apart from the electromagnetic theory. This theory aside, independent evidence for a physically active space was not forthcoming and, they say, this is an important issue for whether ontologies of successful theories should be retained by their successors. And regarding the successors, they enlarge, there is no compelling reason to retain items in the ontologies of successful predecessors if either there is no independent evidence for the items or the items are not essential for comprehending their principle laws or theories. Theories as such are supported also by recalling Poincaré's point that "important connections between earlier and later theories might [well] exist."[24]

Precisely, "In his 1936 Presidential Address to the Chemical Society [later the Royal Society of Chemistry], Nevil Sidgwick more forthrightly *rejected* the view that 'when a new discovery is made, it shows the previous conceptions upon the subject to be untrue.'"[25] Indeed, Sidgwick said that "if 'to-day's scientific ideas show those of yesterday to be wrong, we need not trouble about them, because they themselves may be shown to be wrong tomorrow.'"[26] This view, as expanded on later, brings to mind the famous aforesaid principle of *pessimistic* induction. The induction, which holds that future theories will likely be falsified since all past ones were, is replaced in later discussions by an *optimistic* induction.

22. Ibid., 615.
23. Ibid.
24. See the debate between advocates of Thomas Kuhn and those of verisimilitude per Shan's "The Structure of Scientific Revolutions." §2–4.
25. Ibid., emphasis.
26. Ibid.

This induction aside for now, the above scenario suggests a scientific realism where success strictly implies truth: By common sense, how could theories be fully false if they yield systematically true predictions of phenomena? How could phenomena not be reflected truly by theories, roughly, if they systematically predict, manipulate, and create new phenomena (à la Ian Hacking) in given domains? Talk of the domains via succeeding historical theories being ever truer suggests a development of mature theories in the history of science such that the attacks on a robust realism, suggest Rohrlich and Hardin, must contend with theories being cumulative. A neglect of the commutativity of these theories by anti-realists was done "by invoking questionable theories of meaning and reference [or those posited by Larry Laudan] by enlarging the domain of discourse to include theories which belong only to the history of physics and chemistry but are not incorporated into physics and chemistry" and "by attaching disproportionate importance to transient episodes in a development of the mature theories."[27]

Theories in the history of science as they evolved are not herein simplistically held to be trouble-free in regard to scientific realism. But realism is surely no more problematic, and probably less so, than other epistemologies or philosophies of science. Scientists who are seminal anti-realists such as Kuhn or Feyerabend have proposed radical notions of either incommensurable paradigmatic theories or theories accepted by consensus to which truth is relative and where observation is theory-dependent; the dependence making senseless any historical progress that includes Einstein's theory being truer than even pre-Socratic theories. And theory-dependent observation was not even addressed by the proponents of empirical adequacy, of which the anti-realist anti-metaphysical pragmatic instrumentalism was a predecessor, which was evidently inspired mostly by the unfamiliar subject matter of contemporary physics.[28]

This physics was unlike the classical one that portrayed a world amenable to ordinary observation. Since this observation-friendly physics was followed by an arcane physics of the quantum and relativistic theories, and since these theories bore on a "history of epistemology" that "*is* the history of the philosophy of science,"[29] the new laws begged for

27. Ibid., 616.
28. Cf. Hesse, "Laws and Theories," 404–10.
29. Suppe, "Toward a Metaphysical and Epistemological Realism," 717.

an epistemology that excluded implausible ontologies. A Modern Square of Opposition was evidently used, in lieu of the Aristotelian Square, where contradiction only was accepted and true universal law-like *A* and *E* propositions implied only false contradictories that had existential import![30] This import holds when a proposition's "truth depends on evidence for the existence of things in a certain category . . . ."[31] Reality *per se* was no longer a truth-condition for "truth." "Truth" meant pragmatically that theories are true if they truly work. This anti-realist approach is indebted to Kant's idea of *pragmatisch* for avoiding what became known as a K-K Thesis: How do we know we know?

Scientific knowledge presupposes what is not known to be true; a truthless metaphysical causal principle that is a *synthetic a priori* judgment. This judgment does indeed undercut scientific knowledge as surely as admitting of *not* knowing that there exists a given door would undercut the claim of knowing that the door is open. Insofar as the judgment *qua* causal principle is *a priori*, the principle is presupposed prior to experience for coherent scientific inquiries and cannot be known to be empirically true. And insofar as the principle is *synthetic*, with different subject and predicate concepts, the principle is not logically true. A central point: "Truth" cannot be restricted to the logical and empirical when this results both in well established (systematically predictive) theories having their evident truth undercut by a truthless causal principle and in these theories being no truer than patently false theories. Having already noted how theories may commonsensically have truths limited to various domains, we now note that the methodology in this essay roots epistemology in our self-conscious experience of reality.

Theory-Dependence vs. Depending on Observational Truth

That observation is not necessarily theory-dependent or even theory-laden is certifiable by our observational consciousness of mind-independent *things themselves* apart from any concepts. And by virtue of our incontrovertible awareness of both the *things* and our consciousness, we are aware that our conceptual interpretations of the *things* have degrees of veridicality. The veridical observations are explicated by a phenomenology that appeals to an unfettered experience of ourselves and reality. Along with a

---

30. Cf. Jacquette, "Subalteration & Existence," 191–213.
31. Green, "Tutorial—Existential Import," 1–2.

common-sense modal reasoning wherein true observational predictions strictly imply true theories, this phenomenological contact with reality is the footing for a realist epistemology. The epistemology inescapably enhances W. H. Newton-Smith's *The Rationality of Science*, one of the most venerable defenses of a robust scientific realism. The assorted approaches to realism herein will hopefully resolve some of its most complex epistemological problems in today's philosophy of science, such as how either naked-eye or instrument-aided observation, in being theory-laden, can be approximately true by being infused with a non-conceptual consciousness of reality. How reality really *is*, apart from concepts, begs for an explanation of a concept-free observation. An observation-grounded epistemology, which is itself based on a phenomenology that is prior to truth, is required that explicates how theories can truly reflect what reality is really like, roughly, apart from our will, wish and thought.

Thought is not related by Hume and Kant to our consciousness of it nor, thus, to our implicit awareness of freely choosing to think or not think. Rather, thought is either an association of ideas induced by internal sensations (Hume) or interpretations imposed *a priori* on a material of experience by the mind's categories (Kant). For Kant, free will is merely a possible reality (*noumenon*) and the mind's categorial structure *structures* the appearances of reality. So while there is no presumption of knowing reality, there is a pretension to knowing about our mind! Either the mind's categories or internal sensations, by amounting to truth-conditions for "truth," resulted in anti-realist problems about "truth": 1) while a pursuit of "truth" may be avoided by stressing the success or empirical adequacy of theories, this view of theories must still contend with problems of theory-dependent observation. But this observation in presupposing theory cannot confirm that very success. And aside from the stress on success or adequacy, 2) "truth" is said to have its truth-condition in either discordant groups of scientists or scientific paradigms to which truth is relative. Though this relativism is incoherent because *a-priori* assents to contradictory truth-claims are self-refuting, a less troubling weak realism, which accepts a reality of theoretical entities in lieu of true theories, overlooks other serious problems.

Truth in Science Informing an Ethics That Fulfills Our Nature

Consider how truths in ethics, art, and politics are related to science after making a compelling case for scientific truth. While this truth may seem to be an ideal norm-free "paradigm knowledge-yielding enterprise,"[32] notably in physics, the enterprise involves various normative or value-laden disciplines. There are disciplines such as a plausible naturalistic ethics rooted in scientific descriptions of our psycho-biological nature (by a modal-logic proof of a normative first cause). And political science as a science presupposes a causal principle that is suspended insofar as politics bears on rights and responsibilities. Also, even physics cannot be divorced from values; values presupposed even by asserting that one theory is good or better than another by virtue of their comparative truth. Consider these norms after reiterating challenges to scientific objectivity.

The objective truth of a given theory is related to phenomena that respond systematically in law-like ways to theoretical entities by testing. Testing, which is systematically successful, implies a reality of the entities, according to weak realists. Yet these realists disregard not only that there cannot be entirely false theories in terms of which the successful law-like behavior is understood but also that theory-dependent observation, which they largely ignore, rules out non-dependent observations from which the reality of theoretical entities can be inferred. Also, Popper's truth-functional falsification is not faced. Here, the conditional $T \rightarrow P$, where T is a theory and P a prediction, means that while $\sim P$ entails $\sim T$, T is not inferable from P. For there is the logical possibility that a theory can be either false or true by true predictions. In order for predictions to both have an epistemic import and escape knowledge being limited to knowing only that theories are false per Popper's falsification method, my methodology includes reasoning from predictions that are true to true theories by a modest modal logic. This logic is not limited to the *logically* possible. Rather the logic accepts that the conceivable can nevertheless be an epistemic impossibility.

This weaker sort of impossibility commonsensically supports a strong scientific realism. The reasoning for this robust realism, which is illuminable without any technical formalities, bears on a recent

---

32. Suppe, *The Structure of Scientific Theories*, 716. While Suppe eruditely supports this virtually received view of scientific knowledge, this knowledge is argued herein to be mistakenly bifurcated from ethics, art, and politics. Part of the problem, for sure, is a dogmatic acceptance of the naturalistic fallacy.

history-of-science conference. Thus, although the conference contested scientific realism by overlooked "cases where historical actors had significant explanatory/predictive successes with a theory now rejected,"[33] the future rejection of a present-day *mature* theory would not be believable by virtue of an *epistemic impossibility* of that theory being entirely false when it makes systematically true predictions. How could the predictions obtain if the theory was completely false even if the falsity is *logically possible*?

How can phenomena in a given domain not be reflected truly by a scientific theory, at least approximately, if the theory steadily predicts phenomena? Phenomena and theory are methodologically comprehended logically and phenomenologically. Phenomenology does not conceal phenomena by either a Kantian structured mind or, more modestly, mere concepts. For there is a non-conceptual observational consciousness that, infused into a consciousness that is conceptual, begets an objectivity of conceptual observation. And observational predictions that are systematically true may now, given a neutral touchstone with reality, strictly imply true theories. *Pari passu* if theories can be true and if "truth" can be ascribed to the causal principle, because the principle is understood as a modal conditional, this principle strictly implies a first cause that St. Thomas thought he had proved.[34] And my revitalized proof in the essay herein affords objective truths of theology, ethics, art, and politics that Thomas undoubtedly intended; his intention supposing a strong realism. There is this realism for ethics wherein the first cause, as an inferable supreme norm, created our psycho-biological nature as it ought to be. So there is no is-ought naturalistic fallacy in holding that the "good," whether in ethics, art, or politics, is that which fulfills our psycho-biological nature; politics being largely the institutionalization of ethics. The ethics, art, and politics, which stem from proving a first cause, is expanded on in chapter seven,[35] after investigating in depth how a simple modal logic and existential phenomenology secure scientific truth.[36] This truth is distinctively rooted in a phenomenology explicated by Hazel Barnes.

---

33. Shan et al, "Scientific Realism and the Challenge," *Conf. theme*.
34. See Trundle, "Thomas' 2nd Way," 145–68.
35. See Trundle, "Art as Certifiably Good or Bad," 39–50.
36. See Trundle, "20th-Century Despair," 101–23.

2

Realism Rooted in Our Observational Consciousness

One of the last essays of the late Hazel Barnes was "Consciousness and Digestion: Sartre and Neuroscience" (2005). This essay was a Sartrean analysis of the Nobel prize winner Gerald Edelman on the biological "underpinnings to consciousness" where the metaphor "digestion" concerns, among other things, "the fact that digestion is not identical with the physical organs that produce it any more than consciousness is [reducible to] its neurological underpinnings."[1] A reduction to these underpinnings not only renders senseless the concept of "truth," because truth is not ascribed to phenomena but rather to our conscious statements about phenomena, but also a tenable understanding of science that relies on notions in existential phenomenology such as our incontrovertible self-consciousness. A consciousness of reality of which we are also conscious, that is, is a necessary condition for a robust realism that is shown herein to have opposing positions that are untenable, if not incoherent. Oddly, despite an incoherent relativism often associated with Sartre, the realism has a source in his *Being and Nothingness* (1943).

This book was translated with an extensive lauded introduction by Hazel Barnes, later on my Ph.D. committee, who indorsed my phenomenological approach to scientific realism because it *adapted* Sartre's notion of our consciousness of reality to both supporting scientific realism and showing that the thesis of theory-dependent observation was false. This false account of observation led to an epistemic relativism that, ironically,

1. Cannon, "Hazel E. Barnes 1915–2008," 90–103.

was frequently associated with Sartre. Thus, although Sartre's book introduced his technical account of existential phenomenology to Europe after World War Two, the book was misidentified as one that puerilely trumpeted the cliché "existence precedes essence." Essence as truth or meaning was typically taken to be relative to individual choices in an absurd, paradoxical, and hellish world, which is a world where people in bad faith are awash in sadistic and masochistic behavior. This behavior influenced esoteric novels, film, and theater, but evidently not the public or most philosophers in America until late 1964.

Consciousness and Central Critics of Existentialism

In 1964 while at Miami University (Oxford) I heard Dr. Raymond E. Olson, an esteemed philosophy professor whose aim to reconcile religion and science is similar to mine,[2] ask a symposium speaker who had cited the cryptic "existentialism" to please explain briefly what that ". . . ism" is about. Other attending philosophers turned their heads eagerly back toward the speaker in shared curiosity. The curiosity was voiced just a few months before *Life Magazine* helped to popularize both existentialism and the iconic Sartre by its piece "Sartre and Existentialism: A Spurned Nobel Prize Brings the World's Attention to a Lonely Philosophy of Despair." This despair and Sartre are not sappily eulogized herein and fault is found with many inferences he draws from his own studies of consciousness. Consciousness is *no thing* (*néant* or *nothingness*) insofar as it is not a phenomenon that is subject to science. Rather than being subject to science, consciousness is that which is presupposed by science for its coherence; a point expanded on after further exploring both critiques and defenses of the unique existentialism advanced by Jean-Paul Sartre. Sartre and others, such as Albert Camus, did give visceral voice to a despair (*angst*) in the wake of mass murder and the most murderous century in human history, traumatizing multiple millions of persons mentally, spiritually, and physically.

---

2. Dr. Raymond E. Olson is revered by me and many others. Professor Olson was aptly memorialized: "He and his wife helped found the honest and intimate Oxford Community Church. Ray supported not only the practice, but also the scholarly study of religion. He conscientiously maintained consistency between his religion and his scientific and philosophic interests." See Paul et al, "Memorial Statement for Raymond E. Olson," 1–2.

Even so, many Anglo-American academics either relegated the "philosophy of despair" to a pseudo-philosophy or regarded Sartre as flagrantly sexist. The accusation of sexism was often made by evidence disregarding (bio-denying) feminists[3] who both held that Sartre's ideas were indebted to his mistress, Simone de Beauvoir, and sought to estrange Beauvoir from Sartre. One of Sartre's female defenders quipped: "I have heard Margaret A. Simons, the dean of Beauvoir scholars in the United States, say that she hates [Sartre], and at times she refuses even to say his name"; adding sarcastically, that "the energy necessary to pull one philosopher out from under another one, with whom she has chosen to be buried, requires vigorous effort if not actual violence."[4] The violence refers to the brazen disregard of Beauvoir being so in love with Sartre that she got in bed with him after he died. "'Death had closed its hand around me; it was no longer a metaphysical scandal, it was . . . our arteries,'" Beauvoir presaged in 1954 when Sartre was hospitalized.[5]

After that hospitalization years later, she laid beside Sartre's corpse. "'I asked to be left alone with Sartre,'" said Beauvoir, "'and I wanted to stretch out beside him under the sheet [but a] nurse stopped me. . . . I lay down on the sheet and slept a little. At five o'clock, some orderlies came. They . . . carried him away.'"[6] A vain effort by feminists to "divorce" her from Sartre by stating that Sartre's *Being and Nothingness* was either adapted or indebted to her early existentialism is denied straightforwardly by Hazel Barnes. Barnes says that "The significant question is whether Beauvoir in 1927 did, in fact, as Simons claims, 'define the major themes . . . of Sartre's "Being and Nothingness."'"[7] Barnes retorts curtly, Beauvoir "*did not*. . . . Simons has been misled by purely verbal resonances and ideas much too vague to have the significance she ascribes to them."[8] Despite Hazel Barnes being one of the most preeminent women philosophers of the twentieth century (also praised as a "real lady" by her colleagues, being a full professor in three disciplines at UC Boulder and having a prestigious scholarship named after her posthumously—the most high-status "single faculty award" that recognizes "the enriching interrelationship between

---

3. Cf. Koertege and Patai's *Professing Feminism*, xv: Feminists "were oblivious to the tenuousness of the [evidence-ignoring] doctrines that were so widely held."

4. Holveck, "The Birth of American Existentialism," 7–16.

5. Brown, "The Last Days of Jean-Paul Sartre" 70.

6. Ibid.

7. Barnes, "Response to Margaret Simons," 29–34.

8. Ibid, emphasis.

teaching and research"[9]), I can say by both her work and working closely with her that she was not besotted with an ideological feminism.

The feminist critiques were boosted by other strange bed-fellow foes, some in once Nazi-occupied Eastern Europe. These European foes viscerally despised existentialism after World War II just because its pre-war related phenomenology in Husserl, Heidegger, and others was largely German. Though not German, Sartre had studied under Heidegger who was "banned from teaching by the University of Freiburg's 'de-Nazification' hearings in 1946."[10] Others scorned illogical moods (*angst*) and a phenomenological self-consciousness that, not being mind-centered, alienated Anglo-American philosophers who were at times dogmatic, if not ideological. "Amidst this tangle [of A. J. Ayer, Merleau-Ponty, Jean, Ambrosino, and Bataille that took place in 1951 at some Parisian bar]," states an historian, "one finds Bataille's statement that an 'abyss' separates English from French and German philosophy, the first recorded announcement of the analytic-continental divide in the twentieth century."[11] Though this century's divide often led to existentialism being grudgingly relegated to a "service course" for keen undergraduates, graduate courses in existentialism tended to be excluded derisively. This derision occurred since existentialism was misjudged as either meaningless by positivists or senseless by analytic philosophers, in terms of self-refuting verification principles, in many secular research universities that were dominated by the positivists or their heirs.

One heir is the late Robert Turnbull who I heard call himself a "not naïve logical positivist," suggesting he was sympathetic with positivism despite the self-refuting nature of both its later liberal and conservative verification principles (the latter principle being self-refuting since it was not itself empirically or logically true/false and the former since no evidence counted against *its* falsity; bringing to mind Popper's falsification principle).[12] When Turnbull became the new chair of philosophy at Ohio State University in 1970, he informed all department associates down to the majors (including myself) that faculty having scholarly interests other than a positivist-analytic focused philosophy (e.g., philosophy of

9. Chancellor of UC Boulder, "Hazel Barnes Prize," para. 1.
10. Peters (ed.), *Heidegger, Education, and Modernity*, 148, fn. 53.
11. Vrahimis, "'Was There a Sun Before Men Existed?'"
12. In specifying the logical possibility that theories can be false or true by true predictions, Popper held that only *false* predictions that counted against theories are epistemologically significant for science.

religion) were invited to go elsewhere.[13] Other interests averse to the new philosophical focus included existentialism. Like many of his concurring colleagues, even so, Turnbull was witty, charismatic, and humorous; echoing a point made by Frederick Suppe about many of the preeminent positivists: While waiting for an elevator at a philosophy convention many years later, Turnbull asked me about my interests. Telling him that my interests included the philosophy of science, he amusingly quipped "Oh good, maybe you can explain why this damn elevator won't come up!" And although his sense of humor contrasts to the legendarily intense Ludwig Wittgenstein, whose early *Tractatus Logico-Philosophicus* was a positivist Bible and who later pioneered analytic (linguistic) philosophy, it was amazingly appreciated by the 1970s that Wittgenstein actually esteemed the phenomenologist Martin Heidegger's ideas of dread and nothingness by way of one of his closest students.[14] And thus the trendy allegations of senselessness speedily faded.

Faded crazes of vilifying existentialism, if not phenomenology, in the Anglo-American positivist, analytic, and feminist traditions are now reinforced by a "reification fallacy." This fallacy is leveled haughtily by a critic who contends that their backers may say "that *analytic reason* is inapplicable to their philosophies, but I think this is nonsense."[15] The "nonsense" is that abstract concepts like "dread" and "nothingness" are treated *inter alia* as something concrete. But a concrete immediacy is evident in Sartre's concept of nothingness by our irrefutable experience of ourselves as being implicitly aware *of* our direct consciousness of something *as not being* that thing (or anything we are directly consciousness of): Consciousness is not literally nothing. In sum, the inapt criticism follows in the wake of other critiques such as feminist accusations of sexism (denied by many famous female philosophers), and a reputed meaninglessness of key existentialist ideas by logical positivists, especially by A. J. Ayer in *Language, Truth, and Logic* (1936); the criticism waning when it

---

13. This rejection of the philosophy of religion is curious, given Turnbull's final rank of Major as a US Army Chaplain after his BD (Bachelor of Divinity) in 1943 from Oberlin College. Does this bring to mind, by contrast, Wittgenstein's admiration for Kierkegaard? Or did Kierkegaard bear only on what *cannot* be said? See Hull, "Biography," para. 1.

14. The student, famously, is Norman Malcolm. See, for example, Malcolm's *Ludwig Wittgenstein*, 59.

15. Cf. Maller, "Problems with Reification," 1, emphasis. Also, the positivists' criticism of these concepts as meaningless was undercut by their self-refuting verification principle, both the conservative and liberal interpretation.

later became public that Wittgenstein's respectful remarks about ideas such as *angst* were sanitized, by his own devotees, from his piece "On Heidegger on Being and Dread."[16] The dread aside, Sartre's analysis of a direct consciousness of which we are also conscious bears profoundly on perennial problems in the philosophy of science. Though my linking science to that analysis is not always faithful to Sartre, what he says affords novel inferences that resolve thorny problems in the philosophy of science. Scientific realism is now considered by beginning with Sartre's basic assessment of how reality *itself* is revealed by our self-consciousness.

Existential Phenomenology and Classical Criticism

Sartre's existentialism is illustrated nicely by Eleanore Holyeck who commented on Hazel Barnes' autobiography *The Story I Tell Myself* (1997). In Holyeck's "The Birth of American Existentialism: Hazel E. Barnes, a Singular Universal," she maintains that Barnes' "central philosophical discussion stresses the notion of a singular universal, which she prefers to call 'a unique universal' (*Story*, xii), i.e., a conscious existing pour-soi [for-itself] who makes free choices and is, therefore, self-creating and self-determining in the situation in which she finds herself."[17] Whereas a self-conscious existing pour-soi as both freely choosing and self-determining classically reflects Sartre's existentialism—much of which I have held herein is not implied by his existential phenomenology. Yet, this phenomenology does both posit existing things of which we are conscious and holds that we are indirectly conscious of this consciousness.

Self-consciousness as such (as against Sartre's existentialism) is faithful to the basic phenomenological analysis of Sartre. Sartre's critics are mostly those in the Anglo-American positivist tradition who think that if we have free will, this fact must be concluded in a sound deductive proof based on external evidence. Bertrand Russell, for example, stated that "there may be very excellent arguments for free will . . . I have never heard."[18] Rest assured, alas, that his heirs will ever hear that argument for free will. For its certified reality is not reliant on abstract proof. To

---

16. See Wittgenstein, "On Heidegger On Being and Dread" (30 Dec 1929 at Moritz Schlick's place) 80–83. See also Malcolm, *Ludwig Wittgenstein*, 59, fn. 4 for Heidegger's *angst* about there being anything existing rather than *nothing*.

17. Holveck, "Birth of American Existentialism," Article excerpt, para. 1.

18. Russell, *Autobiography of Bertrand Russell*, 70.

seek it is to miss the point both of founding free will in our immediate phenomenological experience and that we are already implicitly aware of our freedom to seek or not seek that proof. The absurdity of such a proof aside, Sartre's phenomenology may be clarified by holding up a book and asking someone: "Are you not *aware of* your observational consciousness of this book?" Sartre would say more detachedly that "a direct consciousness of it is that of which there is an indirect awareness"; this, over saying that "*my* direct consciousness is that of which *I am* aware" in order to avoid our self-awareness being associated with an "I" that includes the infamous "I think" of Descartes' "thinking self"—the paradoxical if not contradictory divide from a full-bodied ordinary self, nonetheless, being even more obvious.[19]

With this disclaimer, my language is often used because it resonates more suitably with our ordinary talk about consciousness. Consciousness involves our *direct consciousness* of something other than itself and our *indirect* consciousness (awareness) *of* that direct consciousness.[20] Thus, although consciousness as such is a unity without a sub-consciousness since the latter could not communicate with the other consciousness and vice versa, says Sartre, there is a sort of "duality" in which we are implicitly aware (conscious) of both our *direct consciousness* of something and that this thing is not our consciousness. Otherwise, we could not be *aware of* our being conscious. And being aware of our consciousness appeals to the integrity of our experience, a mark of existential phenomenology. A classical criticism is that if the thesis of this self-consciousness is true, we should be able to be directly conscious of our indirect awareness. While this criticism may seem logical, the awareness is not in fact that of which we can be conscious. And so the thesis is false. Indeed, this logocentric criticism labels our self-consciousness experience of ourselves, abstractly, as a thesis rather than granting that the experience reveals unassailably an immediate awareness of our consciousness of *something*. Moreover, the *thing* of which we are directly conscious cannot be our indirect awareness on pain of there being no awareness of the direct consciousness.

---

19. For a possible reasoning *a posteriori* to paradoxes of our consciousness, see Trundle's "Aristotle *Versus* Van Til and Łukasiewicz," 323–44.

20. Sartre, *Being and Nothingness*, li–liii. Reducing either consciousness or self-consciousness to a *phenomenon* is often a mistake made by neuroscience philosophers, of not scientists.

From Critics of Paradox to a Paradoxical Consciousness

The phenomenology in this essay holds that something of which we are directly conscious may include virtually anything other than our consciousness—our consciousness being *no thing* (*nothing*) that we are indirectly aware of, from external things and our emotions to causal effects on our bodies and behavior. Exactly, to be directly conscious of our behavior is, for instance, to be indirectly aware of our freedom to behave or not behave in given ways. Likewise, to be directly conscious of our headache is to be implicitly conscious of having it despite its not being willed and our willing to not have it. While existentialists stress paradoxes and flat-out contradictions that are studiously discounted by rationalistic philosophies, Sartre's stress on *absolute* freedom does itself ignore our seeking to both not suffer the pain, even if vainly, and find relief from the pain that might itself be mitigated causally by various medications.

In sum, medicine's causal efficacy both supports our having a limited free will and contrasts poignantly to Sartre's existentialist notion that we are *absolutely* free. His unadulterated freedom (free will), including freedom from *a priori* norms of reason and right or wrong, results justly in angry criticism by many scientists for whom his position is patently naïve if not outright cruel. Oddly, the cruelty was denied by psychiatrist R. D. Laing, M.D., during his atypical career. His career is criticized, however, by other psychiatrists such as Nassir Ghaemi, M.D. He remarks that Laing "went overboard with the French existentialist ideology that all things psychiatric are about power," Laing incredulously "believing, like his teacher Sartre, that all mental illness was a [freely chosen] creative response to unlivable life circumstances."[21] In spite of these circumstances, Sartre implies not only that when we are happy or sad, or even in love, we are solely responsible for those feelings but also, among other things, for our psychic infirmities. For we could freely choose to have or not have them. So in the absence of any proviso by Sartre, and there is none, if we suffer manic depression (and even in accord with Dostoevsky's *Notes from Underground* I would add *free fall* when we fall or jump from rooftops per Newton's 2nd Law), then the choices to violate or not violate the law of gravity are equally rational. We are not only as rational to choose to suffer as to not suffer the depression but also entirely culpable for either alternative. These alternative absurdities, though, are not inferable from Sartre's basic analysis, much less mine, of our self-consciousness.

21. Ghaemi, "Profiles of the Past," 128.

Our self-consciousness is the precise phenomenological footing for certifying the reality of both our limited free will and a limited causal determinism. This paradox is not held *a priori* but rather inferred *a posteriori* from our self-consciousness experience. The experience renders coherent scientific truths about both our psycho-biological nature and Nature because a causally determined reality is not the condition for "truth" and, hence, does not determine our truth-claims where contradictory claims would incoherently both be true. In "Paradoxes of Human Nature," I argue against a Kantian pseudo-rationality, which reduces free will to a possible reality, in the spirit of Étienne Gilson's criticism of Kant's idealism.[22] This idealism is faulted plainly but profoundly by Gilson:

> When Kant proclaimed that he was about to effect a Copernican revolution by substituting his critical idealism for the dogmatic realism of the Middle Age, the thing he really brought about was the very opposite. The sun that Kant set at the centre of the world was man himself, so that his revolution was the reverse of Copernican, and led to an anthropocentrism a good deal more radical... than any of which the Middle Age is accused. It was only in a local sense that medieval man thought himself to be at the center of things; the whole creation of which he was the destined crown and end... was none the less something outside himself... to which he had to submit and conform himself if he would know anything of its nature. But modern man, brought up on Kantian idealism, regards nature as being no more than an outcome of the [*categorial*] laws of the mind.[23]

The mind, for Kant, is not either informed by or conformed to an experienced reality. Rather, reality as it appears is produced by laws of mind by the mind's *a priori* structure. This structure imposes categories (*categorial* interpretations) on a material of experience. The experience in being categorized as one or many (quantity), positive or negative (quality), related events or concepts (relation), and impossible or possible (modality), means that Kant's idealism tells us about the mind and not about an external reality. This reality, in the spirit of Gilson, is vacuous alike for rationalistic intellectuals who are not Kantians. For they mimic

---

22. See Trundle's "Paradoxes of Human Nature," 181–86: We are paradoxically but incontrovertibly conscious of being both limitedly free and not free (causally determined).

23. Gilson, *Spirit of Medieval Philosophy* 245, emphasis.

Kant by the absurd *a priori* demand that reality conform to their reason.[24] Reason likewise, in terms of Gilson's criticism, is the center of their world when they try to reconcile causal determinism and free will by either relegating the will to a virtually fictional reality (Kant's *noumenon*) or positing Kant's proposed *pragmatisch*. Pragmatism accepts our having free will as true if this truly works in rendering coherent moral praise and blame. This notion of praise and blame, influential today, arises from Kant's practical reason since the notion's not being knowable by pure reason means that we must be practical by acting *as if* we have free will for the sake of a possibly illusory morality.

That a pragmatic morality influences most modern academics who may not have even read Kant is clearly evidenced by a senior astrophysicist at the Harvard Smithsonian Center, Howard Smith. Smith states, without referencing Kant, "Even were a *conceptual* breakthrough to someday prove we do not actually have free will, we may still need to *act as though* we do. Taking responsibility by acting as if there is free will . . . is part of being aware."[25] Precisely, the point is that to be aware incontrovertibly of our behavior is to be implicitly aware of our limited will to either behave or not behave in given ways. Free will is not proven by either some conceptual breakthrough, waiting for discovery, or in some formally deductive manner. Rather, our will is established by appealing to the integrity of our immediate phenomenological experience; the experience of our limited free will, as expanded on shortly, being as necessary for coherent "truth" in *science* as is our limitedly being understood scientifically for an intelligible "truth" in *ethics*! Ethics cannot ignore psycho-biological limitations, such as severe provocation or manic depression, which may mitigate moral responsibility.

While responsibility brings to mind Kant's "moral law within" as against the "starry heavens above" in Kant's *Critique of Practical Reason*, our direct consciousness of things other than itself (from stars to our psychic states) means that our direct consciousness is oriented outward and not inward towards itself. Its not being directed inward towards itself reminds us of our inability to be directly conscious of our indirect awareness *of* that consciousness. For our indirect awareness would already be aware of that direct consciousness—precluding an indirect awareness of our direct consciousness as a phenomenon because there would be

---

24. Cf. Trundle's *Camus' Answer* for a general discussion of this point.

25. Smith, *Let There be Light*, 183. From Trundle, "Paradoxes of Human Nature," 181–86, emphasis.

nothing there. This point reflects a dog-chasing-its-tail dilemma that while an infinite regress may be logically possible, it is impossible empirically; the "empirical" better signified by "in fact" because of a non-empirical (non-corporeal) nature of consciousness. Moreover, in addition to our emotions or cognitive states, consciousness can be directly relatable to external reality. This reality may be understood as reality *in itself*. In itself, reality means, first, physical Nature (Sartre's *non-conscious being*) as this *being is* in itself when we are conscious of it without concepts. This concept-less consciousness does not hide *being* but rather reveals it. Second, reality may be that of which we are observationally conscious in various modes.

These modes of consciousness include three ways of grasping an external reality with increasing epistemic imports for everyday and scientific observation. Reality is graspable 1) as *non-conceptual undifferentiated being* (the most minimal import that is often related to Eastern thought); 2) as a *non-conceptualized differentiated being* with aspects of individuality, extensiveness, continuity and so on per John Compton's "Natural Science and the Experience of Nature" in *Phenomenology in America*,[26] with the potential to "see" something as it is *in itself* but not to notice it conceptually as a given thing; and 3) as something conceptualized—a conceptual consciousness being *infused* by a non-conceptual consciousness of the thing's aspects. This aspectual-conceptual mode affords truth ascriptions to observation claims due to our direct observational consciousness containing a non-conceptual consciousness of the thing *in-itself* because of the thing's aspects such as individuality.

Hence *reality* is not split from *reality as it appears*, as with Kant. There are no Kantian categories of mind that mediate between our concepts and the raw material of an experienced reality, concealing reality from both our sheer observational consciousness of it (of which we are aware) and our conceptual-theoretical interpretations. These interpretations, also, are not divorced from an external reality by internal sensations that are not known to reflect reality, as with Hume. And unlike Hume and Kant, a judicious distinction is made herein between abstract theories of mind and an immediate integrity of our own experience by existential phenomenology.

---

26. The aspects are noticed only conceptually, in the case of John Compton. See Compton, "Natural Science," 90–91.

Consciousness: Unmasking Sophistical Substitutes for Philosophy

Before addressing how a phenomenology of consciousness unmasks new substitutes for philosophy, consider how philosophy's obvious distinction from the substitutes is stymied by Kant's later devotees. The diverse devotees range from theologian Karl Rahner who developed an antirealist "transcendental (Kantian) Thomism,"[27] to physicist-philosopher Edward Mackinnon, who adopts a more subtle neo-Kantian obscuration of reality. This reality is not immaterial *noumena* (*things-in-themselves*) such as the good, self, or God. Rather the reality, backed by Mackinnon, is influenced by the often-ignored Kantian notion of a raw material of experienced *things in themselves*—called "phenomena" when the *things* are categorially interpreted. In rooting this interpretation in foundational concepts, Mackinnon suggests that these concepts conceal reality. A reality masked by concepts, not categories, is neo-Kantian.

The "neo-Kantian epistemology," says MacKinnon, "differs from [the] Kantian in its treatment of categories, or foundational concepts. Where Kant bases categories on a psychological analysis and justifies their necessity by a transcendental deduction, neo-Kantians ground categories in linguistic usage . . . ." Here, the usage of "ordinary language is extended to and restricted in [theoretical frameworks such as] quantum contexts."[28] And not either contextual or ordinary languages are averted by phenomenologists such as Husserl who influenced Sartre, since, says MacKinnon, they "are backing into a . . . private language if they think they can express the pre-conceptual given while bracketing [suspending existence assumptions about] the shared conceptualization of reality *implicit* in any expression of the given"; his assuming that all consciousness is conceptual by speaking consistently of "conceptualizations . . . [that are] *implicit* in any expression of the given."[29]

The given thus understood, nonetheless, is challenged by Rev. Msgr. Robert Sokolowski. Sokolowski, with enviable scholarship from

---

27. Three theological schools compete "in the Catholic Church today," says Norbert J. Fleckinstein: "a renewed, traditional Thomism; the conjugal mysticism of Balthasar, St. John Paul II, Benedict and their 'communio' allies; and heirs of the transcendental (Kantian) Thomism of Rahner and Lonergan." Fleckinstein, "A Theological Style," 1.This said, some notable scholars defend Lonergan's critical realism as the groundbreaking Catholic response to Kant.

28. MacKinnon, "Why Interpret Quantum Physics?" 86–102.

29. MacKinnon (Ed.), "Introduction," emphasis, 68–69.

Aristotle to Husserl and Kant, notes that neo-Kantianism starts at the "roof" in contrast to Husserl who starts at the "foundation."[30] Husserl begins "with the deepest foundations of consciousness" in order to obtain a "[pre-predicative] experience," this experience being the "foundation for categorical and predicative activity" with intellect realizing "itself within . . . consciousness."[31] Consciousness is not understood the same by Sartre and Husserl, but Husserl's [pre-predicative] conscious life brings to mind Sartre's pre-conceptual consciousness.[32] And they may agree that to be directly conscious is to be conscious of something other than this consciousness,[33] from external objects to internal thoughts and feelings, with a profound possibility that something of which we are conscious conceptually is rooted in a non-conceptual consciousness, the latter occurring by itself or as what is infused into conceptual consciousness. Either way, there is an indirect but immediate and invincible consciousness *of* that direct consciousness (a self-consciousness).

Self-consciousness is the *foundation* for metaphysical theory. Oddly, MacKinnon says that John Compton must construct a "theory" on aspects of reality "to discuss the pre-conceptual given" and that is not "different from other theories, though the grounds of accepting, testing, evaluating, and confirming it are different."[34] The difference, though, is immense between theories that ignore our consciousness of something non-conceptually (but circularly suppose the concepts in question to create theories) and theories rooted by existential phenomenology in a self-confirming indirect consciousness (awareness) *of* our consciousness of something. It is neither abstract theory nor a doctrine of private language to say that we can recollect aspects of something we saw non-conceptually, i.e., of which we were non-conceptually aware. The term "aware" is used by the famed analytic philosopher Fred I. Dretske to suggest that a boy can *reflect upon* his previous non-conceptual awareness of his father's workplace to confirm his mother's claim that he *saw*, but did not *notice* the workplace. The boy is able to *reflect upon* his earlier non-conceptual awareness for confirming his mother's avowal that he *saw*, but did not *notice* the workplace.

---

30. Sokolowski, "Husserl on First Philosophy," 3–23.
31. Ibid., 5, non-conceptual consciousness is a comparable foundation.
32. See Embree, "The Phenomenological Derivation," 1.
33. Sartre, *Being and Nothingness*, x; that is, that which is *not* consciousness.
34. MacKinnon, "Introduction," 69, emphasis.

Being able to *not notice* what one is aware of as a given thing joins the phenomenological and analytic philosophical traditions. In the latter tradition (bypassing Hume's reduction of an observable world to internal sensations and Kant's imposition of the mind's categories on observation), Dretske says in ordinary language that "I have occasionally been in such a preoccupied state that as I walked down the street I was ... unaware of everything around me," adding, "It was only after I snapped out of the 'fog' that I realized I had been seeing certain things without being aware of it...."[35] This awareness is related by Dretske to a non-epistemic (non-conceptual) seeing deemed to be vital for objectively true observations that avoid an epistemic relativism in both science and philosophy.

In the journal *Philosophy of Science*, for example, Athan Raftopoulos states viably that there is "a part of observation, which I will call perception [that] is bottom-up and theory neutral. As such, perception could play the role of common ground on which a naturalized epistemology can be built and relativism avoided."[36] The avoidance is noted by Dretske in recalling his landmark book *Seeing and Knowing*. He says "My claim was that there was something called non-epistemic seeing, so that I can [speak without senselessness of seeing] the book on the table ... without even knowing what a book is," as opposed to "seeing [noticing] that it is a book, that's epistemic seeing."[37] This seeing is not undercut by a so-called "Direct Realism," warned against by John Searle, by confusing our taking ourselves to be aware of our experience of the book (*content* of perceptual experience) with our being aware of the book (*object* of perceptual experience).[38] And although Dretske adds that differentiating epistemic from non-epistemic seeing (awareness) is "pretty obvious," it does not seem clear to him, unhappily, that "psychologists and neuroscientists are much interested...."[39]

Not noticing a thing of which we are aware, says Dretske, is a *non-epistemic awareness* (seeing$_n$). A book review on Dretske's non concep tual basis for an objective conceptual seeing (*epistemic* seeing$_e$) says he is "successful" from "standard objections."[40] Overcome objections include

35. Dretske, *Seeing and Knowing*, 11.
36. Raftopoulos, "Reentrant Neural Pathways," S187–S199.
37. See Bøndergaard and Fønss, "Dretske's Last Interview," §6.
38. Ghijsen, review of *Seeing Things as They Are*, 125.
39. Ibid. Neuroscience as a science per se is differentiated later from sophistical neuroscience philosophy.
40. See Aune's favorable review of Dretske's book in *The Philosophical Review*,

the boy's earlier seeing$_n$, when he saw his father's workplace, on which he later reflects. The reflection is based on the boy's earlier non-conceptual awareness of the *aspects* of the workplace; its individuality, extensiveness, continuity, and so on. Sartre holds that if we reflect on our consciousness, we do not encounter either ideas derived from inner sensations (Hume) or phenomena fabricated by a structured mind (Kant) but rather a "consciousness *of* this or that *thing-in-the-world*."[41] Since our conceptual consciousness of mind-independent things in an external reality is grounded in a non-conceptual consciousness of them, and this consciousness *can* occur alone, external things are both observable non-conceptually and conceptually noticeable.

Noticing something conceptually as opposed to a concept-free awareness of it, *via* analytic philosophy that appeals to what it makes sense to say, and an existential phenomenology of our irrefutable experience of ourselves of which we are immediately aware, evidence that phenomenology is alien to ordinary theories of mind. Thus, although the mind involves consciousness, consciousness is not identical to the mind. To think is to be conscious *of* thinking, showing that thinking is not identical with consciousness. While we cannot think without being conscious of it, we can be conscious without thinking; a point missed by Descartes when he muddles mind and consciousness. He says that the demon "can never bring it about that I am nothing, so long as I shall be *conscious* that I am something" wherein the proposition "*I am, I exist*, is necessarily true each time it is . . . conceived in my *mind*."[42] The mind aside, he was already and phenomenologically conscious of himself before his systematic doubt was even begun in the *Meditations*!

The *Meditations* may, for some philosophers, call to mind Kant for whom phenomenologists would be "faced with the impossibility of understanding the sublime state of mind as a consciousness of *something* . . . ,"[43] this impossibility presumably being worsened if a "consciousness of something" *were* a state of mind rather than the mind (or thought or thinking) being that of which we are conscious. Consciousness begs for a distinction from mind. The mind as either essentially the self or a thinking thing is undercut by that thing being precisely that of which he

---

383–88.

41. See Sartre, *Being and Nothingness*, emphasis, 316.
42. Descartes, *Meditation ii*, §3. Emphasis only on "conscious" and "mind."
43. See Clewis, "Review of *The Sublime and Its Teleology*," 106–7.

was already indubitably conscious when Descartes began to doubt. To doubt is to think and thinking, he maintains, has the property of consciousness. "Consciousness, for Descartes, is an intrinsic property of all thoughts," notes L. M. Jorgensen, "by which the subject becomes aware of the thought itself. While this involves reflection, this is not distinct from the thought itself."[44] If thought itself is not distinct from consciousness, however, then is it possible that we can be conscious of something *without thought* in terms of both ordinary-language (analytic) philosophy and an existential phenomenology that both appeal to our immediate and irrefutable experience of ourselves?

This experience of ourselves as a self-consciousness "clearly gives us what is sometimes called a kind of *direct realism* about the world [in the sense of *things themselves*]," says Ron McClamrock, adding that "We see here Sartre's rejection of reality as hidden and unreachable . . . the opaque field of representations which shield us from the real things [that are] the *things themselves* . . . "[45] In accord with these revealed things, a realism of existential phenomenology means that this consciousness is always both a direct consciousness of something other than itself and an indirect consciousness of that consciousness as either *no thing* or not being that to which it relates itself. In not being anything it relates itself to, consciousness is *no thing* (*néant*). *Néant* means, among other things, that consciousness is not anything subject to naked-eye or instrument-aided scientific observation. In seeking to observe consciousness, scientists would be absurdly striving to be directly conscious of their indirect awareness *as* a phenomenon. As a phenomenon, however, their indirect awareness would exclude an awareness of anything. Absurdly, in order for us to be directly conscious of our indirect awareness, this awareness would have to be both what it *is* and *is not*. That is, it would have to be at once both a phenomenon and not a phenomenon: not a phenomenon in order to be aware of itself as a phenomenon of which there is a direct consciousness! There "can be consciousness of a [scientific] law," says Sartre, but "not a law of consciousness."[46] Scientists and pseudo-philosophers who try futilely to treat their own self-consciousness as a *phenomenon*— an immoral masochism of bad faith in a Sartrean ethics (*mauvaise foi*),

---

44. Jorgensen, "Seventeenth-Century Theories of Consciousness," §2.1.

45. Cf. McClamrock, "Final Lecture on Sartre, §1.

46. Sartre, *Being and Nothingness*, lv. Consciousness is called a *nothingness* in order, among other things, to contrast it to *something qua* a phenomenon of scientific inquiry.

suggests that these pseudo-philosophers and scientists are not even pre-scientifically aware of their own consciousness. Rather, they are more like bodily Cartesian automatons than self-conscious persons. Precisely, while treating other persons and themselves in this manner makes one wonder if the philosophical wheel must be reinvented repeatedly (as if there was no history of philosophy), Sokolowski comments appropriately that this treatment of human beings by philosophers is paradoxically non-philosophical:

> [The] most prominent "non-philosophies" of the ancient world are reductive atomism ... and sophistry and historicism, found in the original sophists. The atomists were a kind of *scientific substitute for philosophy*. ... Cognitive science is the combination of neuroscience, computer science, and logic that *some people take to be a contemporary substitute for philosophy*. ... Only first philosophy can deal with such things, and it is the same first philosophy now as it was before and continues throughout the ages. ... Philosophy always has to define and defend itself against these. ... The struggle to do so is endemic to the human condition. Because there is such a thing as philosophy, there also are counterfeits that are played off against it, things that only look like or claim to be philosophy.[47]

The Seductions of Self-Refuting Reductionisms

A reductionist fallacy is appropriately ascribed to *scientistic* claims that everything is entirely explicable by science such as reducing consciousness to a phenomenon and moral sentiments to either psycho-biological states or states of the brain. Similar tired tricks arose before, from the ancient sophists to logical positivists. The fate of positivism, presaging other ploys today, is due to their wannabe-scientific verification principle for reducing sentences such as "x is good" to "I like x" on bogus grounds that the former is *meaningless* in not being logically or empirically true/false and the latter is *meaningful* by describing an empirically verifiable psychological feeling. This conservative version of the verification principle is, of course, self-refuting since it is not itself logically or empirically true/false (the liberal version also being self-refuting since nothing counts for or against *it*). So either reducing moral deliberation to or construing it to be caused because of neurocognitive conditions, or appealing

---

47. Sokolowski, "Husserl on First Philosophy," 2, 9.

to those conditions for otherwise either explaining or explaining away the deliberation, is likewise self-refuting or futile. For neurocognitive deliberations in this case would themselves be explicable by, or reducible to, neurocognitive conditions. In terms of these conditions, "we see that neuroscience and psychology can help to explain *how* [free will] works," notes one neuroscience philosopher, "rather than explain it *away*."[48]

In addition to my discussion below of the epistemological and logical incoherence of denying free will, which is related inextricably to our consciousness, the attempt to explain it away is rebuffed by one of the pioneers of neuroscience. Neuroscientist Wilder Penfield "explained how when the cerebral cortex of a subject was probed, the subject's hand would move. The subject was subsequently asked who moved his hand, and he would reply that he didn't do it, that the neuroscientist did it."[49] There is then the point that "If the physical brain was the cause of all conscious activity such as the subject intending to move his hand, then by probing the brain it should also cause the subjective phenomenon of intending to do something." This was not, however, the case: "the subject clearly knew that he did not intend to move his hand. Penfield concluded that there is no place in the cerebral cortex where electrical stimulation will cause a patient to decide."

Seeking to explain *away* free will by a cognitive neuroscientific inquiry, which would allegedly show that our behavior is causally determined, is to circularly presuppose (as any scientific inquiry) that all events are caused. Or to put it another way, I am one of those philosophers who work on free will who is "frequently irritated by articles by scientists, usually neuroscientists, proclaiming the death of free will . . . the arguments against free will constructed on the basis of the results reported are question-begging . . . ."[50] Begging the question follows because the question ensues how science can establish causal determinism when the determinism is already assumed in terms of the causal principle. The principle even holds for quantum physics because this physics is not indeterministic *per se* but rather deterministic of probabilities. No science in principle can circumvent presupposing that all events have, deterministically, either exactly or inexactly measurable causes.

---

48. Nahmias, "Did my Brain Make Me Do It?" Abstract.
49. Tzortzis, "Has Evolution Been Misunderstood?" §*Naturalism*.
50. See Levy's review of *Is Science Compatible with Free Will?* para. 1.

On one the hand, there is the gambit of appealing to "correlations" of neuronal and mental states in order to avoid their identity that would result in both a reductive materialism and a vacuous notion of "truth"—"truth" not being ascribable to material things but rather to, among other things, statements about those things. The incoherent reductionism is typified by the renowned neuroscience philosopher Paul Churchland when he stated "I remember deciding at about the age of eleven or twelve" that thinking is "just electricity."[51] And attempting to avoid "electricity = thought" sorts of reductionism, by correlating one with the other, puts cognitive neuroscience in danger of being a pseudoscience because, as noted insightfully by Gabriel Vacariu, correlations of neuronal states to states of the mind do *not* presuppose any laws that are proper to science.[52] Even a science as unglamorous as the several-hundred-year-old Newtonian physics, in a domain where Planck's constant is negligible and phenomena do not approach the speed of light, illustrates a stark contrast to the hyperbole of many neuroscience philosophers. These philosophers must contend with the diffident success of neuroscience as opposed to the astonishing success of that physics. The physics affords theoretical state descriptions of physical systems at present times that can be coordinated causally, with uncannily precise predictions, to future states of those systems where logically related systems presuppose laws.

The laws notwithstanding, neuroscience philosophers, who furtively accept a complete causal determinism of neuronal states producing mental states, render nonsensical their own statements as well as science. The atheistic scientist Victor Stenger approvingly notes that a neuroscientist tells us that "'Free will is an illusion.' We don't exist as immaterial conscious controllers [but rather are] physical beings whose decisions and behaviors are the fully caused products of the brain and body."[53] Accepting the body as the only human reality that is causally determined means, however, that Stenger's own truth-claims are themselves determined and not made either freely or consciously; an incoherence enlarged on soon that further exposes neuroscience ploys. The ploys reflect an insincerity illustrated by Stenger in holding the universe could

---

51. MacFarquhar, "Two Heads," 63–64. Is the real problem that the head *qua* mind is reduced to a bodily brain that renders incoherent our incontrovertible consciousness of freely chosen thought?

52. See Vacariu's superb contributions to in *More Troubles with Cognitive Neuroscience*, Introduction.

53. Stenger, "Free Will is an Illusion," para. 3.

come from nothing, not needing a creator, by quoting Lawrence Krauss' *A Universe from Nothing: Why There Is Something Rather Than Nothing*; the latter criticized by physicist George Ellis who stated "It's very ironic when [Kraus] says philosophy is bunk and then himself engages in this . . . philosophy."[54] This bogus philosophy shared by Stenger would better call the "nothing" a "void," notes William Lane Craig, that "is a *physical system* that then undergoes evolution and change according to the laws of quantum mechanics"—both Krauss and Stenger knowing this, so "it is a deliberate misrepresentation of science to say that this is a description of literal nothing."[55]

"Nothing" switched for something that is *knowingly* subject to scientific inquiry typifies the sophistical ploys of many neuroscience philosophers and their enablers. In cleverly backing a materialistic-determinism criticized herein as illogical, it is not illogical to wonder why they go so far off the deep end metaphysically; beyond the "physics" that they so prize. In having critiqued them rationally, there is no *ad hominem* fallacy when we underscore circumstances or motives that may explain their irrationality. Is the irrationality explicable by the following epistemological pathologies?

1) Do the pathologies include an arrogant disdain for the history of philosophy that is triggered by many neuroscience philosophers being smitten with science? An overzealous fervor for science has resulted in a naïvely dogmatic *scientism*. Science is hereby held to exhaustively explicate all of reality where reality consists solely of phenomena that are entirely causally determined. Is there a fear that this deterministic materialism, in being metaphysics and not science, would be undercut by its logical incoherence as shown, for example, in Plato's *Phaedo* 99a-b, St. Augustine's *De libero arbitrio* and St. Thomas' *De Veritate* q. 24, a. i–xv? Indeed, the evident contempt for the history of philosophy collides head-on with Étienne Gilson's humility when he was "professor of the history of philosophy at the University of Strasbourg" in France where he "published the first of six editions of *Le thomisme*, entitled *Le thomisme: introduction au système de S. Thomas d'Aquin*."[56] This openness to the history by the renowned Gilson, which led to his vast achievements, contrast to the gaffes of many egotistical neuroscience philosophers when he said of

---

54. Horgan, "Is Lawrence Krauss a Physicist, or Just a Bad Philosopher?" para. 16.
55. Craig, "The Death of Victor Stenger." Para. 9 of interview, emphasis.
56. Redpath, "An Abbreviated Biography," para. 6.

"this first edition . . . 'The book deserves to survive in this first edition as a monument to the *ignorance* of its author.'"[57]

2) Is there a desire to evade moral responsibility by denying free will? Again, attention to motives is not an *ad hominem* if a position is already shown to be illogical, motives explaining why an illogical position is held. Free will was denied fixatedly by one neuroscience devotee who I and other faculty knew. His denials occurred during the decades he engaged in treacherous self-serving manipulations: attacking reputations of his colleagues in order to obtain his ends and being misleading, if not lying, about what those ends were. His misdeeds, masked by a gregarious façade, benefited both him and certain autocratic administrators. He was used by the administrators to cajole faculty into accepting their agenda and his own agenda was often forced on faculty by them. He thus managed-up to them for power and success, evoking the notion of "successful psychopaths" whose earlier name of "moral idiots" is now assessed by a diagnostic PCL-R (revised checklist).[58] Much of the checklist, despite the issue of whether he is merely bad or mad,[59] reflects clinical traits *prima facie* that he had: glib or superficial charm, unrealistic goals, need for constant stimulation, impulsiveness, grandiose pride, cunning and manipulation, chronic lying, and lack of both remorse and empathy; as many of those who have known him over the years would surely attest (although they may not have tied these traits to the disorder). And although it cannot of course be formally certified here that he is a psychopath, a Harvard psychiatrist said by analogy to President Donald Trump that "anybody, trained or not, can observe speech and behavior [that can

---

57. Ibid.

58. For these classic psychopathic traits, see the discussions throughout Hare and Babiak's *Snakes in Suits* (2007) as well as Voight's "Bad Bosses." Dr. Hare won the *Bruno Klopfer Award* for outstanding long-term professional contributions to personality assessment at the Society for Personality Assessment Convention in March 2016. And for those who suppose that non-experts cannot plausibly make a case that someone prima facie is psychopathic, see the commonsensical counterpoint below by Harvard psychiatrist Lance Dodes.

59. Cf. Begley, "Trump is Dangerous," para. 19–21. Begley notes that psychiatric "theorizing would be entertaining if the subject were, say, a Shakespearean character and not the man with his finger on the nuclear button. The short chapter by Trump's 'Art of the Deal' ghostwriter Tony Schwartz is so surreal (*'facts are whatever Trump deems them to be on any given day'* because '*his aim is never accuracy; it's domination*'), it should be in an Ionesco play [in the Theater of the Absurd]." Emphasis. Trump's relativistic view of facts, as a function of power, brings to mind the infamous Thrasymachus whose power-based sophism was reduced to absurdity by Plato.

be looked up in the DSM-5 and] then see whether he either meets this criteria.... The fact is, he does."⁶⁰ Also, pioneering psychopathy expert Robert Hare leaves wiggle room: Those with "a 'heavy dose' of psychopathic features may pose serious personal, psychological, and financial difficulties for others [but that] even those with a somewhat lower dose may present significant problems for those around them...."⁶¹

3) Do the neuroscience philosophers as such, who are less keen about traditional philosophy than science, aspire to a limelight of the latest hi-tech futuristic fad? This fad is assessed less humorously by one philosopher who refers to "neuro-thugs" for whom artistic *phenomena* include an "fMRI [not beauty] of the beholder," another saying sarcastically that trendy proposals for neuro-this and neuro-that may have potential but "little else as yet"—his fearing having to "open nominations for the *Captain Ahab Award* because of, among other things, obsessive ... *promotion* of neuroeconomics."⁶² Neuroeconomics and neuro-this and neuro-that aside, a question ensues: Is metaphysics facilely dismissible by way of the physical brain? The brain is appealed to in this manner by those who, while evidently enviably educated, still appeal in this odd way in order to establish to the brain's relation to morality. The relationship to morality is made by Joshua Greene, a neuroscience philosopher who has the questionable designation of "social-sciences professor":

> My lab studies moral judgment and decision-making, primarily using behavioral experiments and functional neuroimaging (fMRI). The goal of our research is to understand how moral judgments are *shaped* by automatic processes (such as emotional "gut reactions") and *controlled* cognitive processes (such as reasoning and self-control). Much of our work is aimed at understanding these automatic ... processes in more detailed functional terms. Recent work examines related *phenomena* such as cooperation, punishment, and belief in God.⁶³

60. Devaga, "Harvard Psychiatrist Lance Dodes," para. 17.

61. PCL-R (Psychopathy Check List—Revised) was developed by Robert Hare. See Hare, "The Wall Street Ten Percenters" para. 5. See also Langbert, "Managing Psychopathic Employees," para. 1–21.

62. See Harrison, "Neuroeconomics: A Rejoinder," para. 1.

63. Greene, "Home Page." For Greene's reductive (Hobbesian) materialism that denies free will and reduces mind (and *a fortiori* consciousness) to a material brain, see his submission "His Brain Made Him Do It: Encouraging a Mechanistic Worldview Reduces Punishment."

Should the *Phenomenon* of Neuroscience Philosophy Be Studied?

To say that neuroscience can study the phenomenon of *belief* in God proceeds *pari passu* with saying it can study the phenomenon of *disbelief* in God, not to mention the phenomenon of neuroscience studies themselves. Indeed, why not the *phenomena* of believing that neuroscience will prove that the mind *is* the brain and that everything is entirely caused? Would there be causes of our self-awareness, in neuroscience? Consider neuroscience philosophers Pat and Paul Churchland. In overlooking their incontrovertible and immediate awareness of their own behavior, they were like Kant when he wrote his *Critique of Pure Reason*. As he would have been aware of his freely writing that free will is only a possible reality (*noumenon*)—in effect a mere abstract concept, the Churchlands would be aware paradoxically of their freedom to deny or not deny a reality of free will. Precisely, in this sense they paradoxically also wonder why archaic "*abstract* concepts" like "freedom," the free will of which they would actually be *concretely* aware, concern us rather than our thinking progressively about what causes us.[64]

These causes bear on an ironic link of neuroscience philosophy to psychopathy. Psychopaths would also tend to deny free will, as noted earlier, in favor of our behavior being fully caused. So cause-and-effect statements are used to rationalize their behavior. As the behavior consists of seeing the world "as theirs for the taking, researchers at the University of British Columbia found that they used more causalistic words such as "'because' and 'so that,'" says Lillian Glass, who unmasks deceptive language for the FBI, "since they tend to rationalize their actions with their own logic."[65] This logic may have some exceptions, says neuroscience psychiatrist Dr. James Fallon. Fallon learned that he does himself have the brain imaging pattern and genetic makeup of a psychopath. But unlike many neuroscience philosophers, he regrets he had only a *purely cognitive* appreciation for suffering patients because of his psychopathy, and wishes he had an *emotional empathy*. Contrary to an incoherent deterministic-materialistic metaphysics of Greene, the Churchlands Victor Stenger, and others, Fallon says we can both freely nurture and

---

64. MacFarquhar, "Two Heads," 63–64, emphasis. One might reply, "Really? Existential Phenomenology is abstract? Our immediate, incontrovertible, and phenomenological experience of ourselves is abstract? Just a theory?"

65. Giang, "7 Signs," para. 7.

be nurtured, offsetting a deterministic hard-wired human nature. I "was completely wrong about science, which was a bitter pill... because *I had thought everything was driven [determined] by genetics, biology.*"[66] He did not think nurture mattered but, being open-minded, discovered that if one is raised in a very nurturing environment, one can counterbalance biology. Besides biology, there is "free will. Since finding all this out, I've made an effort to try to change my behavior . . . I've more *consciously* been doing things that are considered 'the right thing to do,' and thinking more about other people's feelings."[67]

This support for feelings, we recall, is by a neuroscientist who holds also that *nature* (biology) can be limitedly offset by *nurture*. This potency of nurture means that Fallon, despite discovering himself to be a psychopath who had earlier stressed only cognition, rejects that free will is an illusion that itself is caused biologically. But we should not restrict ourselves to Fallon's inference that biology does not cause all behavior. For our being limitedly nurtured is interpretable as a theory inferred from experience that, construed as data, affords an inference to the contradictory theory that nurture is an illusion and all of our behavior is causally determined (per an Under-determination-of-Theory-by-Data (UTD) Thesis).

This thesis aside, there are epistemological points that augment Fallon's inference by rendering incoherent the alternative inference of exhaustively caused behavior. Besides this behavior conflicting with our phenomenological consciousness of ourselves, it is the case that if all behavior is caused because a causally determined reality is the truth-condition for "truth" (and how can "truth" not have that reality as its condition if it causes truth-claims?), then thoughts expressed as statements S and ~S would incoherently both be true; including statements by the anti-determinist and determinist. And the determinist view of causality is worsened if "truth" is ascribed to the theory of materialism wherein material phenomena alone are real. For if reality consists merely of matter (with theoretical entities being perhaps sorts of epiphenomena), then there is a *collapse* of even "truth." For "truth" is not ascribable to phenomena but rather only to statements that cannot be reduced to phenomena.

Indeed, this sort of reductionism, as noted earlier, was criticized in one of Hazel Barnes' last essays, "Consciousness and Digestion: Sartre

---

66. Cooper, "Neuroscientist Studying Brain Scans," Transcripts main page.
67. Stromberg, "The Neuroscientist," para. 13.

and Neuroscience" (2005). "The essay provides a Sartrean perspective on the work of Nobel prize winning scientist, Gerald M. Edelman, on the biological underpinnings to consciousness" where the metaphor "digestion" in the title concerns "the fact that digestion is not identical with [cannot be reduced to] the physical organs that produce it any more than consciousness is identical with [can be reduced to] its neurological underpinnings."[68] The underpinnings aside, the deterministic materialism resulting in knotty epistemic problems does not, curiously, seem troubling to others. Some of these tacit deterministic materialists do not reject outright our being causally determined phenomena. In the journal *Cognitive Science* some of them question more subtly, in a seemingly benign manner, "what do people find incompatible with causal determinism?"

> For example, suppose that people are considering an agent in a deterministic universe who is controlled by her fears and passively allows her friend to be bullied. The present results . . . suggest that people think it actually would not be possible for any agent who was in this sort of situation in a deterministic universe to actively work against her fears and take a different path to confront the bully. Perhaps it is this fact about people's judgments that makes them reluctant to say that agents in a deterministic universe can be morally responsible.[69]

Regardless of what ordinary folks judge about moral responsibility in an imagined causally determined universe, where hypothetically "everything that happens . . . is caused in a completely deterministic way by some prior event,"[70] the question ensues of how there can be events of moral responsibility when there is a complete absence of free will that is presupposed by the responsibility in question for its intelligibility? Besides the question being commonsensical—Kant making a big deal about the presupposition, why is there no attention to a foregone conclusion that the agent's defense or non-defense of her friend is a patent effect of a previous cause? It would itself be a cause of effects that are themselves causes of others *ad infinitum* in a universe that is devoid of

68. Cannon, "Hazel E. Barnes 1915–2008," para. 31.

69. Bear and Knobe, "What Do People Find Incompatible with Causal Determinism?" §6.2. This deterministic cognitive science, about which some cognitive scientists themselves have second thoughts, studiously ignores our own immediate, incontrovertible and phenomenological self-conscious experience.

70. Ibid.,

any intentional purpose because the purpose cannot obtain without our self-conscious free will.

Without this free will, how could there be any intelligible moral responsibility, much more coherent moral praise or blame? More importantly, why is there no phenomenological consideration of the moral agent in *our* real non-hypothetical universe? Would not the agent ordinarily be aware of both her fear and of her *will* to defend her friend but, at the same time, be aware (guiltily) of her fear offsetting her will to do what is morally right? Right and wrong and their corollaries of moral praise and blame *are intelligible* in our real universe. While these moral notions allow for our psycho-biological nature being limitedly subject to deterministic causes or causal influences, where depressions may be caused, the notions also involve our having a limited free will of *willing* that we not have the ailments or, per the cognitive-science example, a paralyzing fear to defend a friend. *Pari passu* fear and depression mitigate degrees of moral responsibility such as our having, all things equal, normal obligations to protect our friends and be sociable.[71]

Sociability while suffering sustained depression is a virtual, if not literal, physical impossibility. This does not, however, obviate our having free will such as *willing* to not have various ailments that may result, in turn, in our willing to stop suffering by medication. And although the medication may cause our relief, the relief being caused is consistent with our having free will such as our *willing* to both feel better and be more sociable. In this non-hypothetical real universe, human beings are limitedly both free and not free (causally determined) without the vicious reductionism. This reductionism begets a deterministic materialism that is rejected, for good reasons, by many physicists, biologists, and psychologists. Psychologist Roy Baumeister notes that "psychologists who retain a faith in [causal] determinism must keep this an *abstract belief* and violate it in practice: They must act as if people really make choices, as if multiple possibilities exist for future life . . ." and as if "[d]eterminism is not viable in practice but is an *elegant theory* that people may find appealing as an abstract article of faith."[72] And faith in a causally deterministic materialism (scientific materialism) is rendered senseless, scientifically and

---

71. Cf. Trundle's "Paradoxes of Human Nature," 181–86. This nature is affirmed *a posteriori*, coherently, not incoherently *a priori*.

72. Baumeister and Vohs, "Determinism is not Just Causality," para. 14, emphasis. Sadly, this exhaustive causal determinism, which is logically incoherent, is continually considered plausible.

philosophically, by Rutger University physicist Casey Blood. He singles out neuroscientists (although neuroscience philosophers are emphasized herein):

> Scientific materialism is the idea that nothing exists besides matter. This view is subscribed to by many scientists, particularly it seems to me, neuroscientists. In his book, *Consciousness; Creeping up on the Hard Problem*, the neuroscientist Jeffrey Gray says, "Worse, this line of thought risks leading back to a dualism [physical brain plus a non-physical origin for consciousness] whose rejection is widely seen as a major conquest in contemporary discussions of consciousness." . . . So the question is: Does the current state of physics support the idea of scientific materialism? . . . There is currently no evidence for particles, hidden variables, or collapse in physics. This means there is no support for the idea of a single-version, objective physical reality. As far as we currently know, it could well be . . . that there are many simultaneously existing versions of physical reality. . . . I would say that in spite of what we know of the *neural correlate* of consciousness in the brain, there is also no evidence in neuroscience that precludes dualism. Thus science offers no evidence in support of scientific materialism [or materialistic determinism supposed by many scientists]; it is . . . an article of faith . . . .[73]

The faith seems to be often disguised by neuroscience philosophers as a fact founded in science. The foregoing scientific, philosophical, and phenomenological points against that faith are ignored by many neuroscience philosophers such as Greene. He adds instead that he proposes "a 'dual-process' theory of moral judgment [wherein] deontological moral judgments (. . . with concerns for 'rights' and 'duties') are *driven* by automatic emotional responses"[74] versus "consequentialist moral judgments (. . . promoting the 'greater good')" that are "*driven* by more controlled cognitive processes." But besides these processes of cognition describing neuroscientist James Fallon who diagnosed himself as a psychopath and regretted not having empathized emotionally,[75] the usual academic arguments against the emotional are criticized by Ruth Barcan Marcus. She suggests that those glib stick-figure moral arguments all share a precise pseudo-rational "resolution without [an inexact] residue" where guilt is

---

73. Blood, "No Support for Scientific Materialism in Physics," para. 1–3.
74. See Greene, "Home Page," for this and the next quote, emphasis.
75. Cooper, "Neuroscientist Studying Brain Scans," Transcript.

allegedly inapt and "pangs of conscience are viewed, at best, as sentimental. But ... to insist that there is in every case a solution without [inexact] residue is false to the moral facts."[76] The facts are ignored by Greene. He notes that a tension in moral theory between deontology and consequentialism (one falsely thought tension is that doing the right thing per se conflicts with desirable consequences) "reflects an *underlying tension between dissociable systems in the brain*." He states that many "of my experiments employ moral dilemmas . . . that are designed to exploit this tension and reveal its psychological and neural underpinnings."[77]

Is Neuroscience Philosophy a Philosophy?

What are the underpinnings psychologically and neurologically of this neuroscience philosopher's *own* thought? The thought of Greene, which would be a causally determined phenomenon by his own self-refuting thought, amounts to cliché culture-of-death stuff with its depressing, predictable, *scientistic*, Skinnerian-Walden-Two promise of utopian behavioral manipulation and its naïve metaphysics of "matter alone is real" wherein nothing is alive as life is ordinarily understood. Would not "neural underpinnings" either explain or explain away the very position of this philosopher *cum* social scientist? If his philosophical position is wholly explicable through science (as is neuroscience itself), then his own position is not one of philosophy but rather is itself a phenomenon. Will this phenomenon be studied by neuroscientists and their studies studied by yet others and so forth *ad infinitum*? The infinite regress, in which the studies are not *about* causally determined phenomena but rather are themselves the phenomena to which neither "truth" nor "falsity" are ascribable, does not result from tackling the "easy problems" of consciousness. The regress results in part from ignoring what David Chalmers calls the hard problem. Why "are we subjects, and not just [objectifiable] objects? Why do we have subjective experiences? Descriptions of neurophysiology [as the easy problems] are all third-person—neurons do this, serotonin does that. Yet consciousness is experienced in the first person—'I,' not 'it.'"[78]

---

76. Marcus, *Modalities: Philosophical Essays*, 137.

77. Greene, "Home Page."

78. Egnor, "Materialist Neuroscience," para. 3. Cf. Chalmers, *The Conscious Mind*, ix–x. The "it" is denied and the "I" affirmed, by inference, in the work of Aquinas.

This senseless objectified "it" is denied by Husserl, Heidegger, and Sartre as well as by St. Thomas Aquinas. "Aquinas, if Étienne Gilson's Aquinas is right, shares a *non-humanist* existentialist outlook with Heidegger" and "although Heidegger has a 'negative' concept of finitude, his is unlike other negative concepts of finitude that are either skeptical or in which finitude is an impediment to knowledge."[79] Knowledge is not obstructed in terms of a "purified consciousness" that is confronted by a question of "how the mind 'constructs' 'the world' that it can explore in the immanence of the *I*."[80] If the *I* that is intrinsic to human consciousness were an "it" (phenomenon) unequivocally subject to scientific inquiries that presuppose the causal principle, then this principle would apply indisputably, too, to consciousness. There would be the odd upshot that free will is an illusion. The alleged illusion brings to mind not only many celebrated neuroscience philosophers but also, for example, the incoherent reductionism of both physicist Victor Stenger and psychologist B. F. Skinner.[81] Besides a Skinnerian materialism in which there is no truth since "truth" is not ascribed to phenomena but rather to statements, we recall (without denying a limitedly true causal principle) that this epistemic quandary for the neuroscience philosophy is vexed also by "truth" having as its truth-condition an entirely determined reality where contradictory truth-claims would be equally true because equally caused.

Caused as well would be the contrary claims that all cases of consciousness are material phenomena (understandable *in toto* in terms of the brain) and that no cases of consciousness are material phenomena where both claims would be paradoxically true because their truth-condition—the very condition for their "truth"—would be a deterministic physical reality that caused these neuroscience philosophers to claim whatever they claim. The claim in support of materialism in particular would mean that neuroscientists could not distinguish their consciousness as a

79. Hyde, review of Gilson's *The Metaphysical Presuppositions of Being-in-the-World*, para. 5.

80. Gueguen, "St. Edith Stein on Phenomenology and Scholasticism," 1–63.

81. Neuroscientists raised a strange specter of "free will" at their conference 12–14 Sep 2014 in Atlanta, "NEURO-INTERVENTIONS AND THE LAW." The conference questioned if "neuro-interventions" such as anti-psychotic drugs, should be used "to *make* someone who . . . lacks sufficient capacity into a fully responsible moral agent." The agency notwithstanding, the drugs might be construed as "*causing* persons to be morally responsible." One can appreciate how coherent possibilities may be a slippery slope to an incoherent determinism/materialism. Does not the phrase "cause persons to be responsible" seem as oxymoronic as "causing our freely made choices"? Emphasis.

phenomenon from phenomena they study. Nor in their study could they reason from a phenomenon of consciousness to consciousness as a theoretical entity (the entity being hypothetically inferable from phenomena by way of a weak realism). The realism herein holds that consciousness cannot be grasped as either an empirical phenomenon or a theoretical entity.

That neither this entity nor an empirical phenomenon are that to which consciousness can be reduced is 1) a phenomenological certainty, with implications for what it makes sense to say, by virtue of our immediate and incontrovertible self-conscious experience, 2) presupposed for the intelligibility of phenomena being revealed with an approximate objectivity, which is assumed paradoxically about neuroscience by the aforesaid neuroscience philosophers, by virtue of our non-conceptual and conceptual observational consciousness and 3) presupposed for observations being that by which theories can be corroborated, if not have strictly implied truths in terms of modal logic, whereby it is coherent to both compare theories and speak of their having increasing historical truth. This truth is illustratable by Einstein's theory being truer than Newton's, which was not falsified but restricted to a domain where Planck's constant is negligible and phenomena do not approach the speed of light, since *inter alia* the former theory is effective in both a Newtonian domain of classical phenomena and where phenomena *do* approach the speed of light. In short, in supposing absurdly that consciousness can be reduced to an empirical phenomenon, and by implication to a theoretical entity, the aforesaid neuroscience philosophy is not philosophy but rather a phenomenon for scientific study!

Modern Philosophy Misled into Mimicking Science

Science as an epistemological model for modern philosophy—indeed for the entire history of philosophy as its "paradigm knowledge-yielding enterprise,"[82] has led philosophy afar from fruitful insights. These insights often arose in ancient and medieval thought and bear on how approximately true scientific theories may be strictly implied by true (successful) observational predictions in terms of a common-sense modal logic. This logic is noted by E. A. Moody, for example, who "states that his analyses of 'Aristotle's *De Interpretatione* and *Analytica Posteriora* . . . [exhibit] some acute discussions of logical questions, especially those pertaining to

---

82. Suppe, "Afterword," 716.

modal arguments.'"[83] Some arguments, which include those of Thomas, are relevant to "if-then" statements that are stronger epistemologically than modern truth-functional implications; some of the implications being transposable into modal conditionals the truths of which are related to existential phenomenology.

Consider how this phenomenology allows for consciousness having a profound existential import for things *in themselves* in contrast to pivotal developments in the history of philosophy that influenced, for worse, some peculiar developments of neuroscience philosophy. Philosophy influences science and science has an effect on philosophy, the two-way impacts illustrated by Kant modeling his meditation of British Empiricism and Continental Rationalism on the Copernican Revolution. As this Revolution inverted key concepts of Ptolemaic astronomy by construing the sun as being passive and the orbiting earth as being active, there is likewise an alleged activity of our mind in acquiring knowledge. Knowledge is said to be acquired by the mind actively organizing, synthesizing and interpreting a raw material of experience. Reality is not known *in itself* (*Ding an sich*), according to Kant. Rather as it is interpreted by an *a priori* structure of mind. Kant tells us about the mind but, worsening Hume's skepticism of divorcing sensations from an external reality, nothing at all about this reality.

Reality, for Kant, is grasped as it appears (not as it is *in itself* by our unstructured non-conceptual consciousness), its appearance being determined by our mind whose structure consists of so-called categories. The categories, by acting *a priori* on experience as a prism acts on light, are said to produce judgments such as the causal principle that all events have causes. A causal regularity as such is presupposed universally for intelligible scientific inquiries, a point impressed on Kant's heirs. His heirs, however, inherited a comedy of errors of one unraveling setback after another such as the causal principle not being known to be true *about reality*. Reality was not known to be reflected truly by the principle for those who accepted, and continue to accept, Hume's dismissal of induction.

The anti-induction underscores that the principle's universality, essential for a scientific view of reality, is not validly inferable from *some* experienced events having causes. Causes being universally unknowable was allegedly resolved by Kant making the principle's epistemic status *a*

---

83. See Trundle's *Medieval Modal Logic & Science*, 86–87; Moody's *Studies in Medieval Philosophy*, 376; and Knuuttila's "Medieval Modal Theories and Modal Logic," 505–78.

priori; his situating the *a priori* in our mind: Our mind relates all events to causes by *synthesizing* a raw experience *a priori*, inducing the judgment "all events are caused," which is thus not known to be true about reality. This return to square one is a result of the *synthetic-a priori* nature of the judgment. The judgment "all events are caused," as *synthetic*, has different subject and predicate concepts and is not true logically. And in being *a priori*, it is *prior* to experience and not true empirically. Absent empirical and logically necessary truth, the causal principle was held falsely to be metaphysical and later meaningless; ignoring its status as an alethic modality whose denial is physically impossible.[84]

Aside from the physical impossibility, as noted later, existential phenomenology questions if we are *aware* of an *a priori* cognition, as we are of our thoughts. And if not, why Kant's idealism should not be deemed a defunct abstract theory as much as some theories of neuroscience. When theory clashes with our own ordinary self-awareness, no one but arcane academics would reject their simple experiential awareness in favor of theories; theories tested precisely by our *experiential awareness* and not the *awareness by theory*. In terms of the theory accepted by Kant, the situation is even worse because our mind having a structure amounted to a *ruse* for reconciling rationalism and empiricism, not to either relate theories to a consciousness of reality of which we are aware or resolve issues such as how predictive success may strictly imply true theories (some logicians lament that Kant, in articulating the category of *modality*, failed to re-discover the medieval modalities of modal logic addressed in the classical and medieval periods!).

In the classical/medieval periods there were philosophers who acknowledged our awareness, if not an awareness (consciousness) of our direct consciousness. Our self-consciousness, given Kant's notion of a structured mind, raises the erroneous specter of our consciousness having a structure. If it had a structure like the structured mind that was theorized by Kant and if a "structured consciousness" were that of which we are indirectly aware—the awareness being necessary to affirm we are conscious, then we would be aware of the consciousness but be unable to distinguish its structure from the structured properties, processes and relationships of the phenomena to which consciousness relates itself. But if direct consciousness has no structure, then it has no content that

---

84. The impossibility of the world or universe (universe(s)) not having a cause, which is not itself caused, strictly implies a first cause. Cf. Trundle, "Thomas' 2nd Way," 145–68.

interprets or skews reality. And if reality is not skewed, then consciousness both reveals reality as it really is and is a pure translucency.[85]

As a translucency, consciousness is not held to avoid the issue of existence as does Husserl.[86] Contrary to his phenomenology, existence is not bracketed ("disregarded") in the act of being conscious. In sum, consciousness is not a material phenomenon like a brain or structured cognitive entity, as the mind envisioned by Kant. And consciousness is not a Cartesian thinking thing, either, that deduces a self, God, or external world. One may object that a world which is knowable would be impossible, paradoxically, due to an unknowable consciousness that is *no thing*. This brings to mind a Platonic paradox that specifies our either already knowing or not knowing something: If we already know, then we cannot come to know and if we do not know, then we cannot come to know, either, since there would be no basis to discern falsity from truth.[87]

Though truth is thus founded by Plato in a pre-existing soul that recalls what it already knows, modern rationalists such as Descartes generally agreed that the mind contains that which is necessary to formulate self-evident principles for deducing information about reality. Reality is understood in a paradoxical manner by modern empiricists. They included Hume for whom knowledge, if there is any, would be acquired empirically from our sensations. A reliance on sensations led to *skepticism*, however, since universal truths are not inferable from finite sensations. And denying the sensations by relying on the mind's universal truths led to *dogmatism*, the truths not being known either *a posteriori* or *a priori*. So Kant's solution to the paradox was an *a priori* structure of the mind; *the worst of both worlds!* For the world is not known but rather our mind, ending in skepticism. And his notion that "there is an a priori structure of mind" is not known empirically or logically since it is *synthetic a priori* and thus metaphysical and dogmatic! How are dogmatism and skepticism avoided by existential phenomenology per the Platonic paradox and paradox mediated by Kant? The paradoxes seem to pose a unique problem herein for the analyses of consciousness. For the consciousness in terms existential phenomenology rejects both that consciousness is *no thing*, in not having a structure (or content), and that knowledge is derived from Humean sensations caused by an external reality. How can

---

85. Catalano, *A Commentary*," 34.
86. Boland, "Phenomenology and Philosophy," para. 4.
87. See Plato, "Meno," 363.

reality be revealed to consciousness? If the latter reveals reality as simply *being there*, how can knowledge arise and make the revelation significant epistemologically? An initial epistemological analysis of consciousness has thus far been examined. And this examination is the starting point for an exclusive development of a strong scientific realism. Reality will now be discussed in regard to multiple levels of consciousness.

Scientific Truth from a Non-Conceptual Consciousness of a *Thereness*

Reality as an undifferentiated *thereness* can be the object of direct consciousness. This consciousness is the most primordial level and, as the other levels of consciousness, is always related to something other than itself. Here, reality is not perceived as either a particular thing or collection of things in contrast, for example, to Kant's *a priori* category of quantity in which we allegedly always interpret reality in terms of one or more things. Noticing them as particular things, as F. I. Dretske suggests, involves conceptual activity and this activity is lacking at this most basic level, there being no doubting, thinking, believing, or knowing. And so this sheer consciousness of reality has only a potential epistemic significance; underscoring that physical reality is *coextensive* with its appearances but is *not* limited to them. In surpassing our knowledge of reality, a specter of reality that is revealed by this primal consciousness illustrates, for example, how scientific theories can be *underdetermined* by reality; reality possibly having empirical properties that are contradictory. That is, this elemental consciousness of reality explains how contradictory theories that are empirically equivalent may be inferred *a posteriori*, not *a priori* (incoherently), by a conceptual mode of consciousness in terms of an Under-determination-by-Data (UTD) Thesis.

This thesis, contrary to virtually all philosophers of science and scientists, is perfectly consistent with a robust scientific realism. This realism is one in which reality, for Sartre, is coextensive with its appearances but both is not limited to them and surpasses our knowledge. In Sartrean language, phenomena are reality (*Being*) as it conceptually appears. Appearances are coextensive with *Being* but *Being* is not limited to them. Thus *Being* exceeds our knowledge of them. And while metaphysics queries why existents are as they are, existential phenomenology (phenomenological ontology) describes *Being* itself, the conditions by which there is a world and so forth.[88] The existential phenomenology herein examines *inter alia* different modes of consciousness that provide a foundation for formulating metaphysical or scientific theories that are not vacuous without points of contact with reality. Reality itself is the source of this contact by virtue of a pre-conceptual consciousness of which there is an indirect but immediate and incontrovertible awareness.

An awareness of this fundamental mode of direct consciousness has immediate *ontological* import since reality is grasped as *being there* apart from our will, wish, or thought. Later thought about the *thereness* may result in construing it as an undifferentiated brute existence without meaning. We are in a world bereft of God, says Sartre, based on his inferring the *absolute* meaninglessness of brute existence; inducing his notorious notion of nausea. Nausea need not arise, however, either at the time or later upon reflection when brute existence is differentiated conceptually. A conceptual construal of the primary consciousness upon that reflection, may actually afford objective meanings of things. These things may permit, for example, strict modal inferences from them as second causes to a first-cause God. And this God, as noted later, may be a supreme norm of good by which we can differentiate more or less good things. That these things involve a conceptual construal of a more elemental mode of consciousness does not imply that reality is really all one and the same.[89] Both "same" and its synonyms are unsuitable as ultimate depictions of reality based on this most basic level of consciousness. Consciousness as a pure translucency in all of its modes, however, precludes Kant's distinction of *reality* from *reality as it appears* and Hume's divide of *external reality* from *internal sensations*. So there is no impasse of the perceived corresponding to a conceptualized world. Rather than the world having *a priori* univocal meanings, the existential phenomenology herein primarily posits a *thereness*, as an ontic basis, for potential descriptions that can be true.

---

88. Cf. Sartre, *Being and Nothingness*, 632, 634. Though Sartre does not address a UTD Thesis, he would presumably accept evidence-inferred contradictions. For contradictions and lesser threatening paradoxes, based *a posteriori* on our experience, are endemic to existentialist revolts against a perennial rationalism imposed *a priori* on reality.

89. Barnes, *An Existentialist Ethics*, 237. An atheistic aspect of Sartre's ethics, as noted earlier, does not follow *prima facie* from his basic phenomenological analysis of direct and indirect consciousness. Nonetheless, his analysis of *mauvaise foi* is insightful and penetrating.

True descriptions of a *differentiated* reality can arise potentially from our consciousness of reality as an utterly *undifferentiated mass or thereness*. The formless *thereness*, which does not strictly reflect Sartre's position but is consistent with it, is addressed by the eminent Sartre scholar and existential phenomenologist Hazel Barnes. She remarks that when Sartre "writes abstractly on the fundamentals of his ontology [apart from our consciousness], he states definitively that *Being-in-itself* . . . is undifferentiated mass."[90] Thus, although the higher levels of consciousness with immediate ontic and epistemic import reveal "differentiation, meaning, and plurality for *Being*,"[91] the *Being* at these higher levels of consciousness—which are so habitual as to go virtually unnoticed—do not obviate an amorphous reality of which we can be conscious. This consciousness is further discussed by Barnes who considers our ordinary responses. Since "one's usual responses do not rush in to prevent it, the original encounter of consciousness with the world takes place," she says, "stripped of the overlay of associations—or at least more nearly so than is normally possible."[92] Barnes enlarges on this: "This escape from conceptual habits may come about as the result of fasting, systematic contemplation [as in the East] . . . or a number of other causes as well as through drugs . . . ." Using drugs, meditation, or other methods to obtain a consciousness stripped of its conceptual habits does not, however, reveal the unreality of a so-called world of particular things ("things objectively at hand" per Heidegger's *vorhanden*) that are ordinarily noticed. Consider why this is the case after clarifying a consciousness of *aspects* of phenomena.

The *Thereness* of Phenomena and Its Aspects

The following analysis of aspects of phenomena establishes both that existentialism is not the irrational muddle portrayed by many Anglo-American philosophers and that inferences are validly drawn from an existential phenomenology of *Being* that, reflecting Sartre's position

---

90. Barnes, *An Existentialist Ethics*, 235, emphasis.

91. Sartre, *Being and Nothingness*, xx, emphasis.

92. For this quote and the next one, see Barnes, *An Existentialist Ethics*, 233–35. While her discussion largely uses the word "consciousness," "awareness" is often used here because: "awareness" is more common colloquially, is used by non-phenomenologists who are sympathetic to phenomenology to whom this essay refers, and helps clarify indirect from direct consciousness—as in our indirect *awareness* of direct *consciousness*.

that *Being* overflows its interpretations, are inferences often drawn quite differently from his. My conclusions *mediate* between, not Sartre's but rather, a Sartrean *non-conceptual* consciousness of an undifferentiated reality and reality having differentiated aspects of which we may be *conceptually* conscious (à la John Compton's phenomenology[93]). The aspects of which we are *conceptually conscious*, which includes phenomena having "individuality" and "extension," is a consciousness *infused* with a *non-conceptual consciousness* of those aspects. And in both cases we are indirectly aware of that direct consciousness. My mediation between the Sartrean and Compton positions underpins Compton's idea of an objective *pre-scientific* consciousness (he largely uses the term "awareness"). My mediation bears on a direct awareness or consciousness without concepts that agrees with Sartre's existential phenomenology; explaining why observation is not skewed by being theory-laden or, worse, theory-dependence. The latter, which are theses in the philosophy of science, collide head-on with objective observation and our phenomenological experience.

We experience ourselves as being aware of our *conceptual* consciousness of things. And since things are experienced ordinarily as really being as they appears to be, in terms of aspects such their individuality and independence of what we think, this consciousness is inferably infused with a *non-conceptual* consciousness of aspects that are really there. Indeed, we need not rely on inference since, at other times, we are straightforwardly aware of our non-conceptual consciousness of those aspects. Thus besides the aspects, we are equally aware of a *transformation* from our being non-conceptually conscious of an undifferentiated reality to a reality having those aspects. A transformation to the aspects, which can be induced by boredom or drugs, may be shattered by, say, physical sensations. A sensation of hunger may prompt us to snap into being conscious of the aspects in order get food; recalling that we are aware *of* the transforming consciousness even if the latter is still not conceptual. While the aspects are not always conceptualized, they are revealed by a purely translucent consciousness. *Pari passu* the aspects are literal manifestations of reality that are not noticed as given things by conceptual activity. The activity's absence in our non-conceptual awareness of the aspects, which mediates between the Sartrean and Compton positions, has both immediate ontological import and an import closer

---

93. Compton, "Natural Science," 90–91.

to an epistemological state of noticing things than a consciousness of reality's undifferentiated *thereness*.

The *thereness* of reality bears indirectly on reality overflowing its theoretical interpretations and renders plausible phenomena being underdetermined even by empirically equivalent theories that, while contradictory, may nonetheless both be true (by virtue of inferences *a posteriori* from phenomena to theories in terms of a UTD Thesis). The Thesis reflects Sartre's "transphenomenality of *Being*" where *Being* is "not exhausted by any or all its appearances [because *Being*] always overflows whatever knowledge we have of it."[94] But there is a direct ontological significance of an immediate *thereness* of aspects with profound implications when, for example, the aspects are particular manifestations of reality with a structure; keeping in mind that a structure of the aspects could not be discerned *in themselves* if there was a structure of our consciousness analogous to a Kantian structured mind. And so this mind is not consciousness and this mode of consciousness, given its being a pure translucency, has a potential epistemic import in terms of the aspects informing, or lending themselves to, *conceptually objective* delineations of everyday things. Accordingly, let me reiterate that although I am indebted to Compton for his insightful and cogent case that these aspects reflect our everyday pre- (non-)scientific experience, the experience is not related by him to our *non-conceptual* awareness of the aspects; my arguing precisely that this awareness is infused into an awareness of pre-scientific conceptualized things.

These things as well as phenomena subject to scientific inquiry have a structure typified by the aspects of *continuity, extensiveness, individuality,* and *independence*.[95] Their significance for scientific realism is noted after describing each of them. *Independence* is reminiscent of Sartre's notion of the "coefficient of resistance" whereby the more resistance there is to our will, the more our will is that of which we are aware. We are non-conceptually aware of reality not conforming to our intentions in terms of their contrast to our consciousness of things *being as they are* independently of our will, wish, or thought. Nor does our thought control an aspect's *individuality* which refers to our being non-conceptually conscious of a thing's boundaries (borders, edges, or peripheries).

---

94. See Sartre, *Being and Nothingness*, xx, emphasis.
95. Compton, "Natural Science," 90–91.

Insofar as there are things to which we relate our consciousness (*its* relating *itself*, for Sartre), we relate it to things with boundaries. And boundaries bear on extensiveness. *Extensiveness* means that to be conscious without concepts of something is to be aware of it as occupying a volumetric region of lived space and time. Inasmuch as time and space are lived, we are aware also of the aspect of *continuity*. In presaging the notion of causality, *continuity* refers to a consciousness of things changing or evolving and as being differentiated from a background region to which they are related. In short, we are indirectly but, at the same time, undeniably aware *of* our sheer pre-conceptual consciousness of the aforesaid aspects. These aspects are patently manifest to us by phenomena that change, occupy volumetric regions, have boundaries and "are as they are" independently of our intentions (will, wish, or thought).

Phenomena Seen$_n$ (Non-Epistemologically) in the Analytic Tradition

Intentions related to our conceptual conscious are discussed after discussing how a non-conceptual consciousness of the aspects of something is fortified by comparing it to a current analysis of another philosopher in a vastly different philosophical tradition. This tradition is that of analytic philosophy which was pioneered by the later Wittgenstein. An analysis that reminds us of his appeal to ordinary language is articulated by F. I. Dretske. Dretske's analysis of a non-conceptual awareness is strikingly similar to that of existential phenomenology. He says, "I have occasionally been in such a preoccupied state that as I walked [I was] unaware of everything around me," only after "snapping out of the fog" there being a realization "I had been seeing certain things without being [conceptually] aware of it; that is, I can remember having seen things, but I cannot remember being aware . . . that things were looking a certain way to me."[96] Clearly, "things looking a certain way," despite no *conceptual* awareness, is like an awareness without concepts of things with individuality, borders, regions of occupation, and so forth as noted by existential phenomenology.

---

96. As previously noted, the words "awareness" and consciousness" may be used interchangeably. See Dretske, *Seeing and Knowing*, 11. Dretske's case for being aware of things without concepts, which is the basis for objectivity, is disputed vainly by G. N. A. Vesey for whom all seeing is *seeing as* (noticing conceptually).

The phenomenology, in turn, echoes the analytic account of "snapping out of the fog" and "remembering things looking a certain way." We snap out by intentionally relating our awareness to either different levels of consciousness or diverse things. And "things looking a certain way," as recalled, is explicable also by our being able to remember distinct aspects of things of which we were non-conceptually conscious. This consciousness relies on an indirect awareness; an awareness *of* that direct consciousness, *a recognition of which is needed by F. I. Dretske's, otherwise admirable, analytic account.* This account's tenability is shown by the case of Johnny. He does not either think about or conceptually notice what he sees, as he rides in the back of a car driven by his mother.

The mother, looking in the rear-view mirror, sees him looking out the window where his father works. When he asks why he did not see the workplace, is the mother's reply senseless that he saw but did not notice, it? Where *D* denotes workplace and *S* an agent such as Johnny, Dretske notes that *D*'s looking some way to *S* presupposes merely a sentient agent with a suitable visual ability in which workplace *D* occupies *S*'s visual field. "It presupposes or entails nothing about whether *S* notices *D*, whether he takes, or is inclined to take, *D* to be something in particular, or whether he exploits his visual experience in any way . . . ."[97] The various ways that our visual experience is exploitable, says Dretske, includes different types of thoughts (including judgments, interpretations, beliefs, doubts, regrets and so forth) that may be aroused by the conceptual differentiations of something that we saw. To say that we *saw* something *without* either the differentiation or thoughts, though, is *not to say* something senseless, much less logically incoherent. And it is equally coherent, consequently, to affirm both a non-epistemic seeing (seeing$_n$), noted by Dretske, and, beyond what he addresses, a non-conceptual awareness of which itself we are indirectly aware. Thus, although we cannot be aware conceptually and not be non-conceptually aware, per the previous discussions, we can be aware non-conceptually and *not be* aware conceptually. The latter insight is certifiable by our immediate phenomenological experience since conceptual and non-conceptual awareness are both that of which we are indirectly but immediately and unassailably aware.

Finally, both modes of awareness imply the same insight: A non-epistemic (or non-conceptual) awareness of something, as it is apart from our will, wish, or thought, is *infused* into an observational awareness of

---

97. Ibid., 21.

the thing when it is noticed conceptually. Conceptual observations would otherwise have no known contact with reality or be subject prima facie to our subjective experience. "If one's past experience, one's conceptual categories, modes of classification, and habits of association have any influence on what one believes," continues Dretske, "they thereby have a commensurate influence on what one can see in the epistemic way of seeing [seeing$_e$]."[98]

The Tradition of Seeing$_e$ (Epistemologically)

Seeing in the epistemic mode in which *inter alia* things are noticed implies that what we see conceptually is relative, more or less, to biases of past experience. This experience prompts the inference, says Dretske, that persons with radically different belief systems or cultural frameworks could not see the same things if there were no non-epistemic seeing. The sophisticate and the savage as well as the expert and novice looking at the same thing would see different things. And this is but a prelude to an unadulterated sophism which specifies that our observational truth-claims are relative to our private perceptual worlds.[99] The notion that these worlds are that to which truth is relative is logically incoherent if not trivial.

The notion is trivial if each person's or group's decreed truth is true necessarily since each person or group, respectively, would be the truth-condition for truth. And it is logically incoherent if truths that are contradictory are accepted *a priori*. Not either an *a priori* assent to violating the principle of non-contradiction or the assent to triviality need be accepted, though, to accept a reasonably restricted relativity inherent in other ways of seeing (other conceptual ways of discerning) without undermining the general objectivity of our observational awareness. We can have an awareness that is public, certifiable, impartial, objective and communicable despite clashing worldviews by virtue precisely of a *non-conceptual* awareness, of which we are indirectly aware, of the same events or objects.

Objects actually resembling our observational awareness of them without concepts, as proposed in existential phenomenology, may provoke a skeptical question: How we can *know* that reality is really

---

98. Ibid., 76.
99. Ibid., 76–77.

differentiated as we are non-conceptually aware of it? The short answer is that if we are *not* aware of reality as it really is *in itself*, at least roughly, a sophism returns in which truth is relative to perceptual worldviews of either individuals or groups that precludes the cooperation and communication that do in fact occur; including ironically a communication of the skeptical question. The longer answer is that our phenomenology does not base an abstract theory of reality on either another abstract theory of knowledge or vice versa. Rather, knowledge is based on both a non-conceptual direct consciousness of *something in itself* and an indirect awareness of both that *thing* and consciousness of *it*; where *it* can be conceptually measured against the conceptual consciousness of *it*. That is, in being conscious of something directly, we are indirectly aware both of the thing we are conscious of without concepts and, concurrently, of a conceptualization of the thing. In terms of a conceptualization, the thing conceptualized is thus comparable to the *thing itself* of which we are also indirectly aware: To be indirectly aware is to be aware of a sheer consciousness of something, without concepts, which is infused into a conceptual consciousness of the *thing*.

3

Consciousness and a Robust Realism in Science

Scientific realism, as John Compton says in *Phenomenology in America*,[1] involves conceptually noticing the aspects of things that include their individuality, continuity and so on. Our consciousness of a thing's aspects *without concepts* is, herein, infused into a conceptual consciousness where the aspects are *conceptualized*. The conceptualizations contrast to the thing's having *a priori* essences either by ready-made meanings (myth of the given) or by sensory stimuli causing us to express sentences about what we see, per a radical Humean empiricism of Feyerabend: External stimuli are said to cause sensorial *sentences* recast as true or false *statements* by possibly contradictory theories. Instead of a theory-dependence and relativism, our existential phenomenology posits a robust realism for conceptualizations in science and a weak relativism for everyday things. These things need not be restricted to discourse that is incoherently relativistic where "'good reasons' for belief or action must be 'culturally'" defined by the "external community rather than in the internal logic of the discourse."[2] Or again, relativistic discourse is related by Gábor Kutrovátz

---

1. Noting that after WW II and "the explosion of my father's ambiguous creation [winning the Nobel Prize in physics for helping develop the first self-sustaining atomic chain reaction]," the late John Compton stated that "the world—insofar as I would have any part in it—needed more reflection and more emphasis on the values for which we live rather than the development of scientific knowledge." See his "Natural Science and the Experience of Nature," 89–94. See also Jim Patterson, "John Compton, Charter Faculty Member of Vanderbilt Philosophy Department, has Died."

2. See a classical critique of relativism by Dixon, "Is Cultural Relativism Self-refuting?" 75–88.

to "post-Kuhnian studies of science" which, taken literally, "implies that all . . . aspects of science are relative to the social and cultural context . . . ."[3] The contextual relativism herein, however, is a species of realism that is benignly relative to a culture where the speech truly works.

Inference from Scientific Success to the Success of a Benign Cultural Relativism

Before examining everyday conceptualizations that truly work, consider truly working successful scientific theories. The theories were related hitherto to successful observational predictions and the predictions to a realist reading of truth by a commonsense modal reasoning. This reasoning is illustrated by an epistemic conditional in modal logic: "Necessarily if a theory makes systematically true predictions (P), then the theory is approximately true (T)," denoted $P \Rightarrow T$ where $\Rightarrow$ signifies strict implications. While the implications are based on observational truth and this truth is likewise a basis for truth-claims about everyday things, our routine success in using these things does not exclude the claims being limitedly relative to cultural contexts. Thus, although this contextual relativism does not hold for propositions of physics (where laws (L) comprise a theory construed as a proposition ($L_1 \wedge L_2 \ldots$) that permits a truth-ascription, at least hypothetically[4]), consider how the relativism may permit objective truth but limit our daily conceptualizations.

Conceptualizations of soup cans in Compton's phenomenology would, in our phenomenology, suppose a non-conceptual awareness of a can's aspects. Keeping in mind, as Compton notes, there "seems to be a continuing presupposition of [some] convergence between scientific ontology and the ontology of the prescientific life-world,"[5] the aspects bear on how the can is *in itself* apart from our will, wish or thought (*independence*), occupying a volumetric region of space and time (*extensiveness*), and having a boundary (*individuality*). The individualized boundary

---

3. Kutrovátz, *An Epistemological Cross-Section of Science Studies*, 10, fn. 26.

4. While a mathematical physics should not be an epistemic ideal for all knowledge, its propositions do have uniquely clear meanings, within its proper contexts, wherein physicists who speak different languages, as in the film *Torn Curtain*, can still communicate *via* the propositions of a theory. And the theory can have a truth-value in truth-functional propositional logic when laws (L) are conjuncts of a proposition ($L_1 \wedge L_2 \wedge L_3 \ldots$) where $\wedge$ denotes "and."

5. John Compton, "Reinventing the Philosophy of Nature," 3–28.

relates to the can's flat ends that cause it to sit on the shelf securely or, by its cylindrical shape, to be insecure because under certain conditions that shape may cause it to roll (*continuity*). Continuity and individuality bear also on a background region discernible from the can by the can's metallic top and red front with letters that, when noticed, spell the name of a given soup. The concept of "soup can," much more conceptualized aspects of the can, nevertheless, has an import that is relative marginally to practical purposes; purposes arising in cultural praxes.

While the customs and conventions of different cultures may determine whether "soup can" has a meaning, the meaning is not inherent in the aspects by which that thing is conceptually discerned. Children learn to discern soup cans in our culture as things that contain potentially warm liquid to consume. This consumptive potential may be foreign to aborigines, though, although aborigines can still be said to see non-epistemologically (see$_n$) or, alternatively, to be conscious non-conceptually *of the same thing*! Seeing the *same aspects* of a thing without concepts enables a conceptual construal of the "can" by the aborigine as, say, something to carry water. Recall the film *The Gods Must be Crazy*, for example, in which an aborigine and white Australians can be said, in a sense, to have seen the same thing when they saw an empty "coke bottle" in the outback. They *saw* the "bottle," but *not conceptually* as the same thing. While a thing's meaning may often be relative to diverse cultures, this does not involve either arbitrary practices or conceptual constructions that are irrelevant to how reality *really is*. Indeed, there is a political correctness in the West that advances a social constructionism in which everything, from "gender" to "family," is an arbitrary social construct with meanings entirely relative to cultures.

A Relativistic Political Correctness vs. a Credible Cultural Relativism

Consider a credible cultural relativism after an influential and still prevalent one that flies in the face of all credibility. Where two cultures are designated by Θ and Ψ, a radical social constructionism holds that sentence S can be true in Θ and false in Ψ where "Θ" and "Ψ" determine the truth or falsity of S. That is, S has these different cultures as its truth-conditions. These conditions, we need to stress, are not universal conditions for "truth" such as our psycho-biological nature. This nature is a condition for making *evidenced-based* inferences, for instance, to *S*'s truth-value by medical doctors who must make life-or-death decisions. Rather, "Θ" and "Ψ" refer to cultures that arbitrarily reflect either uninformed opinions of persons or political ideologies, as strictly documented about women's studies by Daphne Patai and Noretta Koertege (the latter studied with Sir Karl Popper at the University of London, is Professor Emerita of Indiana University's History and Philosophy of Science Department as well as Editor Emerita of journal *The Philosophy of Science*).[6] Both of these women pioneered women's studies until, they say, politically correct feminists proselytized social construction as an all-inclusive ideological *Weltanschauung* in order to obliterate any significant psycho-biological differences of men from women. This was aptly called BIODENIAL.

Given the BIODENIAL, one can appreciate the menace to society by social constructionists in higher education who arrogantly and fraudulently endeavor to impose their views on students, from women's health (or ill health) to meanings of the family (anything goes), by a truth or falsity of *S* that they insist is relative to, and a fabrication of, cultures Θ and Ψ—*not* by sentence *S* having a truth-value based on the psycho-biological reality of human nature and the natures of men and women. Happily, from "either a biological or cultural point of view . . . the feminist project of androgyny is ultimately doomed. But that doesn't mean that it can't do harm in the meantime," states Stanley Kurtz.[7] He adds pessimistically, "In America, many boys are slipping behind in school; their sisters are significantly more likely to go on to college" and yet "thanks largely to the influence of academic feminists . . . resources still flow disproportionately to supposedly victimized girls. In the end," he says, "gender won't disappear, whatever the mavens of women's studies hope, but the careers of some bright young men probably will." Will women suffer too? Women will suffer as well as men. Men and women will not only *not* fulfill their psycho-biological natures but also inflict irrevocable harm on their natures. Thus in uniquely explicating how our nature is a

---

6. See Koertege and Patai, *Professing Feminism*, 135. Patai is a Distinguished Professor in the Department of Languages, Literatures and Cultures at the University of Massachusetts. She is renowned for her insights on the politicization of education. In higher education, sadly but unsurprisingly, there were reports of feminists at some universities destroying this book in their libraries. The eminent logician, philosophy professor, and law professor Susan Haack said that *Professing Feminism* could not be glibly dismissed by feminists.

7. See Kurtz commonsensical "Can We Make Boys and Girls Alike?" The following two quotes are from this work.

truth-condition, by both a commonsense modal reasoning and existential phenomenology, one would hopefully reflect on their contributions herein.

Herein, a defense of both a *neutral element* in our awareness of reality, which is free of *conceptual constructs*, and reasoning from success to truth challenges compellingly the "now widely accepted conjecture that [even] mathematics is a social construct," as said by prominent international scholars who add that this fiasco is made worse by the "mind itself [being supposedly] a social construct" and by a "more accepted notion that the self is a social construct."[8] These constructs, they say dismayingly, "seem transparent to persons educated in the postmodern world...." The world in last century or so has witnessed daunting returns to sophistical relativisms, dressed anew, that stem largely from Anglo-American academics who have ignored commonsensical modes of reasoning and, most pointedly, our existential phenomenological experience. This experience goes far beyond the received views of rationalism, empiricism, Kant, pragmatism, logical positivism, and analytic philosophy.

Dretske is a refreshing exception in his analyses of awareness that amplify existential phenomenology. This phenomenology bears fruitfully on an astonishing range of issues that include unique ways for certifying the reality of free will, although free will was oddly argued for by both the atheist Sartre and the theist St. Augustine in his *De libero arbitrio* (*libri tres*). Free will, though, was relegated by Kant to an unknowable thing-in-itself (*noumenon*) along with the self, good, and God. So let me reiterate that the phenomenology herein does not muddle free will and mind in a Cartesian way, much less reject free will in a reductive pseudo-scientific (*scientistic*) way. Also, this phenomenology replaces abstract theories of mind by relating free will to our self-awareness; appealing to the integrity of our own immediate, unassailable, conscious experience.

This experience indicates that the aspects of reality of which we are non-conceptually conscious do not determine a univocal import of things *a priori*. Rather, the aspects are a basis for ascribing *a posteriori* a certain significance to things in different cultures. So while there is a limited cultural relativism, this is not a top-down reasoning like a politically correct sophism. By the cliché "man is the measure," Protagoras and his heirs today hold that conflicting truths are acceptable *a priori* when reasoning from truth-claims to reality rather than, as in realism,

---

8. For this and the next quote see Bauchspies, Van Bendegem, and Restivo's "The Sociology and Philosophy of Mathematics Revisited," 1–3.

reasoning from reality upward to the claims (parodied in the corporate world, when someone ignores the specs, by the words "Don't bother me with the facts, my mind is made up!"). And thus while the import and meaning of particular things such as a soup may be relative to a given culture, in that culture we can still straightforwardly falsify or verify the truth of the truth-claim that, say, there is a soup can on this counter.

Persons in different cultures, nevertheless, are not exhaustively conditioned—much less causally determined, by those cultures to conceptually discern certain things with only a culture's associated meanings; reminding us, by contrast, of the deterministic paradigms (or later, disciplinary matrices) espoused by Kuhn and the sensory stimuli stressed by Feyerabend. Aside from Feyerabend, it is noted that Kuhn "held scientific change to be law-like" whereby we can call this "aspect of Kuhn's historicism *determinist* (in a parallel with Marx)."[9] If the causal determinism of Kuhn and Feyerabend were the case, their own creative ideas would be inexplicable. In echoing Hume's empiricism, which excluded a creativity that presupposes free will (since thinking is a species of sensation and sensorial ideas are caused), Feyerabend illustrates a creative but incoherent idea by holding that sensory stimuli *cause* sensations. And these sensations he says, *cause* scientists to express sensorial sentences that have no truth-values until the values arise by sentences becoming statements because of their interpretation by theories. Theories are also instilled deterministically into students via Kuhn's creative ideas. These paradoxically preclude creativity and imagination by paradigms that cause students to accept various *Weltanschaaungen*.

Weltanschaaungen as worldviews involve the notion that "one can only think what one's language permits you to think, and indeed forces you to think."[10] When we think, however, are we not actually phenomenologically aware both of our thinking and our freedom to think or not think? Readers can answer this question for themselves by their own unassailable self-conscious experience. Can anyone doubt that this experiential phenomenology is badly needed in Anglo-American culture, if not its philosophers? This philosophy notwithstanding,[11] creativity is commonsensically explicable in terms of our self-consciousness. As to

9. Bird, "Kuhn and the Historiography of Science," Abstract.

10. Wilkins, "Metaphysical Determinism," para. 1.

11. This is to say, with the notable exception of F. I. Dretske and several other eminent Anglo-American philosophers in the pragmatic-positivist-analytic tradition who are noted herein.

be conscious of our own behavior is to be tacitly conscious of our will to behave or not behave in given ways, so too, to be conscious of something is to be conscious implicitly of our will to either signify or not signify the thing in given ways. This bears on imagination. While imagining something is suggested by Sartre to involve an *intentionality of consciousness*, as if consciousness is unrelated to *us as whole human beings*, a less Cartesian-like dualism of consciousness and body is that insofar as we are aware of our intentionally relating *ourselves* to something with one meaning, we are aware also of possibly relating *ourselves* to the thing with other meanings. The meaning of Chianti bottles as containers of euphoric-inducing tart wine is relatable by us to other meanings as well, say culinarily as a flavor for food as well as pragmatically or aesthetically as ornate candleholders.

The candleholder example aside, let there be a brief response to an objection that there is body-consciousness dualism before discussing our freedom from a deterministic culture. Recall that we are said to be indirectly aware of our direct consciousness as both relatable to things other than itself and not being those things. This self-consciousness does not imply a dualism. The purported dualism is avoided by our phenomenological experience since when we are directly conscious of our bodies we are implicitly aware that our bodies are not identical to our consciousness but also that our consciousness functions in a bodily context; in a context of, or backdrop to, consciousness. Consciousness is not experienced phenomenologically as a void, as one isolated half of a dualistic self. A unified self, *pace* Sartre, is evidenced not only by one's own experience of oneself as a unity but also by the anti-dualist way we speak. The "I" of which I speak does not ordinarily refer to a body without consciousness or a consciousness without a body. The body and consciousness may be differentiated *conceptually* but not either *non-conceptually* or when we are conceptually engaged in activity. In this activity, by analogy, St. Augustine suggests that we are aware of our existence as one inseparable life but that, "as a subject for mental exercise," we can be conceptually aware of ourselves as a tripartite separable life of "being, knowledge, and will."[12]

Will is not identical to consciousness, either, but consciousness is a necessary condition for it. In being aware of our consciousness as both related to things other than itself and not being those things, however, our self-consciousness is *free from* a deterministic cultural conditioning

---

12. See St. Augustine, *Confessions*, 318.

as well as a conditioning by either sensory stimuli or scientific paradigms. While neither the paradigms nor stimuli condition us deterministically, this point does not avert habits of consciousness making conceptual distinctions that are typical of a given culture or subculture. In the subculture of a research university, for example, there is the habitual distinctions of books and students slumped in chairs along hallways of which we are also non-conceptually conscious (in terms of their aspects). And we are aware indirectly of being directly conscious of our concepts of particular things in these contexts. Continuous reflection on everyday conceptual activity, though, would make the activity impossible. It would be impossible to successfully stop for a red light when driving a car, for example, if we were always reflecting on our consciousness. Though routine conceptual activity may be mistaken, the mistakes are not often. If they were often, we could not enjoy the successful habitual activities that we do.

Habitual conceptualizations, which are occasionally wrong, can illuminate the defense of an epistemic realism in which reality *is* as it *is* independently of what we will, wish, or think. The *less* we need to interpret what we see by virtue of being repeatedly consciousness of it as a certain thing, the *greater* is the surprise when making a mistake. In being mistaken about our own automobile by entering the wrong one, due to their having similar aspects, we are reminded of our observational consciousness having a touchstone with reality. When reality conflicts with a routine perceptual conceptualization, we are shocked out of being mesmerized by mundane activity. The activity ceases momentarily and we recall that reality has an aspect of *independence*; that there is a basis in reality for distinguishing things of which we are consciousness. This consciousness would never reach a level of permitting our routine manipulation of things, with an assurance they are *really there*, if they were not reflected truly by our conceptualizing consciousness, at least regularly, and if our consciousness could not be occasionally incorrect.

Whether we are incorrect or not about what we observe, we are nevertheless indirectly aware of both our *conceptualizations* of the thing and the non-conceptualized *thing itself*. The *thing itself* is thus *comparable* to its conceptualization by our indirect awareness, explaining why ordinarily there is no doubt about what we see in a way evocative of Wittgenstein's *On Certainty*: One might say "I'm certain it's 3 AM" or "I know it is" only if there is some possible doubt; this, bearing on G. E. Moore's holding up his hand and declaring "I know I have a hand," apart from any doubt and decried as senseless by Wittgenstein. He also criticized as senseless the "I doubt . . ." apart from the "I know . . ." of Descartes. While Descartes starts his metaphysics by a radical doubt ("thinking"), existential phenomenology holds that this thinking presupposes paradoxically his irrefutable awareness of both his direct consciousness of his self and of his doubting). The doubting of Descartes means he was already as aware of his existence as his systematic doubt: There can be no doubt without an awareness of it but there can be awareness without doubt, so doubt is not as basic as awareness. And a self-awareness (consciousness)—an indirect consciousness of a direct consciousness of something without concepts— is that with which metaphysicians should begin their query about reality; where the relation of reality to conceptual activity is grounded. In terms of this grounding there is no err in saying ordinarily that the sun rises. The "rising sun" is rooted in a consciousness of it without concepts. In a conceptual state, that consciousness may be construed as a bright yellow disk and horizon moving in opposite directions.

A directional motion of the two entities involves an awareness without concepts that is infused into our conceptual awareness. So an awareness of the phenomenon's aspects may be conceptualized ordinarily as the rising sun. Whereas saying that the sun is rising in an everyday setting may signify that it's time to get up, wherein getting up and the sun rising can be expressed as true statements, scientists will more carefully conceptualize that of which they are *literally aware without concepts*; not a rising yellow sun or disc but rather a disk and horizon "moving apart," which is verifiable by naked-eye reports in the context of science. Scientific theories often explain what scientists are conceptually aware of in a way largely independent of everyday concepts. Still, these concepts have a success and efficacy which presuppose that everyday activity is rooted in reality due to its aspects being manifest non-conceptually to our direct consciousness of which we are also aware. And this self-awareness (self-consciousness) is the foundation likewise for empirical and theoretical state descriptions of physical systems that may predict, manipulate and explicate phenomena by scientific theories. How theories reflect reality is now addressed.

Relativism vs. a Phenomenological and Logical Support of Realism

The following section spotlights well established (mature) scientific theories by way of, among other things, the accounts of Rohrlich and

Hardin.[13] Here, in terms of our self-consciousness (awareness), theories would be composed of theoretical constructs that are derived both from an observed reality with conceptual activity and this activity from a non-conceptually observed reality. In virtue of reality being composed of things that have the common aforesaid aspects (such as continuity, extensiveness, individuality, and independence), as noted by Compton,[14] scientists can in effect conceptualize something's aspects such that they notice a specific phenomenon. The above-noted phenomenon of a disk (sun) and horizon (earth) "moving apart" illustrates how theories relate to phenomena of which we are *non-conceptually conscious* because it bears on the geocentric and heliocentric theories. Both theories are viable interpretations of the phenomenon per se, rooted ultimately in that non-conceptual consciousness. This led to the theories having an extra-scientific significance for our *conceptual consciousness*. In having this consciousness of the sun in contemplative moods, since the time of the Copernican Revolution, persons have often been induced to be intellectually insecure insofar as we are not at the center of the universe as we had prided ourselves to be.

In summary, scientists can conceptualize aspects of things, of which they are non-conceptually conscious, as distinct observable phenomena. And these phenomena can in turn be conceptualized as theoretical entities, properties, and processes of theories. When taken with theoretical descriptions of physical systems and rules of logical deducibility, the phenomena can be predicted, manipulated, and explicated by mature or established theories.[15] Their use involves coordinating empirical with theoretical descriptions, in a context of higher mathematics, which have concepts clear enough for sound formalizations. Consider how a formalized modal reasoning strictly implies ($\Rightarrow$) a theory's approximate truth after showing how true empirical descriptions are coordinated with a theory and how it can materially imply ($\supset$) empirical predictions e_2:[16]

$$[e_1 \wedge (e_1 \approx t_1) \wedge (t_1 \wedge T_0 \vdash t_2) \wedge (t_2 \approx e_2)] \rightarrow e_2$$

13. Rohrlich and Hardin, "Established Theories" S33–S49.
14. Compton, "Natural Science," 89–94
15. Cf. Rohrlich, Fritz and Larry Hardin. "Established Theories," 603–16.
16. With the caveat that a strict implication ($\Rightarrow$) for the schema below is mine, in lieu of a weaker material implication ($\rightarrow$), this schema simplifies one used by Stephen Körner. See his *Experience and Theory*, 194–95.

To wit: Let e_1 denote empirical state descriptions that, describing physical systems at *present times*, are taken with ($\wedge$) and treated *as if* they are identical to ($\approx$) theoretical state descriptions t_1 ($e_1 \approx t_1$). Then, t_1 is both taken with ($\wedge$) a given theory T_0 and the rules of logical deducibility ($\vdash$) to yield theoretical state descriptions (predictions) t_2. And t_2 is treated *as if* it is identical to the empirical state descriptions e_2 ($t_2 \approx e_2$). All of the latter $[e_1 \wedge (e_1 \approx t_1) \wedge (t_1 \wedge T_0 \vdash t_2) \wedge (t_2 \approx e_2)]$ are the conditional's antecedent. And it implies ($\rightarrow$) the predictions e_2 of the physical systems' states at *future times*.

If *future times* of the systems result in true predictions of e_2 and if e_2 represents the systematically true predictions of T_0, then an approximate truth of T_0 is strictly implied ($\Rightarrow$) by e_2:

$$e_2 \Rightarrow [e_1 \wedge (e_1 \approx t_1) \wedge (t_1 \wedge T_0 \vdash t_2) \wedge (t_2 \approx e_2)]$$

With a proviso that this schema applies to a given domain, the schema can be read "Necessarily if e_2 is systematically true, then it is true that $[e_1 \wedge (e_1 \approx t_1) \wedge (t_1 \wedge T_0 \vdash t_2) \wedge (t_2 \approx e_2)]$"; the latter amounting most relevantly to $e_2 \Rightarrow T_0$, an epistemic modality. And this modality as an epistemic necessity is equivalent to the epistemic impossibility that T_0 is not roughly true when there are the true predictions e_2. That said, recall two points. First, both e_1 and e_2 avoid a relativistic theory-dependence by being rooted in a non-conceptual consciousness of phenomena of which there is an incontrovertible awareness. And so there is a realist construal of the schema. Second, the physical systems' future states are coordinated to the systems' previous states by causal regularities. These regularities underscore the importance of being able to *ascribe truth* to the causal principle by virtue of a common-sense modal logic. Without this logic there is the K-K Thesis (of how we Know we Know) in which scientific truth is undercut by a truth-less presupposed causal principle.

That is, recall the principle's truth-functional version of the principle: "If there is an event (E), then there is a cause (C)" that can be read $E \rightarrow C$ where C is implied by E; allowing for a logical possibility that $\sim C$ when E. This leads to the K-K Thesis of "how we Know we Know" since scientific knowledge would presuppose an unknowable causal principle. This principle would undermine knowledge in science. But scientific knowledge may be sustained by the principle's reformulation as E strictly implying ($\Rightarrow$) C such that $\sim C$ is not believable since it is said reasonably to be physically impossible. Is this impossibility challenged by St. Thomas? Thomas "sometimes states that things are contingent, if their

CONSCIOUSNESS AND A ROBUST REALISM   71

proximate causes are not necessary, i.e., causes which always bring about their effect."[17] The effects that are pertinent to the causal principle, however, are impossible only in the case when there are no causes. And the causes need not be necessary *per se*, notwithstanding their being presupposed for an intelligibility of scientific inquiry.

Finally, the weak symbol → of truth-functional logic, the logic assumed largely from Popper onwards, would typically be used in reasoning to the prediction e_2. This means that it is *logically possible* that e_2 may not obtain ($T_0 \rightarrow \sim e_2$). Precisely, $\sim e_2$ implies $\sim T_0$. And $\sim T_0$ reflects Popper's anti-realist falsification thesis, which is implicit also in Newton-Smith's Principle of Pessimistic Induction. Here, $\sim e_2$ alone yields any knowledge, namely knowing that theory T_0 is false. The falsity is avoided by replacing → with the stronger strict implication after inferring the *epistemic impossibility* that T_0 is not approximately true when e_2 is systematically true, the truth being both rough and restricted to a domain. The domain of Newton's physics, for example, is where Planck's constant is negligible and the speed of light is not approached. Formalized theories are further regarded after enlarging on how *aspects* of phenomena, of which scientists are conscious, bear on testing scientific theories.

Realism Rooted in Aspects of Phenomena

Theories are testable by addressing entities, from gene replication to atomic reactions, which are observationally grounded in aspects of phenomena. Phenomena respond to experimentation but not to our thought and are "ever surprising."[18] Surprise, notes John Compton, means that scientists experience an *independence* of phenomena. To say phenomena "surprise" is to say they can thwart our expectations and that we are *conceptually conscious* of their independence. But independence as a "real property" presupposes as well that a *non-conceptual awareness* of that property is infused into our conceptual awareness. Independence is shown by the scientific measurement in terms, say,[19] of acceleration as meter per second squared (m/s²), density as kilogram per cubic meter

---

17. See Knuuttila, "Medieval Modal Theories and Modal Logic," 505–78.

18. Compton, "Natural Science," 89–94. This and next two paragraphs are indebted to Compton, although the aspects he notes are not related by him to a non-conceptual awareness infused into a conceptual awareness.

19. Ibid., 89–94.

(Kg/m³) and electric field strength as volt per meter (V/m). Measurement would be senseless if phenomena were fully a function of our thought because our thought would then suppose a structure that is not distinguishable from structured phenomena. And consciousness itself could be measurable only by the reductive reduction of it to a structured phenomenon subject to scientific investigation (with the caveat that it would be senseless to even use the term "investigator").

A reliance of investigations on independence is related to the aspect of *individuality* that, notes Compton, permits phenomena to be aptly discerned as having a boundary principle or, in terms of parts and movement, a coordinating principle.[20] While operating on the principles requires a conceptual awareness of phenomena, their truly having the boundaries supposes that the conceptualizations include an awareness of the boundaries being *real* without concepts. Otherwise observation-theoretical concepts would be imposed on phenomena, making them indistinguishable from the concepts. This is the case for skeptical anti-realisms. They ensue from a thesis of theory-dependent observation wherein, for example, Popper holds that the observation statement "This paper is white" presupposes "This is paper." This in turn presupposes a conditional like "If this paper is dropped, it would not break." The latter allegedly begs for theories about "break" and "paper" (where paper that drops does not break because of its elastic and viscoelastic properties[21]).[22]

In point of fact, however, observational statements bearing on paper do not presuppose theory. Rather, a relatively true theory, in the least, presupposes a concept-neutral element in observations of phenomena having properties such as boundaries. The boundary principles also permit identification and consequently, according to Compton, the principles allow for scientists to distinguish one phenomenon from other similar phenomena, notwithstanding their changes and transformations; transformations being stipulated for conditions of invariance, sought scientifically, illustrates the feature of individuality.[23] Individuality, continues Compton, is connected to why scientific theories typically address the primary qualities or essential attributes of many kinds of different phenomena.

20. Ibid.
21. Alava and Niskanen, "The Physics of Paper," 669.
22. Cf. Popper, *Conjectures and Refutations*, 387.
23. Compton, "Natural Science," 89–94.

Phenomena having boundaries means that phenomena occupy a lived region of space and time that, says Compton, denotes the aspect of *extensiveness*. Extensiveness allows for experiencing phenomena as volumetric and dimensional. And Dimensionality taken with phenomena transforming (per the aspect of individuality) result in continuously new perspectives from which phenomena can be studied by either naked-eye or instrument-aided observation. This point explains, notes Compton, why physicists often insist that a theoretic construct prove essential in two or more logically independent experimental-theoretical contexts to warrant regarding the construct as really representing any given phenomenon.[24] Phenomena are thereby conceptually perceived as either evolving or as having coordinated processes that are designated by the aspect of *continuity*. Though the continuity of something in terms of the thing's either evolving lawfully or having coordinated change involves only conceptual observation in Compton's analysis, his analysis in my essay is extended to emphasize as well that the coordinated change and processes are that of which scientists are non-conceptually aware. And this direct non-conceptual awareness is infused into a conceptual awareness, of which the scientists are also implicitly aware, that conceptualizes phenomena. Phenomena being conceptualized in this manner explains phenomenologically how the continuity is really a part of physical reality.

Phenomenal Continuity and Causal Principle: Rescuing Realism

In sum, an experienced reality, says Compton, is characterized by phenomena having lawful relations among variables that correspond to pervasive structural features and regularities.[25] The regularities in particular beg for follow-up points: The regularities are related inexorably to a causal principle (all events are caused) presupposed by scientific inquiry for its intelligibility. This intelligibility notwithstanding, the causal principle is held by Kant and modern philosophers he influenced to be a *synthetic-a priori* metaphysical judgment. In not being known to be either empirically or logically true, the judgment undercuts the truth yielded by scientific inquiry. For again, this inquiry would afford alleged truths that

24. Ibid.
25. Ibid.

presuppose what is not known to be true, namely the principle, because of a K-K Thesis that questions "how do we Know we Know?"

First, however, professed dilemmas such as the aforesaid K-K Thesis ignore that, as enlarged upon later, the causal principle may actually have an unusually strong truth by virtue of a common-sense modal reasoning. Let this reasoning be expanded upon by stressing that while it is *logically possible* that an event has no cause, an event's not having a cause is *physically impossible* where this impossibility can be transposed into the necessity: Necessarily if there is no cause (~C), then there is no event (~E), represented variously as $Nec(\sim C \to \sim E)$, $\Box(\sim C \to \sim E)$ or $(\sim C \Rightarrow \sim E)$. Second, the causal principle is not merely a principle that stems from our conceptual consciousness of phenomena having evident causal regularities, these affording predictions of a physical system's future state that are coordinated to a previously described state of that system. More exactly, the system's conceptualized regularities are themselves grounded more primordially in our sheer consciousness of phenomena, without concepts, having a *continuity* that helps to explain an *objectivity* of the entire scientific enterprise.

Thus far this chapter has shown how the scientific enterprise relies on experienced characteristics of phenomena that include their continuities of change, structural features of volume and dimension, boundary principles, and an unresponsiveness of phenomena *ceteris paribus* to our will, wish, or thought. This section, although having examined a continuity of phenomena and causal principle, referred for simplicity to phenomena as that of which we can have an *awareness*. Since the word "awareness" would usually be replaced by "consciousness" in Sartre's terminology, this terminology is now employed to express more formally the aforesaid aspects of phenomena. The phenomena *in themselves* are discerned initially by a direct non-conceptual observational consciousness, of which we are indirectly conscious, by virtue of which that self-consciousness and our intellect are able to objectively conceptualize phenomena. So, phenomenologically, our pre-conceptual direct consciousness of phenomena of which we are indirectly conscious, *is prior to* all empirical and theoretical truth. Truth has its foundation in that self-consciousness. And this consciousness allows for the immediate ontological and potential epistemological footing for conceptually discerning phenomena upon which scientific theories are developed and to which they refer. Given reference by theories to phenomena with their observational *origin* in manifestations of reality of which scientists are initially conscious, without concepts, how can direct and indirect consciousness contribute to understanding the role of observation and imagination in the history of science in which all major *mature* theories were superseded by later theories?

A Realist Phenomenology of the History of Science

With a caveat that the following brief outline of an historical development of major or mature theories is more colloquial than formal, let me note at the outset that the outline is not intended to interpret the history of science in ways in which do Sir Karl Popper, Thomas Kuhn, or Paul Feyerabend. Nor is the outline comparable to even more cautious scholarship in line with realism, such as the revered work of William Wallace and Stanley Jaki.[26] Rather, my outline humbly suggests that traditional explanations of growing scientific knowledge agree with the notion, as articulated in this essay, that scientific theories make reference ultimately to aspects of phenomena *in themselves*, even if no phenomenology of any sort is acknowledged, for deciding how reality is to be conceptually distinguished. Recalling Compton's insight that there "seems to be a continuing presupposition of [some] convergence between scientific ontology and the ontology of the prescientific life-world,"[27] it is reasonable to suppose that dissimilar theories would *have in common* a pre-conceptual awareness of phenomena, even an initial major theory such as Aristotle's would have reference to that phenomena within certain *mutual* domains of experience despite his theory's supersession by later mature theories such as Newton's. Whether by naked-eye or instrument-aided observation, the theories would have recourse ultimately to common aspects of phenomena. Phenomena of which Galileo was non-conceptually conscious, consequently, was the same or similar consciousness *ceteris paribus* as that of Aristotle's despite the different conceptualizations.

Consider the conceptualizations of Aristotle. He assumed that the natural state of a body is at rest and force is required to keep it in motion ("body" used rather than "phenomenon" presumably because "phenomenon" is used by Kant's idealism to reject the idea that appearances reflect how reality really *is*). This anti-realism aside, physicist Douglas Giancoli

---

26. See in general, for example, Jaki's *The Limits of a Limitless Science and Other Essays* and Wallace's *Philosophy of Science and Philosophy of Nature in Synthesis*.

27. Compton, "Reinventing the Philosophy of Nature," 3–28.

notes that Aristotle's theory of motion was *not* replaced by Galileo's theory because Aristotle's theory was false.[28] Our ordinary awareness of moving objects on a plane indicates they will stop if not continually pushed. The need to push for sustaining the motions of objects was thus limited to an awareness of terrestrial phenomena. But while the phenomena of which Aristotle and Galileo were aware was the *same* phenomena non-conceptually, *different* conceptualizations of that phenomena by Galileo's theory explicated far more phenomena.

By phenomena *imagined* in an experimentally unattainable condition in which there was no friction and interpreting friction as force (Einstein saying famously that imagination is more important than knowledge),[29] Galileo argued that objects continue in motion with a constant velocity when there are no contrary forces. The forces being *imagined* to be necessary for objects to cease moving is explicable by existential phenomenology: Galileo was directly conscious of his envisaged "objects" as well as implicitly aware of his *freedom* to envision them in different ways. Or put another way, Galileo was implicitly aware of choosing to be directly conscious, not of objects as they *in fact appear*, but of his visualizing objects as they *do not appear* but actually *might be* if there is no terrestrial friction. Friction interpreted as being force, according to Giancoli, influenced Newton whose first law of motion essentially restated Galileo's insight.[30] Whereas that insight bore explicitly on only objects in motion, he adds, motion as well as rest were included in Newton's law which specified that bodies continue in their state of rest or uniform speed in a straight line unless compelled to change that state by forces acting on them. This first law was related to the second and third laws in the sense that Newton continued to question what would occur if

---

28. Giancoli, *Physics: Principles with Applications*, 37–38, to which my outline is indebted. The analyses from Aristotle to Newton's kinematics is rephrased to underscore that although they had *different* concepts, they had the *same* non-conceptual awareness. There is a sense in which we see the *same* things despite *different* cultures or *Weltanschauungen*.

29. An epistemological principle specifies that to assert that a proposition is true is to be able to say what "truth" is. *Pari passu* to speak of imagination is to be able to what imagination is. In this manner, existential phenomenology is significant insofar as it affords an explanation of a scientist's imagination; imagination being more important than knowledge according to Einstein.

30. Giancoli, *Physics: Principles with Applications*, 37–38. This and the next paragraph paraphrase his discussion in order to render substantive my discussion of a non-conceptual consciousness. This notion of consciousness supports objective observation in contrast to observation that is theory-dependent.

forces are exerted on bodies. An important point about these bodies, for existential phenomenology, is that a direct consciousness of the imagined bodies by Newton included his being indirectly aware of his *freedom* to question quite differently the envisioned consequences of forces exerted on bodies. Though his implicit awareness of imagined bodies behaving in different ways would not resolve which way was correct, this awareness accounts for Newton's creative thought about various possibilities and his openness to experimental results regarding other laws.

Scientific Truth Involves Paradoxically *Both* Free Will *and* Causal Determinism!

For Newton's second law, the speed of bodies decrease when force is exerted in opposite directions and increase when exerted in the same. So force yields acceleration which is directly proportional to net applied force.[31] Force causing certain effects is philosophically odd since this finding follows a scientific inquiry that presupposes that all events are caused (causal determinism). Determinism per se conflicts with Newton having free will. His free will, however, is *as* necessary for the intelligibility of his scientific inquiry *as* causal determinism. Thus, the determinism is often alone stressed such as when it is said that "advancements in neuroscience, psychiatry, neurology, and related fields of inquiry have shaken the presumption that humans are capable of moral decision making by showing that many aspects of human psychology correlate with localized activity in the brain, thus raising the possibility of biologic explanations for all human behavior."[32] But behavior that is both determined and freely willed are realities of which we are irrefutably conscious. This consciousness is clearly illustrated in forensic investigations of suicides and homicides when persons fall from buildings (related to Newton's second law $f = ma$ as free fall by way of $mg = md^2s/dt^2$ where m denotes mass, g gravity, d distance and t time). In spite of whether persons are pushed or freely jump, gravity *deterministically causes* their fall with precisely predictable forces of impact.[33]

---

31. See ibid., 37–38 for these Newtonian developments.
32. Gligorov, "Determinism and Advances in Neuroscience," 489–93.
33. Cf. Reiss, "Epistemic Virtues and Concept Formation in Economics," 170: "'$mg = md^2s/dt^2$' is a model (an either linguistic or abstract entity) that represents the law of free fall (a fact or pattern of facts or power that obtains in the real world)."

The impact aside, evidence would include considerations of weather the persons were either screaming "No, no, no" as they fell (hinting at homicide and the *will to live*) or shouting "All my problems are over" (signifying suicide and the *will to die*). And besides free will being presupposed for coherent scientific truth-claims since otherwise contradictory claims would incoherently be equally true if truth has for its truth-condition a causally determined reality, free will is necessary also for the intelligibility of scientific creativity. For creativity bears on what *is not* but *could be*. In terms of Kant's *a priori* categories of mind that allegedly interpret a raw material of experience, for example, one category is quality by which this experience is interpreted positively or negatively. The negative would be stressed by the existential phenomenology since we can both be aware of *what is the case* and aware of *what is not the case* but *might* or *should be the case* (relating to creating new scientific theories and ethical behavior respectively).

Our behavior as freely willed, at least limitedly, is certifiable by our invincible awareness *of* our conscious experience. The latter means that scientists, unless they are *automata*, are indirectly aware of their observational consciousness without concepts that is infused into their conceptual consciousness of phenomena. An apt inverse ratio is that as phenomena are *increasingly* grasped in the history of science by esoteric mathematized theories, the theories are related *decreasingly* to the phenomena that scientists are directly conscious of; with a caveat that a reality composed of particles with "no hard properties . . . until they are observed," per standard equations of quantum mechanics, faces new "surprising experiments with fluids [that] has revived old skepticism about that worldview . . . one that never gave up the idea of a single, concrete reality."[34] Reality as it appears, even so, is based on our nonconceptual consciousness of aspectual phenomena. And in spite of the ratio, this consciousness does indeed bear on *objective observational predictions* that, when they are systematically successful, strictly imply the truth of even the most mathematically intricate scientific theories!

In conclusion, all of the foregoing agrees with a robust realism in which there is an extra-mental reality that is increasingly known by ever-truer, mature scientific theories. The foregoing disagrees that these theories would be possible if reality is grasped reductively as consisting of corporeal phenomena that emit sensory stimuli which somehow cause us

34. Wolchover, "Have We Been Interpreting Quantum Mechanics Wrong?" paragraph 2.

to interpret them as specific phenomena. All of the preceding agrees that phenomena as understood by idealism is correct when it admits that we are consciousness of an intelligible world, where "world" involves conceptual constructs. The preceding disagrees that these constructs are caused by an *a priori* structure of mind. All of the above agrees that our mind does not have truth-values imposed by different cultures on its thoughts expressed as statements. The above disagrees that these statements have coherent truth-conditions for possibly contradictory truth-claims.

All of the foregoing agrees that conflicting truth-claims in terms of an Under-determination-of-Theory-by-Data (UTD) Thesis, which admits *a posteriori* of contradictory theories, is consistent with the theories truly reflecting reality. The foregoing disagrees that reality cannot have truths about it yielded by scientific inquiry because the inquiry is undercut by an unknowable causal principle. All of the above agrees that this principle is actually a true modal conditional: In terms of this conditional, the causes are strictly implied by the effects. The above disagrees that these effects necessarily having causes implies that we lack free will because there are causes of consciousness. All of the above agrees that consciousness is a necessary condition for our free will but disagrees that this will is absolute. And all of the foregoing disagrees that we are absolutely causally determined: We are both limitedly determined *and* free, paradoxically, which is necessary for an intelligible ethics and science.[35] All the preceding agrees that a philosophic understanding of the scientific enterprise requires an existential phenomenological explication of our being conscious of reality *itself*. Avoiding this reality's concealment averts key objections to realism: from Hume's internal sensations excluding knowledge of an external world (much more knowing there is a world) to Kant's *a priori* structured cognition that interprets only a raw material of experience, which excludes free will, and neuroscience philosophy that often reduces self-consciousness to a causally determined phenomenon.

---

35. Cf. Trundle, "Paradoxes of Human Nature," 181–86. Paradoxes and outright contradictions are addressed also by Trundle's "Aristotle *Versus* Van Til and Łukasiewicz," 323–44.

4

Science and Observation Infused by Theory

The notion that observation is infused by theory (theory-dependent), which excludes objective observational truth and a truth of theories, was initiated by the philosopher of science Sir Karl Popper. So rooted was Popper's position in received-view philosophy from the mid to late twentieth century that I could not get an article published in the 1980s that, while lauding his countless contributions, exposed his skillfully veiled anti-realism: both his irrational avowal that observation is theory-dependent and his inspiring the anti-realist theses of Kuhn and Feyerabend. The unabashedly embraced theory-dependent observation and incoherent relativisms. The relativisms of Kuhn and Feyerabend (Popper's relativism being much more surreptitious) are admirably critiqued by W. H. Newton-Smith in his *The Rationality of Science*.

But although *The Rationality of Science* is among the very best works on scientific realism in the last several decades, its erudite case for a weaker thesis of observation's theory-*ladenness*[1] failed to show how the *ladenness* is consistent with an observational *concept-free* touchstone with reality *in itself*. Reality *in itself* is herein that of which we are conscious and that which is *infused* into theory-laden observation. These points about observation serve to explain how observational predictions can be *true*. And the infusion of the one consciousness into the other, taken with modal logic, affords saying that systematically true predictions of theories strictly imply their inexact truth. How is this truth uniquely de-

---

1. Cf. Buzzoni's "Mechanisms, Experiments, and Theory-Laddenness," 1–17.

fensible by existential phenomenology? Even with this phenomenology, after all, knotty epistemological problems with any realism resulted in both those very relativisms and theses of theory-dependent observation.

Observational predictions presuppose several modes of our direct consciousness: a *non-conceptual* consciousness that reveals how phenomena are in themselves and a *conceptual* consciousness, which includes a concept/theory-neutral contact with reality, into which that non-conceptual consciousness is infused. This infusion is manifest to us by our *indirect* awareness of the following: An indirect awareness of our non-conceptual consciousness of aspects of phenomena—when we are indirectly aware of phenomena being *seen* but not noticed conceptually; our indirect awareness of our non-conceptual consciousness included in our consciousness of conceptualized phenomena; our being implicitly aware that our consciousness of phenomena *is not* the phenomena that are disclosed as *real existents*; and being indirectly aware both of our mental images of phenomena (*phantasms* for St. Thomas[2]) and of the phenomenon so that its comparison by our intellect to the image enables the image's accuracy to be gauged, although the images are not necessary for conceptualizations of phenomena.

The existential phenomenology in this essay avoids arcane theories of mind, from Descartes to Hume and Kant and their heirs. They bogusly split science from other sorts of knowledge and persist in plaguing philosophies of science.[3] The scientific realism in this essay relates logically the truths in science, theology, ethics, art, and politics. This realism complements a classical realism of Aristotle and Thomas. Before tackling Thomas, consider in this chapter and the chapter following how metaphysics has failed to prevent theory-dependent observation in which "truth" cannot have as its truth-condition an observed reality. Reality as thus construed has resulted in an epistemic relativism and a recourse *inter alia* to either weak realisms or pragmatic stratagems in order to evade observational quandaries that undercut tenable scientific theories.

Theory and Theory-Free Observation

Theory's relationship to a theory-free observation, which is a central thesis herein, bears logically on Anglo-American logical positivism that

---

2. See Aquinas, *Summa Theologiae* I.Q. 86.
3. Knobe, "Theory of Mind and Moral Cognition," 357–59.

surreptitiously and contradictorily both *rejected* metaphysics as meaningless and *accepted* a meaningless metaphysics (a verification principle) where an alleged statement/proposition (or proposition *qua* theory) is meaningful if and only if (*iff*) it is either analytic or synthetic (logically true [tautologous] or provably empirically true/false potentially [testable]). This testing, bearing on my later discussion of methodology that questions its limits, raises a specter of theorists who are supposedly "'moving the goalposts' of science and blurring the line between physics and pseudoscience," are said to violate the "imprimatur of science [that] should be awarded only to a theory that is testable," thus excluding "most of the *leading theories of the past 40 years*."[4] This misgiving about verificationism apart, the true/false empirical criterion was met by the positivist's distinction of theoretical from observation terms. The terms "water," "white," and "weight" are observational by being response to sense experience. This experiential responsiveness is said to contrast to the theoretical terms "H_2O," "wavelength," and "mass."[5]

On the one hand, it is not always true that "things with mass are distinct from things with weight," as reiterated in a distinctive way by Miklavž Vospernik in "Measurement and the Verificationist Theory-Observation Distinction" (concluding—wrongly, I think—that "the analysis of measurement does not fully support this distinction [and that this] might have important consequences for the problem of scientific realism"[6]). We try to show that realism does *not* depend on the observation-theoretical distinction. On the other hand, that distinction, although false, is not meaningless even per the defunct verification principle. The principle is not violated because the distinction is *synthetic*, not assumed *a priori*, and is claimed to be inferred *a posteriori* from experience. This experience was said so convincingly to render distinct terms such as "mass," which do not respond to touch or sight, and "weight," which does, that to say even today that theoretical entities are observable, and thus real, often evokes zealous opposition, if not denigration as a howler.

The howler did indeed have its inception in logical positivism. The "positivists were *anti-realists* about so-called 'theoretical entities,'" confirms Curtis Brown, adding dryly that "electrons" did not refer "to tiny particles too small to see" and that "'theoretical terms' do not refer to

---

4. Wolchover, "A Fight for the Soul of Science," cf. entire article.
5. Schwandt, "Theory-Observation Distinction," cf. entire article.
6. Vospernik, "Measurement," 95–117.

unobservable entities."[7] That taking these entities to be real or observable can lead to a howler is indicated by another philosopher of science who states that *criticizing* the "view that theoretical entities are mere fictions often figures only in *realist [portrayals]* of anti-realism and is hardly seriously maintained by any philosopher . . . in the 20th century."[8] And well into the twenty-first century Adam Toon says, "When scientists produce a theoretical model of a system, they ask others to *imagine* that the assumptions they make are true of that system."[9] He adds both that "There is no need to posit any abstract or fictional object of which the scientists' assumptions are true" and that "Learning about a model is not a matter of discovering facts about any object but of discovering what the model prescribes us to imagine."[10] But why must imagined theoretical models preclude unobserved realities of either those models or theoretical entities like an electron? To say that a theory about an electron is true, for example, is to say prima facie that the electron is real; to exclude the reality is prima facie to exclude the truth. But why must this truth be rejected and "make believe" be accepted by devising a stratagem, as he prescribes, that is modeled on a "'make-believe' theory of representation in art"?[11] Art, even metaphorically, need not replace literal reality and truth.

This flight from truth about reality, in science, explains the wanton waning status of theoretical constructs in terms of both epistemology and ontology, as well as a surreptitious influence of the logical positivists and neo-positivists on observation. Since observation terms were ostensibly unchanging, the positivists stressed the significance of those terms over terms of theories and theoretical entities that changed. The change would make theoretical terms less reliable in regard to both their real existence (ontology) and statements about them being roughly true (epistemology). But the positivists never foresaw how a declining epistemological and ontological status of theoretical constructs would eventually result in a fading status of observation terms. Could a positivist primacy of these terms be sustained when what their depiction of reality seemed increasingly challenged by quantum and relativistic physics; this, in spite of the physics being corroborated paradoxically by predictions whose

---

7. Brown, "Notes on Van Fraassen's Constructive Empiricism," cf. entire article.
8. Andreas' "Theoretical Terms in Science," §Non-realist views.
9. See Toon's "The Ontology of Theoretical Modelling," 18. Emphasis.
10. Ibid.
11. Ibid., 1.

observational status was precisely in question? In question at the same time is the appearance of certain stars that were explained by Einstein's prediction that light is bent by gravitational fields, as oddly portended prima facie by St. Augustine.

Augustine, in countering skeptics who said blasphemously that God permits our deception by oars appearing bent in water, replied that in water that is how oars *should appear*. The appearance begs for a judgment, such as one of an optical theory, for explaining why the oars look as they do in a medium of water; the question ensuing of whether the observation-theoretical distinction was, despite the positivists, one of *degree* (whereby observation terms more or less presupposed theory) or only one of kind (whereby there is the fatal observation-theoretical distinction).[12] The latter was principally one of kind because theoretical and observation terms, says Newton-Smith, evidently operated in entirely different ways.[13] The way that observation terms were held to operate or function is exemplified by the "The pointer is at five," whereas the function of theoretical terms was typified by "Photons have zero rest mass"; a sentence with both theoretical and observation terms being of the sort "Electrons passing through a cloud chamber produce a track on an exposed electric plate,"[14] whereby while plate, track and chamber are observables, they are still understood in terms of theory. Consider how theory and theory-classification extraneous to observation had an impact on scientific realism, a pragmatic instrumentalism and relativism after assessing in more detail what seemed to warrant a sharp division of observation from theoretical terms.

Terms of mature theories and of observation were divided for several reasons. First, pedagogically, the terms are related inversely. Whereas observation terms are grasped by sense experience during the early years of learning language, the language of mathematically complex theories is learned in the later years of advanced education. So although this education is acquired before learning theoretical terms, these terms involve learning how they are interpreted and coordinated with observation terms as well as when the terms of observation are descriptions of diverse physical systems.[15] Second, since these systems are described observa-

---

12. Augustine, *Contra Academicos* (iii, xi, 26).
13. Newton-Smith, *The Rationality of Science*, 20.
14. Ibid.
15. Ibid. Newton-Smith refers to "Eddington and Cottingham when they photographed the field of stars in the Hyades group during the solar eclipse of 1919 in

tionally and observation terms had meanings that were independent of changing theories and theoretical terms, the terms of theories were unstable in contrast to observation terms that seemingly afforded a neutral core to construct and evaluate theories. Theories and their terms arise, for positivism, from meanings of observation terms gained by linguistic experience, although often unconsciously in inarticulate ambiguous ways. This brings to mind Ludwig Wittgenstein, for whom language games of science have more precise terms derived from imprecise but richer meanings of ordinary language; as by analogy a *scalpel* might have its medical conception in an everyday *kitchen knife*. Those who would want rudimentary knives replaced by exact scalpels are like physicists who become misguided metaphysicians if they insist that everyday words be replaced by more precise terms of a scientific theory). Furthermore, Wittgenstein's caution against replacing ordinary words by more precise words of science may be illustrated when, supposedly, he first read one of Freud's works on a short train ride. When he got off, he purportedly noted that Freud must be a genius since otherwise no one could be that confused![16] While strict rules may apply to scientific language, "In general, says Wittgenstein, we don't use [ordinary] language according to strict rules...."[17] These rules imposed on ordinary language raise a specter of the logical positivists who, "gripped by a mistakenly truncated conception of language, tried to claim that many philosophical questions could be dismissed for failing to be congruent with the language of science (as it was then understood)."[18]

Theory and its terms by being *more* exact and *less* fruitful for fostering new language games than ordinary language, as suggested by Wittgenstein, is intriguingly reminiscent of rigorous theories being *indeterminable* (*underdetermined*) by *inexact* observation terms and

---

an attempt to test [Einstein's] General Theory. The salient difference between these activities is the following. In the case of the [observing] one is seeking to produce a true description of the state of a particular physical system at some moment of time. In the [case of theorizing] one is hoping to articulate an interesting generalization or body of generalizations covering the behaviour of all systems of some type."

16. I was unable to recall where I read this about Wittgenstein on Freud, although Freud is mentioned in Malcolm, *Ludwig Wittgenstein*, 39, 51, 100–101.

17. Wittgenstein, *The Blue and Brown Books*, 25. Some analytic/linguistic philosophers say this work marks the middle of a painful transition from the early to the late Wittgenstein.

18. Ross, *Review of* "Seeing Things as They Are," 253.

sentences of sets of data, per Henri Poincaré's famous UTD Thesis.[19] This thesis agrees with Wittgenstein about both the richness of ordinary language and his caution against trying to reduce that language to one of precise science. Scientific progress via the positivist model comes *inter alia* from theoretical laws and terms resulting derivatively from observation generalizations, the latter often arising inductively from our observational descriptions of physical systems. Thus these systems at present times can have their observational descriptions recast as theoretical ones that, taken with theories, imply these descriptions of the systems at future times. Future theoretical descriptions may then be transposed into observational descriptions in order to test theories.

Since theories were held by the positivists to change historically unlike observation language, allegedly, this language was taken to be objectively neutral for theory construction. The construction rests on a neutral ground for evaluating theories such that if T_1 and T_2 imply observational predictions P and $\sim P$ respectively and if $\sim P$ obtains, then T_2 passes a test that T_1 fails. Theories being testable by virtue of the observation-theoretical distinction, fortified by the aforesaid pedagogical and epistemic reasons, was a vital reason for the distinction. Having thus far explained the distinctive reasons, consider why the division resulted in differences of degree and not of kind in terms of the critiques by Hilary Putnam.

Observation-Theoretical Distinctions or Differences in Degree?

While Putnam's early essays defended a robust realism and "did so, moreover, with the aid of arguments from philosophy of language and logic,"[20] he helped to forge the notions of both *theory-laden observation* and the more overlooked *observation-laden theory* that eventually threatened scientific realism. The following claims about these notions of ladenness, from Putnam and Suppe to Churchland, Newton-Smith, and others, were sometimes metaphysical in a neo-Kantian sense of being unverifiable and provisional without relating to either phenomenological experience or empirical certification. The certification aside, Putnam said that if observation terms refer only to observables, there can be no purely observation

---

19. See reference to Henri Poincaré by Worrall's "Scientific Realism and Scientific Change," 201–33. Poincaré held that observational data (expressed linguistically) admits not merely of inconsistency but also contradiction: contradictory theories T and $\sim T$ that are nonetheless empirically equivalent.

20. Norris, "Hilary Putnam on Realism," §1.

term since terms applied to observables can apply to non-observables as well without altering their meaning, say as Newton used the term "red" for theorizing that red light consists of red corpuscles.[21]

Pari passu corpuscles and similar entities that presumably are purely theoretical are related also to observation terms. Terms like "gravitational field" and "electric charge" are patently theoretical and yet also clearly observational because the field can be felt and the charge can be detected by touch as well as observed as a terminal spark. In sum, iconic logical positivists such as Hans Reichenbach and Rudolf Carnap held that observation terms could have context-independent meanings because, "as Putnam puts it, 'there was this privileged class of observation terms—c on this were *blue, touches* and *warm*—which had what he called complete meaning'" wherein one "'could explain the meaning of any sentence in the language if it were [formalized] *a la* logical positivism by some way of relating it to these observation sentences.'"[22] So most sentences that have terms which are non-logical (e.g., not tautologous), says Putnam, refer to both observables and non-observables. And hence there is no natural distinction of so-called observation terms from non-observation terms.

Does this imply, asked Frederick Suppe, that observation terms are entirely indistinguishable? Suppe notes that the previously discussed case against purely observation and theoretical terms does not erase every plausible distinction. *Decreasing* the distinctions as such *increases* an uncalled-for complexity of explicating theories, Suppe reminds us, which is extraneous to the actual employment of scientific theories.[23] These theories should be subject to complex critiques only if the critiques are warranted philosophically. And a philosophical significance of making at least some distinction outweighs the case against it inasmuch as certain distinctions are required in order to capture major differences in epistemological properties of the entities referred to by the terms of either theory or observation. An observation-theoretical distinction of logical positivism, then again, fails to secure those meaningful differences in properties of the entities to which refer the terms.[24]

Whereas terms that are only observational are said to refer manifestly to observables, says Suppe, so-called theoretical terms are terms

---

21. Putnam, "What Theories are Not," 240–51. Putnam's evolving positions in *Philosophy in an Age of Science*.

22. Baggini, "Interview with Hilary Putnam," para. 23.

23. Suppe, "Criticism of the Received View," 84.

24. Ibid.

that arise from theories that may refer also to observables. Observables are referred to exclusively by Darwin's theory, for example, and that theory still employs theoretical terms. And there are terms in observation sentences that have clear epistemic import. This import includes theoretical terms such as "electric charge" that does not invariably refer to observables.[25] Thus, although the observation-theoretical distinction is a prerequisite for capturing an import of theoretical terms, states Suppe, the terms as discerned by positivists is quite flawed in this regard. In this regard as well, Anna Estany notes some ensuing extremes. In contrast to Jerry Fodor and Carl Hemple, who defend objectively neutral observations and the received-view observation-theoretical distinction, for example, she notes that the neuroscience philosopher Paul Churchland maintains that "all perceptual processing is inescapably laden with . . . general knowledge shaped by [or caused by] past experience."[26]

This experiential notion of our personal past that distorts or skews observation takes us from Suppe's reasonable call for capturing a philosophical significance of theoretical terms to the epistemic relativism of *Weltanschauung* (worldview) analyses that are a surreptitious species of the theory-dependent thesis of which Suppe is poignantly aware.[27] He is aware that these relativistic worldviews, which presuppose that our culture, personality, and prior experience exclude the possibility of true observations, pay no attention whatsoever to our phenomenological self-awareness in terms of which our awareness of both something and this thing being distinguished (as against "the 'awareness' and 'thing we are aware of'" being *"the same."*[28]). In this essay, we are indisputably aware of our consciousness of physical reality in a manner independently of concepts and hence of any distorting past knowledge.

Knowledge is disputed largely in regard to the theoretical or "unobservable." Anjan Ckakravartty notes that while a "reality of the observable is now generally taken for granted," for example, an "epistemic status of the unobservable . . . remains controversial";[29] remarking that there

---

25. Ibid., 85.

26. Estany, "The Thesis of Theory-Laden Observation," 206.

27. See Suppe, *The Structure of Scientific Theories*, 125–217, which nicely criticizes the relativisms; often criticizing them aptly as neo-Kantian ways of interpreting the world, *a priori*, less Kant's categories.

28. Ross, *Review of* "Seeing Things as They Are," 239.

29. See Ckakravartty's review of E. Agazzi & M. Pauri, eds., *The Reality of the Unobservable*, 359–63.

is "no more succinct a way of describing the controversy between *scientific realists* and *antirealists* than to say that it turns on the reality of the unobservable."[30] Both unobservable and observable entities in the existential phenomenology in this essay, however, are grounded ultimately in aspects of phenomena of which scientists are directly conscious without concepts.

This non-conceptual direct consciousness is infused into our conceptual direct consciousness. Consequently, given that the observable is related reasonably to the unobservable (theoretical entities, properties, processes, and so forth), there is a concepts-free neutral objectifying element in consciousness of which scientists are indirectly aware. They are aware of phenomena as they really are *in themselves*, although admittedly from particular perspectives and with a proviso that observation-theoretical interpretations can still be underdetermined by the UTD Thesis. Accordingly, while an indirect awareness of the scientists admits of both *conceptually interpreted* observables and observation terms which are theory-laden (that refer to observable entities), these entities do not have theoretical concepts imposed exhaustively on them. Thus, although an unqualified observation-theoretical distinction is unwarrantable, a tenable division of some sort may nevertheless obtain.

Degrees of Theory-Ladenness and a Laden-Free Consciousness

One way an observation-theoretical distinction may still obtain is by construing some observation terms as being less laden by theory than others; a hierarchy in which the least theory-laden observation terms are at the bottom of our perceptual activity and, for bottom-up realist inferences to theory, the most theory-laden observation terms are at the top. This top-down-decreasing ladenness is supported by "evidence [which] shows that perception is theory-laden, but that it is only strongly theory-laden when the perceptual evidence is ambiguous or degraded . . ."[31]—the evidence for theory-ladenness not resulting in "a relativist account of scientific knowledge." At the top where there are the least observation elements, we might speak of *observation-laden theoretical terms* that are minimally

---

30. Ibid., emphasis. Recall that holding the unobservable to be real, but denying a truth of theories in which it is understood, reflects an incoherent weak realism. Emphasis.

31. Brewer and Lambert, "The Theory-Ladenness of Observation," S3.

laden by observation. This observation-theory-laden hierarchy brings to mind W. H. Newton-Smith: As admirably astute as he is, does he possibly sometimes seem to do the following: blur observation reports with theoretical judgments; overlook a self-conscious observation that is theory-neutral; and admit of observation terms laden by theory but not of theoretical terms laden by observation. Even if so, he aptly notes that features of observation terms, which permit pragmatic differences of theoretical content, can be used without drastically relegating those terms to unfeasible kinds and classes.[32]

Apart from latter, that is, there may be the bottom of an observation-theoretical hierarchy where there are the least theory-laden observation (O-) terms. The more an O-term is observational, says Newton-Smith, the following holds: The easier it is to decide about whether the term applies; the less the term relies on instruments for determining its application; and the more the observation term has a meaning that can be understood apart from theory.[33] So so-called theoretical and observation terms, which were once radically divided, now have a terminological suitability wherein *sentences* composed of O-terms may need to be revised due to a development of theories.[34] O-terms are also theory-laden, says Newton-Smith, since an O-sentence, despite being corroborated by different observers, may be revised by appeal to theory. For instance, "prior to the development of modern astronomy, anyone would have said that the stars were yellow..." and those who "not versed in science would still say the same [today]. But on the basis of a highly successful theory of colour and ... an instrument-aided study of the stars we reject those observation reports."[35]

Are O-reports swayed by theories or are theories corroborated by the observation reports? By distinguishing *judgments* from phenomena as they *appear*, St. Augustine suggested that the O-report is true that "Oars appear bent the water." The report about water begs for a judgment based on an optical theory for explaining why, in the medium of water, oars look that particular way.[36] The way that the oars look should, precisely, be predicted by a good scientific theory. *Pari passu* prior to mod-

32. Newton-Smith, *The Rationality of Science*, 26–27.
33. Ibid., 27.
34. Ibid., 27–28.
35. Ibid.
36. St. Augustine, *Contra Academicos*, iii, xi, 26.

ern theories, to put Newton-Smith's point differently, anyone would have said that stars, other than our yellow sun, *appear* white. But naked-eye reports of the whiteness are not rendered false by Augustine's thought, by the developments of such things as instrument-aided technologies, B-V color index and photometry.[37] The photometric theory and other developments should yield predictions of stars looking white from our geocentric perspective! This perspective would result in rejecting O-reports only if they exceed what is actually observed by stating, for example, that the stars not only *appear* white but really in themselves *are* white.[38] Thus, although scientific progress can alter *theoretical judgments* and while Newton-Smith makes profound contributions to the philosophy of science, he seems sometimes to conflate "judgments" and "reports." The reports of observation are at least roughly true if they describe how phenomena actually appear. And the appearances in different theoretical experimental contexts, expressed by O-reports, are exactly how scientific theories tend to be corroborated!

To say the corroboration of theories depends on O-reports is not to say *ceteris paribus* that corroboration obtains when the reports about observables beg (straightforwardly or surreptitiously) for theoretical interpretations or judgments. Distinguishing judgments from O-reports was intended to capture this difference—per the difference, for example, between reporting that "the sun and horizon are moving apart" and judging that "the sun is rising" with its theoretical geocentric presupposition. Having noted this difference which will be discussed later, consider how corroborating theories by O-reports is possible in virtue of the reports giving sentential expression to a consciousness of phenomena that, being pre-conceptual *and* conceptual, is a consciousness of which scientists are also indirectly aware. By this awareness, which is immediate and conclusive even if indirect, scientists can certify both the real presence of phenomena and their substantive features such as *independence* in which phenomena do not conform to either experimental expectations or the intentions of scientists who observe them; *individuality* in which phenomena have detectible boundaries (borders, edges, fringes,

---

37. See Nicolson's *Dictionary of Astronomy*, 50, 161.

38. My dissent from Newton-Smith's denial that O-reports may change since they are rooted in our non-conceptual awareness, is a major shift from my former work. This work includes *Integrated Truth: From Physics to Politics*, and *A Theology of Science*. Non-conceptual awareness (consciousness) seems unique to the existential phenomenology in this essay.

margins, peripheries, and so on) that permit measurements which may be mathematically precise; *extensiveness* in which phenomena occupy a volumetric region of space and time; and *continuity* in which events invariably change, evolve or transform in coordinated ways. These ways are an existential phenomenological foundation for conceptualized causal regularities that can be expressed as a causal principle which is presupposed for the intelligibility of scientific inquiry.[39]

The inquiry of science often yields theoretical constructs that are corroborated by predicted O-reports, a truth of the reports being grounded ultimately in the scientist's pre-conceptual consciousness of phenomena. And the phenomena being interpreted themselves as theoretical constructs, in terms of new laws or theories, are founded upon, among other things, the following: inductions from O-reports of various kinds, by the inferred best explanations (or abductions) from a sufficient number of reports, or by altering theories in order to accommodate new domains of phenomena—as the classical domain was succeeded by a relativistic one in terms of these very reports. New formulations of laws and theories, that is, are based on various sorts of O-reports which stem from observational activity (naked-eye or instrument-aided) such as that which is related to experimental setups. In sum, the setups and inquiries rely exactly on what Newton-Smith calls O-reports that pertain to the least theory-laden bottom of an observation-theory spectrum. This spectrum, from a phenomenological view, involves observation reports with a minimal amount of theoretical content and a conceptual construal of aspectual phenomena. The phenomena include the aforesaid aspects of independence, individuality, extensiveness and continuity. The spectrum's ontological and epistemological integrity, in terms of descriptive truths, does not rely on either a conjectural metaphysics or a metaphysics that is supposedly oriented to physics.

---

39. On limitations of the causal principle, see Sneller, "Synchronicity or Coincidence," §1. Here, some "experiences entail a miraculous coalescence of mutually corresponding events in which variegated elements suddenly seem to 'fit.'" Modern thinking, however, despite being highly determined by an impoverished 'causality,' conceives of this causality as a one-directional chain between two separate events. Whether in its rationalist or empiricist form, Modernity reduces the classical Aristotelian doctrine of a fourfold explanation of change to the idea of sheer *efficient* causality. What gets lost in this causal reduction, is any event's "meaningfulness."

Consciousness That is Pre-conceptual Presupposed by Metaphysics

A physics-oriented metaphysics refers to the so-called metaphysical *judgments* that, following Kant, classically include "all persons are free agents" and "all events are caused" (causal principle). Many philosophers would say that the causal principle is more physics oriented than persons having free will, despite both judgments being supposedly *synthetic a priori* and thus truthless; the Kant scholar Stephan Körner once noted that it was no accident that the word "judgment" was used, precisely because it precludes ascriptions of "truth."[40] Many philosophers may assert also that the judgment of there being a spectrum of increasingly theory-laden O-reports is more physics oriented (friendly) than a judgment holding that truths are relative to conceptual frameworks (*Weltanschauungen*), which amount to epistemic prisons that cause or causally condition us to assert incomparable truths in different frameworks: descriptions of the frameworks *synthesizing* different concepts of "relative truths" and "frameworks" and held *a priori* for, say, explaining why there is no objective truth; wherein in this case there would be no theory-laden spectrum at all since all O-reports would be theory-dependent. This supposed dependence does not merely clash with common sense in failing to explain how we can successfully do even the most routine things such walk to the door, if our discernment of physical reality is blocked *in toto* by our observational consciousness having no concept-free touchstone with what is really *there*.

Our being unable to know what is really *there* would also both eliminate *any* corroborable *theories* by O-reports and preclude their playing any role whatsoever in formulating theories. The theories could thereby have no link to the empirical world that they are said paradoxically to predict, if not explicate and manipulate. Mature theories are able to manipulate, explicate, and predict phenomena by virtue *inter alia* of the theory-laden spectrum. In rising upward, ever rising upward towards theories, the spectrum has ever more theory-laden O-reports that, nonetheless, are rooted ultimately in a *pre-metaphysical* and *pre-conceptual*

---

40. Since the judgments are *a priori*, they are prior to scientific inquiry and the inquiry cannot certify their empirical truth, although this truth is irrelevant for a free will that is a non-empirical *noumenon*. And since they are *synthetic*, the subject and predicate terms are different so they are not analytic (logically true); despite the judgments having their possible truth established by either modal logic in the case of the causal principle and existential phenomenology in the case of free will.

observational consciousness of which scientists are aware. And there is an awareness by scientists, per our phenomenology, of their *freely* ascribing truth to truth O-reports and not being *caused* to make the reports at various theory-laden levels of the spectrum. The spectrum establishes concretely, consequently, that both *free will* and *causality* are presupposed for explicating the central elements of scientific inquiry.

Scientific inquiry raises an intoxicating historical query: How could Kant avoid an implicit awareness of his own free will to either write or not write paradoxically that free will is only a possible reality in his *Critique*. When writing his *Critique*, was he entirely unconscious of concocting the idea of *noumenon* as a clever gambit to mediate in between a Cartesian rationalism in which a dualistic free will is *affirmed* dogmatically and a Humean empiricism in which free will is *denied* with an ensuing skepticism? Was he not aware of freely choosing to mediate between a skeptical Empiricism that reductively reduced consciousness to a truthless metaphysics and a metaphysical rationalism where consciousness and mind were conflated? In conflicting with our common-sense experience of ourselves, how could today's philosophy of science escape Kant's un-Solomonic compromise that cut the philosophical baby in half? This cutting in half of the biblical story of two women who claimed the same child as their own refers to Solomon who ordered a baby cut in half with one half for each woman, one of them crying "stop!"; the genuine mother being apparent. Apparent also is that some compromises are equally injurious. These include those that are made by Kant. Genuine answers to enduring profound questions on free will, self, and God, which bear perennially on our lives, were *set aside by Kant prima facie for a game of compromising between* two conflicting philosophical views that themselves also conflict with our irrefutable awareness of ourselves and the world.

The world of which we are aware and our awareness of ourselves renders doubtful, what seems to be, the impracticable notion that *any* O-report by which scientific theories are corroborated can be modified or even overturned by the development of those theories; the *very* theories that themselves puzzlingly depend on reports that *may* also be overturned. For "If any low-level observation report (i.e., a report of an observation framed using O-predicates) may be revised," says Newton-Smith, "how do I know that the particular reports which I rely on in making my theory choices now will not in fact need revising?"[41] And

---

41. Newton-Smith, *The Rationality of Science*, 28.

although he answers his own question by saying that our being unwarranted in having absolute faith in any particular reports does not either mean or imply that we are not justified in having a "general faith in the low-level O-reports we are inclined to make,"[42] making this in faith is founded fittingly on our "success in coping with the world [that] gives us grounds for this general confidence. If such judgments were not by and large reliable, we should not be still here to make judgments."[43]

Metaphysics, Modal Logic, and a Phenomenology of Observation

With a caveat that judgments in coping with the world are not theoretical interpretations as "interpretation" was used previously but rather that which bears on either low-level O-reports or ordinary observational judgments,[44] Newton-Smith's appeal to their success for having a reasonable confidence in their approximate truth is supported by both a common-sense reasoning of modal logic and our existential phenomenology. In terms of this phenomenology, the success of both observation reports and the judgments is explained by our non-conceptually consciousness of phenomena *in themselves* and their being revealed or disclosed to us, from limited particular perspectives, by the sheer translucency of consciousness.

This consciousness *without concepts*, which is based on our own immediate and irrefutable experience of ourselves, is *infused into* a *conceptual* consciousness of phenomena. And although the phenomena of which we are consciousness involve concepts that may be culture- or theory-laden, they can be described by low-level O-reports and ordinary observational judgments both of which can be roughly true about the reality. And in terms of a commonsensical modal reasoning, Newton-Smith's attention to the general success of observational reports and judgments, for coping successfully in life, is strongly analogous as well to our being justified in more formally ascribing truth to scientific theories due to *their* predictive success. For although it is *logically possible* that a

42. Ibid.
43. Ibid.
44. For evident differences of "theoretical judgments" from "appearances," wherein the appearances can issue in true observation (O-) reports, see the previous reference to St. Augustine in his *Contra Academicos*, iii, xi, 26.

theory is not approximately true when it is successful in making systematically true predictions in a given domain, it is an *epistemic impossibility*. And this impossibility may be recast as the necessity of an epistemic modality in elementary modal logic.[45] This logic yields "Necessarily if systematically true predictions are made by a theory in some domain (*P*), then in this domain that theory is roughly true (*T*)" where this modality denotes $Nec(P \rightarrow T)$ or $P \Rightarrow T$.

The modal conditional $P \Rightarrow T$ means, for example, that if *P* is true, then the truth of *T* follows necessarily and it is impossible for *T* to be false. Central to this inference is an idea in modal logic of *strict implication* that is sandwiched between logical entailment, which is stronger, and material implication that is weaker wherein the weaker implication happens when *p* implies *q* by the truth-functional *material implication* $p \rightarrow q$; the symbol $\rightarrow$ reading "if ... then," which is true if and only if *q* is not in fact false when *p* is true. And stronger than strict implication is when *p* implies *q* in terms of the *logical entailment* $p \vdash q$, whereby the symbol $\vdash$ is used here to denote a valid inference such that *q* being false when *p* is true is logically impossible. This impossibility specifies that $p \vdash q$ is necessarily true by *q* following logically from *p*. In this manner strict implication pertains to modal logic and the logic marks a boundary of material implication from the stronger entailment.

Per entailment, there are cases where *q* is not entailed by *p* but $p \rightarrow q$ is too weak epistemologically to capture a relationship. A relationship that is too weak is precisely why the famous logician Irving Copi said that symbols for material implication, such as $\rightarrow$, "must not be thought of as representing *the* meaning of 'if-then', or *the* relation of implication" since most conditionals "assert more," his admitting that the weaker symbol "ignores part of the meaning of most conditional statements."[46] The statement "If Jane enjoys some music, she'll enjoy the Big Bopper," for example, allows for a factual or reasonable possibility that Jane will not enjoy the Big Bopper even if she enjoys some music. But stronger conditionals can specify, per Copi's point, that ~ *q* may often be impos-

---

45. While the *epistemic* modalities herein explicitly refer to truth, *alethic* modalities such as "It is impossible for something to disappear" bear on reality without that reference, The lack of this reference reflects Walsh's *Metaphysics*. See Trundle's general discussions in *Medieval Modal Logic and Science*.

46. See Copi's *Symbolic Logic*, 16–17. Given the dogmatic received view of logic at the time, Copi is nothing less than courageous in his critique of restrictions to truth-functional conditionals.

sible when *p*. In addition to *epistemic* modalities, there are *alethic* ones about physical impossibilities such as "If Jane was conceived, then there were prior biological processes." Given the reproductive nature of human beings, it is patently irrational or more than unreasonable to admit of a possibility that there were not the biological processes when she was conceived. Thus, although her conception as such is *logically possible*, it is *physically impossible*. This impossibility can be recast, additionally, as a necessity of the form $p \Rightarrow q$.

While $P \Rightarrow T$ that denotes true theories strictly implied by successful predictions more formally relates success to truth than true observation reports related to our "success in coping with the world,"[47] held by Newton-Smith, his insight is a huge contribution to common-sense reasoning. And he is commendable not only for his erudite critique of the untenable observation-theoretical duality but also for pioneering the idea of an ever more theory-laden hierarchy of observation, proposing in the process an hierarchal base where lie the lowest low-level theory-laden observation reports whose minimal theory content affords enough observation to corroborate a theory. I submit, though, that theory corroboration is nevertheless imperiled. For any low-level observation report is alterable, on his view, by developments of scientific theories that do themselves rely *circularly* on observation reports.[48] Reports that corroborate the developments, therefore, are themselves falsifiable *ad infinitum* by ever more developments. And these developments in terms of the existential phenomenology in this essay, depend on observation reports that are not comparably alterable.

The inalterability of the reports is certifiable by scientists who appeal to their own awareness *of* their observational consciousness. This is a consciousness of how phenomena are *in themselves* apart from concepts, the awareness of which scientists can confirm by intentionally observing phenomena without concepts (bracketing by Husserl and seeing non-epistemologically by F. I. Dretske).[49] Also, the consciousness without

---

47. Newton-Smith, *The Rationality of Science*, 28.

48. Ibid.

49. Seeing$_n$ (non-epistemologically) is seeing or being aware of physical reality as it really *is* in itself apart from concepts. And this seeing is infused into a conceptualized epistemic seeing$_e$, rendering approximately objective our conceptual observational awareness. See Dretske's *Seeing and Knowing*, 11, 21, 76–77. In often replacing "see" with "awareness," Dretske's analysis combines the approaches of analytic philosophy and existential phenomenology in regard to issues of perception.

concepts infused into their conceptual consciousness of that phenomena. That is, phenomena have substantive structures, via the aforesaid aspects such as continuity and *independence*,[50] which can be described truly by virtue of observation reports being rooted in a pre-conceptual and conceptual consciousness of which scientists are irrefutably *aware*. In finding expression in terms of low-level observation reports to which approximate truth can be ascribed, this *awareness* provides a phenomenological basis for an epistemic bedrock that permits theories being corroborated. The corroboration is unavailable to positions based on metaphysics even if, as noted earlier, the metaphysics is "physics friendly." Thus, although Newton-Smith concludes that we need not seek an epistemic "bedrock sought by some proponents of the O/T distinction,"[51] his denial of that distinction begs for a neutral element in low-level observation reports on pain of their not being certifiably low-level when the way reality really *is* continues to be obstructed by concepts.[52]

An inability to explain how concepts do not necessarily obstruct a neutral observational touchstone with physical reality, if not a complete neglect of this foundational problem, bears profoundly on the failure of even attempting a defense of realism by most Anglo-American philosophers in the rationalist-empiricist-Kantian-positivist-analytic tradition. So scholars in this tradition such as Fred I. Dretske and Newton-Smith, who brilliantly addressed these concerns early on in innovative but different ways, are persons whose positions are not only exceptional but also extraordinarily helpful as stepping stones to solutions of those problems.

When one problem seems to be largely resolved such as the observation-theoretical distinction by approaches such as Newton-Smith's, though, other problems invariably surface as to whether or not theoretical terms refer to existing theoretical entities and if in fact these entities are unobservable, whether or not their reality can still be defended on behalf of a strong realism. "In building a stronger form of realism," notes Newton-Smith, "evidence for the truth (or approximate truth) [of a theory] is evidence for the existence of whatever has to exist for the theory to

---

50. Compton, "Natural Science," 90–91.

51. Newton-Smith, *The Rationality of Science*, 28.

52. My criticism of Newton-Smith, wherein I affirm a relatively unchanging epistemic bedrock of low-level O-reports because they are rooted closely in our consciousness without concepts (theoretical or non-theoretical) is a change from my previous books and articles.

be true (or approximately true)."[53] He states that to ascribe approximate truth to a theory, while mandating one's ontological commitments, is not to be committed to a reality of a given theory's theoretical entities having to be *ontologically like* the entities that we experience. This experiential disclaimer agrees with, if not is an understandable approach for avoiding conflict with, the *idee recue* that theoretical entities such as the electron (if they are really real) are unobservable. No one could blame any seasoned philosopher of science for seeking to avoid even the *appearance* of being vulnerable to the so-called "howler" that befalls those who daringly say they saw a theoretical entities (electrons) in electron microscopes; though Maxwell Grover held that the "continuous transition between what we see through 'ordinary spectacles . . . an ordinary window pane' and 'temperature gradients,'" including a use of "microscopes and telescopes," shows both that the relation of observable to theoretical entities "is vague and arbitrary" and that inasmuch as "there's no logical connection between observation and existence, there's *no reason* to believe that unobservable things do not exist."[54] The existence of theoretical entities may not only be plausible but also limitedly observable, moreover, if observations being theory-laden proceeds *pari passu* with theoretical entities also being observation-laden.

Observation-Laden Theory: Can Theoretical Entities be Observed?

Instrument-aided observation as well as observation by the naked-eye, per a received-view philosophy of science, continues to reflect the dogma that only theory pervades observation. Is the notion of *observation-laden theory* (as opposed to theory-laden observation) excluded since groundbreaking theories such as relativistic physics and quantum mechanics have seemed to render false our common-sense ordinary observations of physical reality? Realism is actually still viable, however, by virtue of perennial insights that include those of St. Augustine. Augustine suggested that observations beg for distinctions from their interpretations

---

53. Newton-Smith, *The Rationality of Science*, 38

54. See Klus. "Should We Trust Theoretical Science?" §4. There being no "logical connection between observation and existence," which implies that "there's no reason to believe that unobservable things do not exist," proceeds *pari passu* with accepting the possible existence of the devil, angels and God.

by theories; that theoretical truth is corroborable only by veritable observations.[55]

Observation-laden theories are admittedly implied by, if not central to, the relativisms of some historians "(e.g., Kuhn, 1970) and sociologists of scientific and mathematical knowing (e.g., Barnes, Bloor, & Henry, 1996)" who show "there exists an interactional relationship" of theory to observation such that "if observation is 'theory-laden,' theory is 'observation-laden.'"[56] This *ladenness* is more than reasonable if theories are to have any relationship to an observed reality. We have equally shown, even so, that *observation-laden theories* are still rooted in a theory-neutral consciousness of reality, via existential phenomenology, which is the necessary foundation for either a weak or strong realism. And a realism in which observation relies on theory as much as theory on observation not only needs to be appreciated for speaking unequivocally of degrees and not of kind about the observation/ theoretical terms but also results in an amazing point: The mutual relation of theoretical and observational terms means that we might credibly say that, *pace* the received view, some theoretical entities are at least limitedly observable since the entities observed are observation-laden. That this ladenness is provocative is illustrated by Peter Bokulick of the Dibner Institute at MIT for the History of Science and Technology. "When I first saw the newspaper headline announcing that the top quark had been 'observed' at Fermi lab," he says reflectively, "my thoughts immediately turned to debates over the *theory-laden character of observation* [not *observation-laden theory*] and to . . . what sort of 'observation' might have actually occurred in this case."[57] In this case the answer is, precisely, that scientists held they had observed an observation-laden theoretical entity.[58]

In any event, to say that an entity of a given theoretical language is laden by observation is still to admit of observation being the ontological bedrock to which theories must have final recourse. By recourse is meant that theories do not arise out of nowhere and nothing but rather from observation. So although new observables may be discovered by novel technologies and these often arise from theory development, this development as an evident growth of ever truer theories involves both their

55. St. Augustine, *Contra Academicos*, iii, xi, 26.
56. Roth and Bautista, "Transcriptions," 51–76. Emphasis.
57. See Bokulich's review of Kent W. Stanley's *The Evidence for the Top Quark*, para. 1, emphasis.
58. Cf. Physics editors, "Scientists Take Next Step," para. 1–7.

corroboration by observation and observation as an essential source of ground-breaking advancements of theories. Theory development can be induced by old theories that afford new technology, as the cathode ray tube afforded experiments that led to J. J. Thomson's theory of electron which was said to cause observed scintillations.[59] They had appearances that were explicable by existential phenomenology in which Thomson's non-conceptual consciousness of the phenomenon *in itself* (its distinctive aspects such as individuality and continuity) was infused into his conceptual observation of what are called "scintillations." In regard to these scintillations, an essential point about the epistemological bedrock that Newton-Smith rejects and I accept is that the *same* scintillations would have had to be observed by other scientists for duplicating Thomson's experiment and potentially accept electrons as real by virtue of their causing the phenomenon (as the phenomenon's reality warranted the inferred reality of their cause per the aforesaid causal explanations advanced by Cartwright; despite an increasingly better account of electrons from Thomson to theories of today).

Today, the scintillations would appear the same in the same experimental setup. And although setups change, there is no change *per se* of the appearances expressed by either observational reports or predictions (descriptions) but rather of the appearances' theoretic interpretations. In sum these interpretations attach to theories tested by observational descriptions to which truth is roughly ascribable. And ascribing truth to observational descriptions plays a decisive role for a robust scientific realism that is based both on observations confirming an approximate truth of theories and on a common-sense reasoning of modal logic from their success to truth. A truth of the observations and theories depend, in the end, on a non-conceptual consciousness, of which scientists are aware, which is infused into their conceptual consciousness of distinctive phenomena.

Observation Expressed by Existential Phenomenology Is Not a Theory[60]

In sum, our indirect awareness of our direct consciousness is what is meant by our being self-conscious. This consciousness uniquely supports

---

59. Newton-Smith, *The Rationality of Science*, 38.
60. Theory versus phenomenology is discussed by Efremov et al in "Glucon and

scientific realism, not by another abstract metaphysical theory, but rather by appealing to the integrity of one's own immediate conscious experience. The experience in terms of science stresses that scientists are *aware of* their conceptual consciousness of phenomena in experimental setups or otherwise. They are thus irrefutably aware of the following: that phenomena are *not* their consciousness (being conscious *of* phenomena is to be conscious of not being them); that phenomena are revealed as they really are *in themselves* apart from our will, wish or thought; and that they are aware that their thought may skew the appearances of phenomena by either cultural or scientific concepts. But besides these concepts being distinguished from the phenomena by their awareness, they are implicitly aware of their *non-conceptual consciousness* of the aspects of phenomena (individuality, independence, extensiveness, and continuity). And observational conceptions, of which scientists are aware, explains how errors or accuracies of the conceptions can be gauged by their comparisons to the aspectual phenomena *in themselves*; the latter being distinguishable from the conceptions. Also, the conceptions explain why a subtle cultural relativism does not arise when scientific conceptions are mathematical, or otherwise precisely conceived, and expressed as propositions whose meanings are unambiguous. Regardless of an ambiguity of ordinary language, extolled *ceteris paribus* by Wittgenstein, there is a soft cultural relativism which does not affect formalized propositions in terms of which theories can have laws (L) construed as a proposition, for example ($L_1 \wedge L_2 \wedge L_3$), to which truth is ascribable; although not by a present-day truth-functional propositional logic.[61]

While that logic was often challenged by Wittgenstein, he held that language involves a *lebensform* (form of life) as one's culture or whole of one's social practices, meaning that "claims had a certain hold over our actions, but not . . . like a *law of nature* would."[62] A law of nature expressed as a proposition (say for Newton's second law $f = ma$), whose truth is not skewed by culture, contrasts to many ordinary sentences in different

---

Qurak Distributions in Large N_c QCD," 183–86. Here, "phenomenology" is used differently from "phenomenological data" employed typically in different contexts of science.

61. Cf. Stiftung, "The Form of Our Life with Language," para. 1: "It is peculiar that Wittgenstein uses the expressions 'language' and 'form of life' in a distinctively first personal way."

62. Wolf, "Philosophy of Language." §3b. This article on language is a very insightful.

cultures such that sentence S might be true in Θ but false in Ψ where the latter symbols are cultures to which S's truth is relative. Keep in mind that this relativism, nonetheless, is a *species of realism* insofar as *different cultural meanings* imposed on a thing's appearance do not obviate the appearance having its roots in a non-conceptual consciousness of the *same thing*. In terms of Dretske, for example, we noted that persons influenced by different cultural frameworks could not be said to see the same thing if there were not any non-epistemic (non-conceptual) sorts of seeing.[63] The import of this seeing aside, if the relativism *ignores* the non-conceptual seeing by specifying simply that statement S may be assigned different meanings that entail different truth-values, these values follow necessarily and the relativism is logically trivial. And if a non-trivial version says that S_1 and S_2 express proposition p with an extra-cultural universal meaning (say interpreting $f = ma$ for a pendulum as $mgsin\theta = -m\, d^2s/dt^2$),[64] then to say S_1 might be true in Θ but S_2 may be false in Ψ is to say that p with the same meaning and truth-condition, which is Nature and *not* culture, can nonetheless have different truth-values. These values, however, render logically incoherent the relativism. And so the relativism as Newton-Smith would hold, without a non-conceptual consciousness, is unintelligible if not trivial.[65]

This triviality, if not the incoherent relativism that Newton-Smith famously criticizes,[66] begs for a concise distinction from the cultural relativism discussed herein. There must be a reminder that the relativism above is actually a *species of realism* since sentences S, S_1 and S_2 as well as proposition p alike express truth-claims based ultimately on a conceptual consciousness of phenomena being infused with a non-conceptual consciousness of the phenomena as they are *in themselves* from given perspectives. That is, anything seen is seen from a perspective, but this fact does not counter the phenomenological realism. This realism is centered on an existential phenomenology of observational consciousness that brings to mind, and is strongly analogous to, an analytic philosophical analysis by Dretske's notion that a non-epistemic awareness of something

---

63. See Dretske's *Seeing and Knowing*, 21.

64. See Díez and Lorenzano,"Are natural selection explanatory models a priori?" 786–809, where there is discussion of free fall f = ma becoming mg = md²s/dt² and mgSinθ = - md²s/dt.

65. Cf. Newton-Smith, *The Rationality of Science*, 34–36.

66. See Nanay, "Entity Realism and Singularist Realism," 1–19.

seen (*seeing*$_n$) is infused into an epistemic awareness of that thing seen (*seeing*$_e$) that affords an objectivity to what we say we see.

Without our seeing non-conceptually, persons with radically different cultural frameworks or belief systems could not be said to see the same things. The sophisticate and uncultured looking at, or being conscious of, the same thing would see different things. And this is but a prelude to an unadulterated sophism in which our truth-claims are relative to entities that include cultures. The notion that cultures are that to which truth is relative is indeed incoherent if not trivial: trivial if each culture's truths are true necessarily since cultures would be truth-conditions for truth; logically incoherent if contradictory truths are accepted *a priori*. Not either an *a priori* violation of the Principle of Non-Contradiction or the problem of triviality need be accepted to accept a restricted relativity inherent in other ways of seeing (other conceptual modes of discerning) without undermining an inexact objectivity of our observational awareness. This awareness is shared, public, and objective, despite varying worldviews (*Weltanschauungen*) that are *conceptual*, by virtue of a *non-conceptual* awareness of the same events, processes or objects. And although an epistemic objectivity alien to epistemic relativism is advanced by pragmatic approaches, such as the thesis of "empirical adequacy" (stressing successful theories rather than their truth), we noted that truth can be *strictly implied* by predictive success for a strong scientific realism. This realism is established uniquely herein by a sensible modal-logic reasoning, expanded upon soon, as well as by an existential phenomenology of observational consciousness of which we are also incontrovertible aware.

Our self-awareness was ignored by the most valued philosopher of science in the twentieth century, Sir Karl Popper. His disregard of a direct consciousness of which he was irrefutably aware (like being aware that one can see well only by wearing the glasses for which one is *ably* looking) is attributable to the unfortunate impact on him by Hume's radical empiricism. This empiricism is said to have influenced Albert Einstein because Einstein "admitted that Hume influenced the development of his special theory of relativity."[67] This relativity notwithstanding, Einstein still admitted also that there can be no "conceptual definition" of Hume's distinction of internal sense impressions from internal ideas derived from them precisely because the definition would rely

---

67. Cf. Slavov, "Empiricism and Relationism Intertwined," 247–63.

circularly on the impressions in question; Einstein saying "aside from, circular definitions."[68] And beyond these definitions being problematic, Einstein, in contrast to Hume, criticized the "*insinuation* that a concept . . . is something metaphysical (and therefore to be rejected)."[69] Finally, although Einstein said that "From Hume[,] Kant had learned that there are concepts [e.g., "causal connections"] which play a dominating role in our thinking . . . ," Einstein suggested that Kant, if not Hume, could have easily sidestepped skepticism if he had said more modestly that thinking is necessary for grasping "the *empirically given* [versus private sense impressions and '*categories*'] *necessary as . . . elements of thinking*"[70]; rather than thinking being imposed *a priori* on an amorphous raw material of experience via *a priori categories*. And on top of these categories, the *synthetic-a priori* judgments are criticized by Einstein as "an error" by being dependent on "sensory experience"; although this experience is more against those who "still adhere to the errors of 'synthetic judgments *a priori*.'"[71]

In sum, the strange philosophical bedfellows of Kant's idealism and Hume's radical empiricism continue to obstruct a recognition both that there is an observational consciousness of the *empirically given*, as Einstein put it, and that there can be strict implications from successful theories to their truth. Before further examining these obstructions to truth, consider how "truth" for Popper is both the surreptitious source of a continuing epistemic relativism, by his direct impact on Kuhn and Feyerabend as well as their present-day heirs, and an ongoing but unrestrained challenge to realism. The professed realism by Popper, notwithstanding his furtively fathering an antirealist relativistic theory-dependence, is strange in light of his unbridled alarm over a post-rationalist society; a society that should concern everyone who cares about "civilization" and the "serious deterioration of the standards of scientific discussion."[72] Popper was wrong about that discussion deteriorating. For the paradoxes,

---

68. Einstein, "Reply to Critics," 673. This book with the cherished *signature* of Raymond E. Olsen was kindly offered to me among other books by his wife, which is why I chose it in late March 1969 only weeks after his sudden death. The late Robert Harris, Philosophy Chair at Miami University, noted aptly in a poignant memoir that "we are reminded that life is greater than our understanding."

69. Ibid., emphasis.

70. Ibid., 678. Only "*empirically given*" is emphasized.

71. Ibid., 678–79.

72. See Sir Karl Popper's *Quantum Theory and the Schism in Physics*, 156.

about which he was so alarmed in quantum physics, were both seriously considered and rightly accepted by virtue of following *a posteriori* from experiments and not *a priori* by relativistic interpretations imposed on phenomena. And Popper was wrong, as right as he was about other issues, in assuming that he did not contribute colossally to the irrational relativism which he so ironically loathed.[73]

---

73. Cf. Trundle, "Aristotle V. Van Til and Łukasiewicz," 323–44.

5

Theory-Dependence
A Relativism Founded by a Famous "Realist"

Until this point many knotty epistemological challenges to scientific realism were analyzed, disputed, and many overcome, both logically and phenomenologically. Now investigated in more detail is the immense influence of the most famous self-avowed realist of the twentieth century, Sir Karl Popper. We will seek to show that in fact Popper was *unwittingly* a veiled anti-realist who ironically, more than anyone else, influenced explicit anti-realists for whom reality is not discoverable (the dearth of discoverability notwithstanding, his castigating the relativists "in *The Open Society and Its Enemies* for moral irresponsibility by virtue of his being "a moral realist . . ."[1]). This *moral realism* was, strangely, certifiably not complemented by Popper's pseudo-realism in science. The alleged scientific realism was defended largely by a commonplace notion of truth-functional logic that, while notoriously limited, was unabashedly lauded as the "logic of scientific discovery." Any discovery in regard to reality, however, is a patent illusion regardless of the popularization of that logic.[2] This logic of *falsification* actually afforded an apologetics for succeeding epistemic relativists in order to assail any weak or strong form of realism. Furthermore, these anti-realists, who were indebted to Popper, *understood* him better prima facie than most mainstream philosophers of

---

1. Cf. Popper's rebuke of relativism, despite dramatically advancing it, is not only not disputed but noted explicitly by Jarvie in "Popper's Philosophy," 284–317.

2. Berezow, "Falsification," para. 1–8. Emphasis.

science and scientists who are not avid anti-realists but bought into the chimera that he really was a realist.

A chimera of the realism avowed by Popper is evident by his metaphorical comparison of reality to the murky bottom of a swamp that is never reached by lowered "observational pillars."[3] The pillars and swamp are indeed tied to Popper's rejection of induction via Hume's critique. Despite this critique, Popper's position came to rely, paradoxically, on induction (as when he holds that the more *improbable* are predictions of a law or theory is, the more *probable* is the law or theory's truth). The irony of what I call his inverse-probability is captured also by Deborah Mayo who notes that "even if a hypothesis is highly *corroborated* . . ." Popper "regards this as at most a report of the hypothesis' past performance and denies it affords positive evidence for its correctness or reliability."[4] And Grattan-Guinness notes how Popper rejects that "theories are proven to be true by the accumulation of 'confirming' instances, or at least that" it is "steadily more probable."[5] The inductivist may say that the claim "*all* gold is malleable" is inferable *from* "some observed gold is malleable" (the latter, some say, being essential to gold). But to speak coherently of any observed gold is to know, says Popper, a presupposed theory of gold; the theory going beyond observation by its universality that refers to the swamp-bottom reality.

This covert challenge to realism is overlooked by those who are bamboozled by Popper's reassuring realist similes and self-avowed scientific rationality.[6] Thus, although a rationality of science backed by Newton-Smith neglects to articulate a theory-neutral element in observation, he astutely exposes Popper's pseudo-realism by noting that it may be "attractive to many because they do not succeed in thinking themselves into the system."[7] The system seems *as if* observation statements can test theories, but this stance is not at all the "Popperian picture."[8] The actual picture is of observation being ungrounded, planting a covert *seed* for the up-front relativisms of Feyerabend, Kuhn and those they inspired such as the social-constructionist relativists. Truly, divulging the true picture

---

3. Popper, *The Logic of Scientific Discovery*, 111.
4. Mayo, "Peircean Induction," 299–319.
5. Grattan-Guinness, "Karl Popper and the 'The Problem of Induction,'" 107–20.
6. Cf, Gattei, *Karl Popper's Philosophy of Science*, para. 1–15.
7. Newton-Smith, *The Rationality of Science*, 62.
8. Ibid.

of Popper was, for me, felt quite viscerally. A professor on my Ph.D. dissertation committee objected so vociferously to my denial of Popper's realism that committee member Hazel Barnes phoned me long distance, after encountering this professor in a hallway, to alert me about his irregular behavior prior to my final oral exam—there being two previous ones, with two committee chairs quitting, because of the obstructions. Oddly, Dr. Barnes said that this person gave *no* reasons why my argument was wrong after she asked.[9]

Anti-Realism Arising Paradoxically Out of Popper

There is no intention of underrating Popper's prodigious feats that earned him international honors. The honors range from science, pedagogy, and political theory to his being one of the few scholars who have influenced scientists and even courts of law; although Susan Hack notes that "Popper's philosophy of science is signally inappropriate to [a recent] Court's concern with reliability," adding that when he "describes his approach as 'Critical Rationalism,' it is to emphasize that the rationality of the scientific enterprise lies in the susceptibility of scientific theories to criticism, i.e., to testing, and potentially to falsification, *not* in their verifiability or confirmability."[10] Nonetheless, the analysis in this essay is fresh insofar as it stems from an existential phenomenological criticism of his supposed scientific realism. Thus, although Popper clearly professes that scientists should aim at true and explanatory descriptions of physical reality, reality is held to be so elusive epistemologically that scientists are never justified in a realist sense of ascribing "truth" to theories. Theories are not known to be true in the sense of reflecting how reality really *is* even

---

9. Nor were reasons given at my oral exam, although tensions due to this person led some members to ask the Department Chair Robert Rogers to attend my exam. After the exam, with my graduation on hold, Rogers told me and some other members that this person's behavior was "highly irregular" and that he should be removed from the committee. When I later phoned him, as asked, he said that this person threatened to stop a vital colloquium series if he was removed. He and other members who evidently did not want to offend him, nonetheless passed my thesis with *no* demands to alter it, in a later meeting with my *new* Committee Chair James Kimble. After his death, Kimble was eulogized for defending the vulnerable at a memorial in 2003. After 2003, with the need to be cryptic at this point, there is the need also to investigate illegal and immoral connections to a female attorney who graduated from the UC Boulder Law School.

10. Hack, "Disentangling *Daubert*," 25–36.

approximately. This refusal by Popper to acknowledge even an inexact truth of theories may seem reasonable due to a *Principle of Pessimistic Induction*. This induction per Newton-Smith specifies that since every major theory in history has been superseded within several hundred years, it is reasonable to suppose that any theory now or in the future that is thought to be true will both turn out to be false and be superseded by another theory that will itself be superseded and so on.[11] This supersession of false theories assumes Popper's truth-functional $T \to P$, where T is a theory and P denotes even systematically true predictions, results in the fallacy of affirming the consequent when T's inexact truth is inferred from a truth of P.

A *Principle of Optimistic Induction* that I propose and refer to later, however, advances an epistemic modality for inferences to an increasing *inexact truth* of major historical theories. Though these mature theories have a truth restricted to given domains as they are superseded, the inexact truth applies to ever larger domains for a notion of expanding knowledge in the future. So subsequent mature theories pertain to previous domains and are applicable to ever more phenomena into the future. This optimistic picture of future growing truth reflects a potent verisimilitude in contrast to Popper's bogus gambit of an increasing "truth-likeness" of theories. Since theories are not subject to any inductive reasoning, for Popper, who defers to Hume's denial of true universal propositions since they "transcend experience,"[12] theories are not comparably *true* on Popper's account and it is incongruent with my optimistic induction. To wit: although this induction is based on a theory being roughly true (T) when it has systematically true predictions in a domain (P), $P \Rightarrow T$ where T's falsity when P is an epistemic impossibility, Newton-Smith's pessimistic induction is based counter intuitively on a truth-functional logic where it is logically possible that a theory is entirely false even if its predictions are systematically true.

Popper on Problems in the Philosophy of Science

The optimistic and pessimistic principles, in regard to the future of theories, both admit hypothetically of rational theory choices inasmuch as some theories are in fact more *successful* than others as is manifest by

11. Newton-Smith, *The Rationality of Science*, 14.
12. Popper, *Conjectures and Refutations*, 54.

their historical supersessions. The epistemological significance of the supersessions, however, is incomprehensible on Popper's position. His position not only rejects there being good reasons for claiming that one theory is truer than another, since their supposed success is "confirmed" by observations that circularly presuppose theories (and the theories thus not having observable successes related *logically* to their inexact "truth") but also begs for the explicit recognition that even low-level observational statements do not have any touchstone with reality whatsoever. And hence his position is inconsistent with those statements having any knowable truth. That is, the denial that truth is ascribable to even low-level observation statements, which are similar to the aforesaid O-reports at the bottom of an increasing theory-laden hierarchy, effectively excludes also the truth of so-called "basic observation statements" that purportedly falsify theories. *Pari passu* these falsified theories are thus so "observationally challenged"—to provide a politically correct euphemism for science in a way reminiscent of Popper, that Popper's own position cuts off theories from their corroborative failures and, therefore, from any possible falsification!

If falsification is bogus, then there are catastrophic effects for both the epistemic status of scientific theories, which lose their status as theories, and the ontological status of theoretical entities that lose their status of being real. Moreover, the signature notions in Popper's position of theory *falsification* (versus a verification of theories being knowably true) and *verisimilitude* (their supposed increasing truth-likeness) in being patently untenable brings to mind Barbara Billauer who falsifies "Popper's thesis of 'falsifiability' using scientific examples."[13] She points out as well that "Popper's refusal to respect the *'why'* of science, (i.e., the mechanics of scientific discovery and causal connections) enables him to build thought-castles in the sky where he ensconces his mythical principality of science . . . ."[14] More untenable than even his notion of scientific theories being falsified is calling Popper a scientific realist because realists, while they may be grateful for his forcing them to refine their stances, had to sacrifice too much time in both defending common sense and struggling to surmount many sophistical hurdles systemic to his anti-realism *as well as* the epistemic relativists that he inspired. Consider in more detail exactly why his signature notions are derisorily indefensible after analyzing

---

13. Billauer, "Admissibility of Scientific Evidence," 21.
14. Ibid., 57.

more precisely why basic observation statements have an unintelligible connection to theory. We shall see in greater detail *inter alia* that, on Popper's account, scientific theories are not only presupposed by observation statements, so that the statements can only be said to falsify theories on pain of a vicious circularity, but also that there is universality of the theories that purportedly precludes there knowable truth.

Scientific Thesis of Falsification Faultily Founded

Though theories should comprise true—or at least inexactly true descriptions of reality, according to Popper, Popper denies that reality or anything else can count as criteria for ascertaining their truth. A fundamental reason for this skepticism about scientific theories is that these theories are composed of universal law-like propositions about a possibly infinite set of entities at all times and places such that a hypothetical two-law theory, to which "truth" is putatively ascribable, is denotable as a compound proposition $(L_1 \wedge L_2)$ where $\wedge$ reads "and."[15] But scientists cannot determine the truth-value of more than a finite amount of basic observation statements, says Popper, where these statements are existential in the classical Aristotelian sense of referring to existing observable phenomena in the specific spatio-temporal region. In a given region k in Popper's parlance, for example, no finite amount of basic statements of the form "some Θ_s are Ψ_s" admit of valid inferences to the universal law or law-like proposition L_1 or L_2 expressed as "all Θs are Ψs" (per the Aristotelian Square of Opposition). So no sum of basic statements such as the statement "this gold is malleable," per Popper, is construable as "some gold is malleable" for inferring validly the universal law or law-like proposition "all gold is malleable."

The proposition that "all gold is malleable," to be precise, would have to be inferred inductively. But following Hume, whose denial of induction is accepted without reservation by Popper,[16] we do not have any universal experience in the sense of experiencing all of anything such as gold. And even if all gold had been experienced, how could that be known? In other words our ability to know only that a universal law or theory is false and not that they are true, from the standpoint of logic, is the foundation of his famous *The Logic of Scientific Discovery*

---

15. Newton-Smith, *The Rationality of Science*, 47.
16. Popper, *Conjectures and Refutations*, 54.

wherein universal laws or theories are to be tested only by attempting their falsification. This falsification as a allegedly novel "logic," however, merely specifies the common logic of truth-functional reasoning where although a true prediction P made by a theory T does not imply T's truth in the conditional $T \to P$, a false prediction $\sim P$ can test (falsify) T as illustrated by the conditional $\sim P \to \sim T$. This mundane logic as proposed by Popper, however, was foretold by a pre-modern logic of the Aristotelian Square of Opposition.[17] Here, from the truth of an existential proposition "some Ss are Ps," which can be certified observationally, we cannot validly infer a truth of the unequivocally universal proposition that "all Ss are Ps." But the latter proposition is inferably false (falsified) by the *false* existential proposition "some Ss are Ps." Consequently, where the subject term S denotes "gold" and where the predicate term P represents either "rigid" or "non-malleable," the proposition "some gold is non-malleable," if certified observationally, would be able to test (falsify) the universal proposition that affirms a malleability of gold.

How Falsification is Un-grounded by Observation

Referring to gold either existentially or universally, notwithstanding gold's apparent observability (and thus its being an observation term *prima facie*), is on Popper's position to both know and be able to stipulate formally what gold is theoretically. This deference to theories, when theories are untestable, is bewilderingly empty and contrary to common sense. It seems senseless indeed to hold that if children play in the winter and utter "this is ice," then their talk amounts to *prattle* unless they both know and are able to specify what "ice" is, say in terms of a theoretical physics of ice as "Ice Ih" and its melting point, density, and vapor pressure.[18] The consequence of this nonsensical reasoning is that basic observation statements that ostensibly falsify (or test) theories do themselves presuppose the very theories that depend for their tests on other theory-dependent observation statements that also presuppose theories and so forth *ad infinitum* such that empirically groundless theories are tested paradoxically by theories that are equally groundless.

---

17. Cf. Beziau and Gan-Krzywoszyńska (eds.), "Handbook of the World Congress," lines 1–87.
18. Petrenko and Whitworth, "Ice Ih," 10.

In replacing the notion of "theory" with that of "law" that is also universal, a fatuity of the irrational reasoning becomes transparent when Popper holds that the statement "'Here is a glass of water' cannot be verified by any observational experience" since the "universal terms ['glass', 'water'] 'denote physical bodies which exhibit a certain law-like behavior.'"[19] *Pari passu* the behavior, which is law-like, is related logically to the universal law "all crows are black" which may be falsified by the prototype basic statement "Here is a white crow" where "crow" and "white" are universal terms that presuppose laws or theories that themselves beg for testing by other observation statements which also presuppose theories and so forth in an evident regress *ad infinitum*. And in this dog-chasing-its-tail falsification, which foreshadows the anti-realist relativisms of Kuhn, Feyerabend, social constructionists, and others for whom our seeing or observation depends exclusively on theories, theories are no more tenable than the theory-dependent observation statements on which they depend, and the statements are no more plausible either than the theories on which they depend.

A dependence of observation exhaustively on theory whereby there is no theory-neutral touchstone with reality and wherein not either true predictions or inferences to true theories are possible, notwithstanding a common-sense reasoning expanded on later, is not a pedantic problem without appalling results both in education worldwide and in the world of applied or practical studies. These studies *ceteris paribus* are informed by and should follow from well-tested theories. This stress on theories reflects Aristotle for whom theoretical sciences are superior to sciences that are inferred, which are practical, because *less* changeable principles of theory are the cause of *more* changeable practical applications (*Metaph.* 6.1, 1026a 15). And appreciating that the applied precepts are more mutable than theory is a matter of wisdom. This wisdom contrasts to Kant whose *Critique of Practical Reason* was his very "refuge" from the theoretical *Critique of Pure Reason* in which "knowledge . . . is possible *a priori*, though only from a practical point of view."[20] This practical view resulted in, among other anti-realisms, pragmatic and relativistic approaches to the theoretical. These theoretical sciences, in point of fact, are able to handily defend a robust realism.

---

19. Popper, *Conjectures and Refutations*, 387.

20. Kant, *Critique of Pure Reason*, 25. While *theoretical reason* should be presupposed by *reason that is practical*, as structural engineering presupposes theoretical physics, practical reason became a proxy for the theoretical.

As this realism serves to explain how theoretical physics led to a physics of applied engineering, applied studies such as business ethics and women's studies beg for comparatively unchanging theories: theories of truth (epistemology) and reality (ontology). These must themselves be based on existential phenomenology as a basis for applied and theoretical knowledge. In terms of this knowledge, Aristotle's voice rings down the vistas of time: Our studies should start with the most familiar thing, ourselves.[21] A stress on our self-consciousness is avowed by Victor Caston in "Aristotle on Consciousness," with parallels to Sartre and Husserl, where Aristotle's "direct realism" relies on the perceiver being *conscious* that "the perceptible object . . . is independent of any perception of it."[22] And this perceptual realism is augmented by St. Thomas for whom a perceiver would be "*conscious* that it is himself who understands."[23] This understanding is ground zero for realism. The appeal of realism to our personal conscious experience contrasts poignantly to all of the conjectural pedantries and relativisms of Popper, Feyerabend, Kuhn, and their post-modern heirs.

Observational Truth Undercut by Relativistic Paradigms

Points of either agreement or disagreement between Popper and Kuhn are discussed as a backdrop for examining Kuhn's radical epistemic relativism. The review of Popper's relativism will focus afterward on issues germane to the problems of scientific realism. This realism is rejected by Kuhn when he says, for example, that he and Popper *accept* a "revolutionary" process by which theories radically replace theories and *reject* science progressing by accretion (which is peculiar for Kuhn to profess, given Popper's prescribed "verisimilitude" of increasing truth-likenesses of theories in their historical development).[24] This anomalous development aside in the case of Popper, both Popper and Kuhn highlight the role played in the revolutionary process of older theories failing to satisfy challenges posed by experiment, observation and logic. Finally, Kuhn and Popper are opposed to a number of the most characteristic

21. Cf. Trundle, *Ancient Greek Philosophy*, 243.

22. See Aristotle's *On Perception and Perceptibles* 6 446b.

23. Aquinas, *Summa Theologiae i*, 76, emphasis. His use of "consciousness" is significant.

24. Kuhn, *The Essential Tension*, 267.

positions of classical (received view) logical positivism. In contrast to the positivistic observation-theory distinction, for instance, there is an essential deficiency of any distinction whatsoever.

The failure to distinguish observation from theory in the sense of holding a *theory-dependent* observation that excludes observation being even *theory-laden* by degrees is, according to Popper and Kuhn, to reject observational truth-claims about reality in contrast to the positivists (which belies both they and the positivists being overridingly like-minded in overlooking consciousness as explored by existential phenomenology). Furthermore, with mischievous social and political implications, Popper and Kuhn insist that scientists should aim at *inventing* theories which explain phenomena as real objects.[25] But this aim, in being expressible as a *synthetic-a priori* Kantian judgment, which cannot be known to be true, reflects the vacuous realism of similar metaphysical "regulatory principles." And these principles notwithstanding, the words *inventing* and *reinventing* something such as either theories or persons anticipates an epistemic relativistic post-modern social constructionism.

The social constructionism is advanced "by politically correct academic feminists"[26]—the iconic feminist Helen Gurley Brown being "a product, for instance, of her own *reinvention* from a 'mouseberger' [unexceptional woman] into the subject of 'Sex and the Single Girl,' unapologetically working and sleeping her way out of the steno pool and into an advertising career."[27] Further, inventing or reinventing theories is, as elaborated on later, a signature trait of the post-Popperian relativism. One form of this relativism is advanced by Feyerabend and has immensely influenced feminist epistemology in Women's Studies in terms of Feyerabend's fatuous, if not facetious, "epistemological anarchy"; Frederick Suppe notably dismissing Feyerabend as an insincere scholar when he, unlike Kuhn (Kuhn said jokingly to be a "born-again realist" after a *thousand epistemological cuts*[28]), declined to defend his anything-goes

---

25. Ibid., 269. Explanation is a typical trait of realism and rejected habitually by anti-realists as superfluous to the scientific enterprise.

26. Patai and Koertege, *Professing Feminism*, 135–36.

27. Trundle, "America's Religion," 3–20. This issue for the *Journal for the Study of Religions and Ideologies* was sponsored by the U.S. State Department and included in the unique book on American religion, *Religion, Culture & Ideology in America*, edited by Drs. Sandu and Mihaela Frunza.

28. See McPherson's "Needed: A Nobel Prize," B7, as well as Horgan's "Profile: Reluctant Revolutionary," 40, 49.

anarchical epistemology, which he so audaciously espoused, at an international conference.[29] This critical conference reminds us of Popper, if not Kuhn and Feyerabend, who refers to observational "pillars" lowered on a swamp whose bottom is never reached; a metaphor for an observable physical reality. Popper, Kuhn, and Feyerabend alike reject any notion of science *proceeding logically upward* from existential propositions, which refer to some observed phenomena, to universal propositions for which non-theoretical terms are transposable into terms that are theoretical. How can a false non-theoretical existential proposition, which is not grounded in an observable reality, imply its false universal counterpart? Not either falsification or verification are possible; notwithstanding the mainstream position on Popper among philosophers of science that "science could not be positively verified, but was instead about otherscientists testing and failing-to-refute hypotheses . . . ."[30]

Paradigms as Creations by Sophistical Heroes in Science

Since the aforesaid notion of the theoretical has no intelligible relation to physical reality as it really *is*, there are several plausible ways to construe the idea of created or invented theories. Theories as paradigms tend to amount to *Weltanschauungen* (worldviews) that are imposed *a priori* on reality. Here, reality is said to be reflected truly by the worldviews even if, incoherently, they are contradictory. Or scientific theories may merely be a means for molding reality via the dictum that "man is the measure of what *is*" per the sophist Protagoras (and as adapted to the superior man or *Ubermensch* by Nietzsche[31]), if not the combative Thrasymachus. The latter would relegate theories to *glorified opinions* (recalling Plato) wherein, for example, "might makes right" on the relativistic *a priori* assumption that contradictory claims can both be true about justice since "justice is nothing else than that which is advantageous to the stronger"

29. See Suppe, *The Structure of Scientific Theories*, 636.

30. "Science is fundamentally self-regulated by the integrity of individual scientists: therefore young scientists must develop their personal qualities, as well as learning their subject." See Charlton, *The Winnower*, para. 3.

31. In relating Kuhn to a relativism of Nietzsche, radical (gender) feminist Kathryn Parsons maintained that a moral or social or scientific paradigm "is not merely something through which we see the world. . . . [The paradigm] shapes the facts of the human world." Nietzsche had held in effect that there are no facts, only interpretation. See Parsons, "Nietzsche and Moral Change," 186.

(the stronger saying *x* is just, and it *is* just, until the weaker become the stronger and *x* then becomes unjust).[32]

The "unjust" and "just," and "truth" itself, are allegedly relative to either whoever has power or whatever causes our thoughts, such as different cultures, so say the sophists such as Thrasymachus and Protagoras. Though they are iconic sophistical heroes to their relativistic heirs, they are ostensibly disdained by Popper. He holds, however, that scientists inventively create theoretical conjectures and attempt to falsify them by observation statements. But these statements presuppose theories that beg for further statements to falsify those theories and so forth *ad infinitum*. This *ad-infinitum* impasse issues in a relativistic theory-dependence that inspires contemporary sophistical heroes in science such as Popper and Kuhn. Kuhn's relativism combines the worst of two worlds.

One world involves a paradigm (worldview) that is created by super scientists who, interpreting reality *a priori* with no self-regulating reference to experience *a posteriori*, is the measure of how reality really *is*.[33] How it really *is* in different historical periods, however, is instituted individually by creative heroic scientists. These scientists reflect Nietzsche's notion that there are only interpretations of reality and no facts. Apart from facts, they create conjectural but revolutionary worldviews to which truth is wholly relative. The other world involves a relativistic worldview being viewed erroneously as reflecting reality as it really *is*, apart from our will, wish or thought, by science students who are causally conditioned by the received worldview. And via the worldview, scientists come to regard what was previously deemed abnormal as respectable "normal science." Singular scientists come to mind, from Aristotle to Einstein, who imaginatively solved enigmas.

Enigma solving, for Kuhn, should supplant science's supposed "aim" of obtaining truth. Attaining truth was the vacuous vision proposed by Popper, given that theories are only inferably false. This falsifiability "formulated by Karl Popper," S. T. Asma states skeptically, "nicely rules out the spooky claims of pseudoscientists and snake oil salesmen. Or does

---

32. Plato, *Republic* 338c.

33. Cf. Ankey and Leonelli, "Repertoires: A post-Kuhnian perspective," 18–28. A fine discussion of post-Kuhnianism. The authors note that "philosophers of science have hitherto paid little attention to collaboration, and more generally the social organization of research, as *lenses* through which to think about and analyze scientific change." Emphasis.

it?"³⁴ "We are all living in the vast gray area," he answers, "between leech-bleeding and antibiotics" that elude glib falsification.³⁵ The falsification, Kuhn argues, should be supplanted by the more subtle prescience of science being an enigma-/puzzle-solving enterprise. The enterprise has practitioners who share scientific criteria that, for a group in a given historical time, determines when the puzzle is solved. And when it is not solved, the worldview is not normally suspected but rather its practitioners. By virtue of the practitioners' prominence, on Kuhn's view, astrology is not a science because it cannot be falsified but because it has no puzzles to solve and so there is no science to practice.³⁶ Recall that the practice, for Kuhn, adopts a theory-dependence begun by Popper; despite the dependence being spun differently. Popper's notion of observation statements presupposing theories has theories, per Kuhn, replaced by theoretical paradigms that can be contradictory. Also, the paradigms are imposed *a priori* on reality such that reality as observed instrumentally or by naked-eye is colored exhaustively in a way similar to, but worse than, looking at the world through differently colored lenses. These lenses call to mind Kant's idealism where our cognition imposes *a priori categorial* interpretations on reality with a caveat that the "idealism" in Kuhn's case is a mass-induced mental *Weltanschauung*.

Science Skewed by Popper's Furtive Foundation in Hume

With a reminder that the *Weltanschauung* analysis is held by Kuhn and the theory-dependence by Popper, the purported puzzle-solving nature of science embraced by Kuhn still results in Kuhn's rejection of Popper's point that historical superseding theories bring about scientific communities that learn from their mistakes. This mistake-based learning is compatible with Popper's notion of historically increasing truth-likeness of theories (verisimilitude), although (1) the latter was shown herein to both be vacuous and conflict with Kuhn's view that major historical theories amount to incomparable *Weltanschauungen*, and (2) "Kuhn wants to show that scientific progress is not cumulative, that is, an accumulation of scientific knowledge."³⁷ This lack of knowledge aside, the main mistake

---

34. Asma, "The Enigma of Chinese Medicine," para. 4–5.
35. Ibid.
36. Kuhn, *The Essential Tension*, 272.
37. Cf. Aulfig, "Paradigm and Incommensurability," para. 6–8.

of Popper's idea of superseding theories, for Kuhn, is that the old theories made faulty inferences such as that since *all observed* crows have trait x, *all* crows have x when $\sim x$ might actually obtain and be explained by the more cogent inferences of a new law or theory.[38] Curiously, though, Kuhn's criticism centers largely on the problem of induction that, being *overtly* denied but *covertly* affirmed, results even so in Popper's position having fatal paradoxes. The paradoxes do not merely result *covertly* from what I call an "inductive inverse-probability thesis" where true but improbable predictions imply a probable truth of laws as opposed to Popper's *overt* anti-induction stance. This stance also contrasts to his *covert* inferences from facts to conjectural laws that proceed *pari passu* with a verifiable inexact truth of the laws if they make systematically true predictions.

The predictions having this epistemological significance were outshined by the pejorative influence of Hume's radical empiricism that rejects induction for either formulating or confirming theories. Theories rid of any induction was Popper's outward position. This position notwithstanding, Kuhn overlooks the most glaring question about Popper: Could Popper be unaware that he *even more* overtly held that all observation is theory-dependent? There is a manifest dependence of observation on theory in regard to not merely all observed crows having trait x, where x presupposes a theory. Also, the theory-dependence bears even more devastatingly on basic observation statements for supposedly falsifying laws or theories such as "this crow has trait $\sim x$" that *itself* presupposes a theory. Did Kuhn miss the conspicuous point that, despite Popper's stress on bold conjectures (allegedly apart from induction), induction-related observational facts are bogusly held to be the empirical foundation for inferring conjectural theories? The theories allegedly have basic observation statements as falsifiers. At the same time these falsifiers do themselves presuppose theories that beg for further falsifiers that presuppose more theories and so forth *ad infinitum*. In ignoring this regress, Kuhn misses the profound point that both he and Popper not only overlooked but also worsened knotty epistemological problems such as a sham theory-dependence of observation. This observation, stressed by Popper himself, led appallingly to tortuous decades of relativism with unspeakable harm to society and higher education, especially by way of a

---

38. Ibid. Kuhn no less than Popper has trait x presupposing theory (theory *qua* paradigm).

relativistic political correctness that continues to ignore physical, biological, and psychological realities.[39]

These realities, due to a pervasive political correctness where the *correct* can be false *empirically*, are often studiously ignored by educators in the human and natural sciences as well as in the fine arts and humanities. Given the esoteric nature of the problems such as theory-dependence, these educators might most fruitfully first consider how scientific theories are related to both a common-sense modal reasoning, grounded in ordinary language, and their own immediate, incontrovertible and phenomenological awareness of their theory-free observational consciousness. Is it not dismaying that both their and our own self-conscious experience goes virtually unacknowledged in the mainstream philosophy of science? How can either science or the humanities overlook this theory-independent experience when this experience involves precisely our *always being* indirectly conscious of our consciousness? And while our self-consciousness has been studied for over a century by different approaches, the approaches are omitted most obtrusively by Paul Feyerabend. Unlike most mainstream philosophers, he, like Kuhn, was persuaded in a positive way by Popper's theory-dependence and deference to Hume's extreme empiricism. With a caveat that realists do not seek absolute truth and that Popper's influence on Kuhn and Feyerabend is still ignored, others have linked the three. In an essay in *Nature*, "two British physicists fretted over the public's growing antipathy toward science," says John Horgan. This is blamed on "philosophers who deny that science discovers objective, absolute truths. The essay featured photographs of three 'betrayers of the truth': Karl Popper, Thomas Kuhn and Paul Feyerabend."[40]

A Humean Empiricism that Fed Feyerabend's Fire

The anger that aroused Feyerabend's daring call for an anarchical spread of unconventional theories is similar to Daniel Dennett's disgust with philosophy, around the same time, because of its "narrow insularity" when he was a graduate student in the 1960s. "It was comically cautious . . .

---

39. The relativism, deplored ironically in Popper's *Postscript*, 156, led to a political correctness, which vexed all societal and educational institutions where what is *correct* may be false *empirically*.

40. Horgan, "Was Philosopher Paul Feyerabend Really Science's 'Worst Enemy,'" para. 1. Emphasis.

miniature little piecework stuff. I thought it was dreadful."[41] The dreadfulness was even suggested by Bertrand Russell when he remarked that "The most influential school of philosophy in Britain at the present day maintains a certain linguistic doctrine to which I am unable to subscribe. ... The doctrine, as I understand it," he adds, "consists in maintaining that the language of daily life, with words used in their ordinary meanings, ... has no need of technical terms or of changes in the significance of common terms. I find myself totally unable to accept this view."[42] Instead of this stifling view, there was fervor for Feyerabend's epistemic mayhem that was manifest by new-left ideologues and radical feminists who, until Feyerabend's anarchy and Kuhn's paradigms, found refuge in both the Sartrean cliché "existence precedes essence" (as measured in Protagorean fashion) and the outdated relativisms of Marx and Nietzsche. In our high-tech scientific age, the more updated and prestigious philosophers of science were met with a sigh of relief as evidenced by ubiquitous listings in *The Philosopher's Index* to Nietzsche and Marx before the late 1960s but, afterward, to Kuhn and Feyerabend until today.[43]

The ongoing intellectual flirtations with these philosophers of science, despite these flirtations resulting in a post-rationalist atmosphere that alarms any "thinker who cares for ... civilization,"[44] as decried by Popper, belies the contributions to our civilization's demise by both Popper and Hume's outdated radical empiricism to which is beholden the position of Feyerabend. Consider how Feyerabend's position affects current thought after noting how his theory-dependent relativism relates to the relativism of Kuhn that was nurtured by Popper; this, despite Popper being denigrated in "Consolations for the Specialist" (1970), penned by Feyerabend, from a Kuhnian point of view. Reference to that view reveals once again why academics have not noticed, if not been in denial of, Popper's copious influence on today's anti-realism.[45] The anti-realism is far more anarchical, says Liz Williams, with Feyerabend for whom "it's impossible to develop any set of methodological rules by which scientists

---

41. Baggini, "Daniel Dennett," para. 16.
42. Jones, "Analytic Positivism," Preface.
43. Cf. also Parsons, "Nietzsche and Moral Change," 186.
44. Popper, *Postscript*, 156.
45. Preston, "Paul Feyerabend," §5. In this article, a disassociation from Popper is proposed by noting that Feyerabend held that "Popper's Critical Rationalism would inhibit scientific progress...."

work: ad hoc, rule-breaking postulates are the order of the day."[46] She adds sardonically that "We seem to be heading at full speed towards epistemological relativism here, and indeed," she continues, "not only does science fail to proceed according to fixed principles, but it doesn't deserve its epistemic privileges, either. Far out! So if your preference is for Feyerabend over Popper, astrologers might be on to something, after all."

Anarchical Fires Fueled by Think-Tank-Like Conjectures

Though few philosophers and scientists have recognized that Popper is actually a *faux* realist, our being indebted to Newton-Smith for this erudite exposure, many more acknowledge Popper's influence on Kuhn and Feyerabend. An ongoing thesis of this essay is not just Popper's influence on them but also that his furtive support of theory-dependence fueled the mischievous relativistic anti-realisms of Kuhn and Feyerabend, they in turn influencing radical (gender) feminism, political correctness, and various sorts of post-modern ideologies such as social constructionism. The typical view of Feyerabend, by contrast, is quite different than my take on the connection and its devastating impact on Western culture. For example, Frederick Suppe does not regard Popper as in any way inducing Feyerabend's relativism when he notes that they both agree about theories not being confirmable, that observation terms are not independent of theory and that theories must be proliferated for a growth of alleged scientific knowledge.[47] The stress on knowledge being propagated by think-tank like conjectures in the case of Popper (despite his falsification), however, does indeed *foreshadow* Feyerabend's anarchic epistemology where theories would flourish in an entirely unstructured and non-institutionalized way.[48]

The way in which theories would thrive is similar to thriving societies. These societies thrive because of a healthful unorthodoxy which undercuts an "establishment" that would frustrate creative discoveries that

---

46. Williams, "Karl Popper," para. 10.

47. Cf. Suppe, *The Structure of Scientific Theories*, 170. Suppe is a remarkable philosopher. This, despite Popper not being included among anti-realists or seen as influencing the theory-dependence advanced by Feyerabend.

48. In defense of Feyerabend, one scholar says "what critics have taken to be radically 'anarchistic' defenses of pseudoscience are... principled defenses of the epistemic integrity—and hence authority—of science." Cf. Ian Kidd, "Why Did Feyerabend Defend Astrology?" 464–82.

do not allegedly kowtow to cookie-cutter formulas fostered by an oppressive majority. The majority as a tyranny was, of course, warned against by John Stuart Mill. And thus it is foreseeable that in the essay version of Feyerabend's *Against Method* ("Against Method: Outline of an Anarchistic Theory of Knowledge") where his "'epistemological anarchism' was revealed for the first time [Feyerabend] claimed to be applying the liberalism of John Stuart Mill's *On Liberty* to scientific methodology."[49]

There is no methodology as such in the very anti-establishment approach to science that is posited by Feyerabend. In regard to Feyerabend, there is a superficial similarity to the Sartrean dictum "existence precedes essence" wherein essences as truth/ meaning is created spontaneously and by free choice of will. This post-rational received-view interpretation of Sartre's existentialism (exploited by New-Left students and post-modern social constructionists) ignores that essence in Sartre's *Being and Nothingness*, while not identical with its being produced by our intellect, is compatible with its production by our intellect via an *idea* of a phenomenon (or *phantasm* in Thomas' metaphysics) of which there can be a direct consciousness of which we are indirectly conscious. For example, the medieval scholar Fr. Henry Carr states that, according to Aristotle and Thomas, there is not only no "idea without a corresponding phantasm, but that furthermore the corresponding phantasm must always accompany the idea in consciousness"; his adding that whenever "we are conscious of an idea, the idea's sensible representation must be present also in consciousness."[50]

A non-conceptual observational consciousness of which we are indirectly aware can, via Sartre's basic analysis of consciousness, reveal an external object from a certain perspective as it really is *in itself*. And the revelation can occur without either any idea or sensible representation. But representations of the objects of which we are conceptually conscious, which is infused with the non-conceptual consciousness, may afford the intellect's inference to essences. And essences in the intellect of which there also can be a direct consciousness of which we are

---

49. Preston, "Paul Feyerabend," §1–6: a methodology against a despotic majority.

50. Carr, "The Function of the Phantasm," 179. Among other positions, Fr. Carr was Superior of St. Michael's College (1915–25), Superior of St. Basil's Seminary (1925–28), Founding President of the Institute of Mediaeval Studies (1929–35), General Superior of the Basilian Fathers (1930–42) Principal of St. Thomas More College (1942–49), lecturer at the University of British Columbia from 1951 including the years at St. Mark's College, UBC, 1957–62. See Kirley's "Father Henry Carr and Catholic education in Canada."

indirectly aware, per Sartre's phenomenology, are far more similar to an Aristotelian-Thomistic view of how observations are related to essences (or to theoretical entities) than to their being arbitrary fabrications of the intellect. The intellect aside, Aristotle, if not Thomas, is an explicit predecessor to phenomenology, its being "launched by Edmund Husserl in his *Logical Investigations* (1900-01)," notes D. W. Smith, when two "different lines of theory came together in that monumental work: [psychological theory and logical or semantic theory] (Interestingly, both lines of research trace back to Aristotle....)"[51]

Aristotle's disassociation from phenomenology by anti-realist views has its source in either a mischievous post-rational spin on Sartre or an incoherent post-modern relativism such as a social constructionism. Both ignore human consciousness. In terms of our self-consciousness, there is an existential phenomenological realism wherein Sartre reasons that the "essence is *more than* a mere name that we give for convenience to a haphazard series of an object's manifestations—a position [that is] termed 'nominalism.'"[52] So while Sartre says that "an apple has many perspectives [of which we can be conscious both non-conceptually and conceptually], we ... recognize, in the perception of any one of these perspectives, that all the aspects belong to a *true* totality, 'apple.'"[53]

A Sartrean Phenomenology that Secures Thomism

That a Sartrean existential phenomenology could bolster some basic elements of Thomism would seem outlandish to the vast majority of philosophers.[54] Actually, however, my case for this boost is partially preceded by Stephen Wang's *Aquinas and Sartre* (2009). Before I address why a Sartrean phenomenology strengthens both a realism and the notion of our voluntary nature as held by Thomas (as well as Aristotle), including their rejection of a deterministic materialism such as that of Atomism, consider some points made by Wang. He states that "There are some profound similarities in the thought of Thomas Aquinas and Jean-Paul Sartre" and that his purpose "is to show that these two thinkers, despite their many differences, have a common philosophical understanding of

---

51. Smith, "Phenomenology," §3.
52. Joseph Catalano, *A Commentary*," 23.
53. Ibid.
54. See my article "Sartre on Being," 135–62.

the nature of human freedom."[55] He adds that there are not only "some points of contact between Aquinas and Sartre, but that their approach to a number of key philosophical issues—centered around the question of freedom—is almost identical."[56] The identicalness is said to center on "what happens when we face a choice."[57] Thus he summarizes:

> The best way to understand their common approach is to think of what happens when we face a choice. When there are different options before me, and I have to make a decision, a number of factors will usually influence that decision. Three of the most important factors are undoubtedly who I am, where I am, and what I am seeking. In other words, my personal identity, the objective circumstances in which I find myself, and the goals I am seeking will all have some kind of influence on the choice I eventually make. They make up what we could call the "total situation" that informs my choice. In philosophical theories about human action, it is common to assume that this total situation, once I start reflecting on it, is something stable and accessible. So when I have a choice to make, *I think* about what kind of person I am (what would suit me, what I am interested in, what I am capable of, etc.); *I think* about the objective circumstances confronting me (what is going on here, what needs to be done, what the practical options available are, what the consequences of any action will be, etc.) . . . .[58]

Whereas Wang nicely relates *thinking* to choices, these choices are related herein to our incontrovertible *consciousness* of them. Thus, although Wang comes closer to my analysis when he says "We are conscious of what we experience and aware of this very consciousness,"[59] which echoes my stress on our awareness of our direct consciousness, this self-consciousness is not related to our free will in the way done here. And while Sartre and Thomas are said to agree that "What is extraordinary about human beings is that we can change the way we look at things, change the way we look at ourselves, and change the goals we are seeking—this is what allows us to make a choice,"[60] the reality of our free will

---

55. Wang, *Aquinas and Sartre*, x.
56. Ibid.
57. Ibid.
58. Ibid., x–xi, emphasis.
59. Ibid., 33.
60. Ibid., xi.

is coupled more acutely to a phenomenological awareness of ourselves. To behave in given ways, for example, is ordinarily to be implicitly aware of our freedom to behave or not behave in those ways. When Kant held that free will was a mere possible reality (*noumenon*), for example, was he not aware of his freedom to think or not think that thought? Thought, though, is less basic than our consciousness since there can be a consciousness of reality without thought but there can be no thought without consciousness. Consciousness per se reveals and does not conceal reality by any mode of thought. This supports as such a strong realism. And in appealing to our phenomenological experience of ourselves, there is support for a Thomistic realism, à la Étienne Gilson, and for Thomas himself who appeals to our "introspection" of being "*aware* that in particular situations . . . we might not have acted as we in fact did or that we might not have acted at all."[61] This is one of the reasons Thomas holds "that people have free choice (*Summa Theologiae* Ia, O. 83, a. 1,)."[62] So the essay herein bolsters Thomas' defense of free will. And our irrefutable consciousness of reality as it is *in itself*, of which we are aware, both conflicts with iconic modern anti-realists and upholds a realism of Aristotle and Thomas. Consider how their robust realism has can be based on phenomenology and why it collides head-on with an incoherent deterministic materialism of Kuhn and Feyerabend.

Kuhn and Feyerabend falter in their philosophies of science most essentially by disregarding, in terms of Thomas, the aforesaid introspective awareness. This awareness is simply expanded on by appealing to our self-consciousness: The indirect awareness *of* our direct consciousness of something (other than consciousness) is related inextricably to free will by appealing to our immediate, unassailable and phenomenological experience of ourselves. When we are indirectly aware of our looking at something, are we not also implicitly aware of our freedom to look or not look at the thing? This phenomenological awareness of our free will uniquely undercuts a typical deterministic materialism of the Atomists and most of the sophists, as well, and thus powerfully underscores rejections of that reductionism by Aristotle and Thomas alike. The exercise of their virtue ethics in terms of modern metaphysics, since the time of Kant, presupposes free will. Furthermore, free will and our introspective phenomenological awareness of our free will, are utterly foreign to

---

61. Magee, "Aquinas and the Freedom of the Will," para. 1.

62. Ibid., emphasis. para. 2.

an epistemic relativism of sophism and atomism that foreshadowed the epistemic relativism of both Kuhn and Feyerabend.

They ignore the human subject. While "the human Subject in the immanence of its *consciousness* is the . . . center of all philosophical inquiry" in the Thomistic phenomenology of Edith Stein,[63] which agrees with an existential phenomenology held by Sartre, nothing could be farther from Feyerabend's doctrine of meaning. This meaning is derived from his cryptic notion that an observation language for a class C of observers are sentences that they are *caused* to either accept or reject in reaction to sensory phenomena. How phenomena really *are*, as expressed by conjectures, however, is settled by the consensualism of a majority of C's members (a member of the American Physical society saying that "Theories that disagree with the facts are wrong, consensus or [not]."[64] Those members determine which sentences either are or are not acceptable, which is ironically evocative of the very tyrannical majority that is eschewed but paradoxically advanced by Feyerabend.[65]

Feyerabend, additionally, maintains strangely that sensorial sentences are not statements with possible truth-values. For what we are caused to accept or reject are purportedly only "un-interpreted sentences." Now these sentences, which might be construed as sensorial sentences (à la Hume), might seem odd to professors who profess how a soundness of arguments is related to the truth of statements in courses of introductory logic. These logic courses typically teach that although all statements are sentences but that not all sentences are statements, non-statements include exclamations, proposals, suggestions, commands, and questions. And we ordinarily teach that it is senseless to say that sentences without truth-values are, or could be, true or false: It's false that "Is it cold outside?" The sentences without truth-values, in the case of Fayerabend, stem from a bizarre cross between a radical empiricist theory of mind, which both results in skepticism and conflicts with our self-awareness, and a fabricated linguistic concoction in order to satisfy an anti-realist anarchical epistemology where "anything goes." A whiff of senselessness arises with this sort of talk, reminiscent of Hume's thought, that our thinking is a species of sensation.

---

63. Edith Stein's approach is both Thomistic and phenomenological per Allen's "The Passion of Edith Stein, 6–7.

64. Watts, "Physicists Send Letter to Senate," para. 3.

65. Suppe, *The Structure of Scientific Theories*, 637.

Sensations cannot be a basis for truth. There is a dependence of truth, though, on proliferating theories for ever more interpretations of reality in terms of un-interrupted observational sentences. These sentences aside, the proliferation is not an epistemological anarchy in the progressive open-minded manner that was foreseen by Feyerabend. Rather, the proliferation is fatal to coherently choosing theories, although physicist Karl Sovizol captures an emotional "justified infuriation" behind Feyerabend's anarchy when Sovizol states that "Some physicists 'go wild' and pretend that the transient status of their science reflects final truth of the world," telling "fairy tales about the first three minutes of the universe, short histories of time and what not. This is good for marketing ... and sells well."[66] What is not well is that a think-tank-like torrent of conjectural theories, in Feyerabend's counter extreme, are not chosen rationally by corresponding to reality. For reality, on his view, echoes Hume's empiricism of internal sensations. And the sensations are *not* known to reflect an external reality. So reality is understood circularly by the very sensory phenomena that *cause* us to either accept or reject the un-interrupted sensorial sentences which are in question.

The question in existential phenomenology would be, given that external things *in themselves* are revealed as they really *are*, would not sentences either correspond or not correspond to reality despite what C's members think? What they think, apparently, is the truth-condition for truth; permitting contradictions, a priori. Also, how could sensory stimuli could cause them to accept or reject sentences about phenomena unless (recalling Descartes' futile body and soul dualism) the members resemble soulless mechanistic automata who are not either conscious of phenomena or of their own spoken sentences? Do sentences caused by the members' sense organs comprise a *human activity* of which C's members are conscious? Consciousness encounters "this or that thing-in the world, not my visual or tactile sense," says Sartre: "if I can see or touch my sense organs, I have the revelation of pure objects [because of their objectifications], not of a revealing or constructive activity."[67]

What activity could there be of either the members' sensory organs or observed phenomena that renders coherent phenomena *deterministically causing* us to accept or reject sentences about phenomena? Phenomena are that of which class C's members would be observationally

---

66. See Svozil, "Feyerabend and Physics," 9.
67. Sartre, *Being and Nothingness*, 316. That is, the eye does not see itself.

conscious. And this consciousness, which is direct, would be that which the members of class C are also indirectly aware. They would be *aware indirectly* but also irrefutably aware of the following: their consciousness *of* external things; of these things not being their consciousness; of their freely choosing to observe some things and not others; and of their freely chosen intention to say that the sentences are true when their conceptualizations, formulated into the sentences, correspond to the things of which the members are non-conceptually conscious. This phenomenological notion of consciousness collides head-on with Feyerabend's curious connections to the anti-realisms of radical empiricism, pragmatism and relativistic social constructions.

Constructionism and anti-realism notwithstanding, notable is how an existential phenomenology of consciousness may bypass sensible mental images and phantasms related to Aristotle and Thomas. This is the case at least in terms of a consciousness of something non-conceptually. Here, a thing is *not noticed* as a given thing, per the analytic philosopher F. I. Dretske's non-epistemic seeing (seeing$_n$), versus a conceptual consciousness of something when it is noticed as a specific thing. In either event we are not aware of any activity by either the things we observe or our sense organs causing us to express sensorial sentences. As Sartre suggests, we are aware *of* our consciousness *of* things-in-the-world. The experienced world in terms of existential phenomenology allows for sensible images of which C's members, despite Feyerabend, can be directly conscious. Those images are comparable to the things *in themselves*, by our indirect awareness *of* our direct consciousness of them, for assessing their correspondence. The correspondence is coherent in this existential phenomenology because this phenomenology does not exclude the images while providing a novel way to appreciate the Aristotelian-Thomistic tradition. In synch with this tradition, C's members would be indirectly aware, not of being *caused* to observe certain things, but of doing so *freely*. If they cannot freely observe one thing instead of another because reality is causally determined, then both Feyerabend's own claim that sentences are caused and its counter claim would incoherently be equally true because equally caused. This illogicality would be the case, given that a causally determined reality is the total truth-condition for truth.

Novel Challenges to Phenomenology's Robust Realism

In the end, "truth" ascribable to theories when they roughly reflect reality is defensible by Sartre's phenomenological realism. But realism suffered a catastrophic setback with Feyerabend, Kuhn, and Popper by, starting with Popper's pseudo-realism, there were incrementally increasing anti-realisms. These anti-realisms are reflected cynically not only by pragmatic positions such as Richard Rorty's, who has Cartesian doubts "about any set of empirical claims whatever,"[68] but also by a pragmatic-focused constructivism. Here, concepts are merely useful at best, with no norm to guide ends, which echo Popper's falsification of knowing only "*what it is not*," as foreseen by Ernst von Glasersfeld and Paul Watzlawic.[69] Also, the thesis of theory-dependence adopted by Popper influenced the jumbled relativisms of Feyerabend and Kuhn. Their relativisms and those of the constructivists cannot be replaced by realism merely by showing that their epistemologies are self-refuting, as vital as this refutation is. Nor can their relativisms, in being trivial if not incoherent, be replaced by metaphysical defenses of objective observation being more plausibly theory-*laden* than theory-*dependent*. Denials of dependence on theory via the metaphysics of Rohrlich, Hardin, Cartwright, Hacking, Suppe, and Newton-Smith, as erudite as they are, must bring in other essentials.

The first essential is an existential phenomenology in which theory-laden observation is based on a non-conceptual observational consciousness of which there is an immediate, incontrovertible, and phenomenological awareness. The second is a common-sense modal logic by which the approximate truth of theories is inferable from true observational predictions. While not either the predictions or phenomenological awareness were acknowledged by the aforesaid philosophers, they nonetheless engaged commonsensically in what may be regarded as an Aristotelian-like metaphysics of *ta meta ta physika* (the works after the physics) in the sense that physics has presuppositions and implications that were admirably examined.[70] In particular, the above philosophers forged the path metaphysically for a phenomenological account of how theory-laden observations can be roughly objective and how a reality of theoretical entities may be related logically to the truth of theories. Their truth as related to a reality of theoretical entities raises a specter of com-

---

68. Ramberg, "Richard Rorty (Against Epistemology)," §1–4.
69. Massarenti, "Constructivism," para. 1. Emphasis.
70. Editorial Staff, "Metaphysics," para. 1–2.

mensurability, verisimilitude, and scientific method as notions that need further study for the right return to a vigorous scientific realism.

If this realism is embraced by physicists, then these physicists face at least three problems. The first problem, says Fritz Rohrlich, is "the careful specification of the validity limits of every theory and model used . . . ."[71] This essay bears on the problem in terms of ever growing historical domains of success that strictly imply increasing scientific truth (per a principle of optimistic inference). The second problem, states Rohrlich, is that "the coherence relationships . . . must hold between two theories of the same physical system but on different cognitive levels . . . ."[72] These levels are ruminated herein in terms of superseding theories that include previous domains and that achieve predictions, explications, and manipulations of phenomena beyond the prior theories. And the third problem is an "ambiguity in the ontology of two different formulations of empirically equivalent theories."[73] The theories refer to an Underdetermination-of-Theory-by-Data (UTD) Thesis that even Newton-Smith, as insightful as he is, seems to have taken too seriously. He says that some weak UTDs may permit resolutions and that "there is no *a priori* guarantee that there is such a unique total theory of nature."[74] At the same time, Newton-Smith adds that "We have to entertain the thought that there might be [a] massive *UDT*, by which I mean that there could be a pair of incompatible evidentially equivalent total theories of nature."[75] And by this response, he says, "we drop the assumption that there is a matter of fact at stake with regard to any undecidable empirical proposition."[76] Furthermore, "We relax the ontological ingredient in realism [sentences of theories being true or false about how the world really is apart from ourselves] by restricting from the set of sentences to be given a realist construal any undecidable sentence. What in this case we regard as being the truth about the world would be the *common part* of the two theories."[77]

Let the two theories, which are global and contradictory, be read as T_1 and $\sim T_1$. Let us say that these theories have shared elements such that they constitute the theory T_2 (wherein even if T_2 does not arise because

71. Rohrlich, "Scientific Realism," 443–51.
72. Ibid.
73. Ibid.
74. Newton-Smith, *The Rationality of Science*, 41.
75. Ibid.
76. Ibid., 42.
77. Ibid., emphasis.

there is no common core, this is no obstacle to a robust realism since a lack of the core does not preclude the theories being evidence-based by data; more on this later). In any event, does not a solution of T_2 arising from shared elements of T_1 and $\sim T_1$ beg the question? Besides T_2, the question ensues of why there could not arise another contradictory theory $\sim T_2$. And could not shared elements in $\sim T_2$ and T_2 result in theory T_3, which is countered by another contradictory theory $\sim T_3$, and so forth *ad infinitum*? The regress need not be troubling to realists who distinguish a logically incoherent *a priori* acceptance of contradictions from those inferred *a posteriori* from data. Reasoning from data to theories, which are empirically equivalent, involves no self-contradiction.[78]

The possibly contradictory theories remind us that reality can have conflicting empirical predicates and that there is nothing self-contradictory in asserting that reality need not abide by the Principle of Non-Contradiction. Non-Contradiction bears on conceivability and conceivability is applicable to *statements about reality*, not to *reality*. In appreciating the difference of reality from logic in this manner, it seems unsatisfactory for Newton-Smith to conclude that "In any event, [a] massive UTD is not a phenomenon we in fact face and, as a theoretical possibility, either response will preserve the core of realism to the extent that there is an overlap in the content of the under-determined theories."[79] His prior responses refer to the theories as weak or modest UTDs, which are actually "notional variants" of the same theory. These theories are said, however, to still allow for a global theory inferred from common parts of two empirically equivalent contradictory theories. In the real event of these theories, though, we have seen that his solution results in an infinite regress. This regressive solution is not only in vain but also unnecessary. Realists can simply accept any UTD that is *evidence based* by virtue of being inferred *a posteriori* from data! And when Newton-Smith says that "If there were nothing in common except the observational consequences, realism on either response would be implausible,"[80] the implausibility is not based on any modal logic but rather on truth-functional logic. This logic cannot address the plausibility of observational consequences, which are systematically true, that strictly imply true theories in given domains.

78. Cf. Trundle, "Aristotle V. Van Til and Łukasiewicz." 323–44.
79. Newton-Smith, *The Rationality of Science*, 42–43, his emphasis.
80. Ibid., 43.

6

A Robust Realism for Increasing Scientific Truth

A robust realism relies largely on inferring increasing approximate truths of *mature* historical theories from their systematic success in increasingly greater domains. And this defense of ever larger domain-restricted inexact truths is not countered *prima facie* by criticisms such as that "both scientists and (realist) philosophers seem to be much too optimistic about the truth which can be inferred from successful predictions" because there are "umpteen examples of scientists making a doxastic commitment to a theory on the basis of its predictive/explanatory success, only to be forced to withdraw that commitment at a later date"; an example in a related footnote stating, "Einstein upon hearing of Bohr's successful prediction of the ionised helium spectral lines: 'This is a tremendous *result. The theory of Bohr must then be right.*' (cited in Pais 1991, p. 154)."[1] But Bohr's *not being right* because of the *result* is irrelevant to a realism that relates *result* to *right* by strict implication when theories are mature, *à la* physicist Fritz Rohrlick and others, and the theories have well-tested systematic successes in specified domains.

These successes, as such, are overlooked by instrumentalism, empirical adequacy, post-modernism, and the major anti-realisms of Popper, Kuhn, and Feyerabend; the latter two posing a strategic threat to realism due to their boldness and novelty. Having noted distinctively that their theory-dependent relativisms were covertly influenced by Popper, despite the vacuity of Popper's self-avowed realism going largely unnoticed,

---

1. Vickers, "Towards a Realistic Success," Intro., emphasis.

this chapter undertakes to surmount some obstacles to *any* realism, via existential phenomenology, that ensue from Popper's veiled notion that all observation language is theory-dependent. His notion of this dependence reflects precisely a recent intertwining of epistemic and historical problems. These include commensurability, verisimilitude, and scientific method. An account of how there can be a strong scientific realism that supports inexact scientific truth will initially considers comparability.

An Increasing Truth of Theories Presupposes Their Comparability

To say that scientific theories are comparable (commensurable) is to say that sound reasons may be adducible for claiming that one theory is better than another, say by being simpler when their predictions are equally successful or, given that success strictly implies truth, by the other theory having more truth. Given this connection to truth, commensurability bears on verisimilitude whereby one might say commonsensically that Newton's physics is truer than Aristotle's. For if their theories were incomparable, which implies that no *mature* theories are comparable, then there could be no coherent talk of an historical sequence of major theories having ever more truth. This ever greater truth implies that the truth of a theory in the historical sequence is inexact. A significance of the notion of progressing inexact truth is best gleaned by recalling a diametrically opposite view. Kuhn, for example, is said by William Devlin and Alisa Bokulich to have rejected "the traditionally accepted notion of scientific change as a progression towards the truth," substituting instead "the idea that science is a puzzle solving activity, operating under paradigms, which become discarded after it fails to respond accordingly to anomalous challenges and a rival paradigm."[2]

These paradigms, which were held nonsensically by Kuhn to be incommensurable and sensibly by Frederick Suppe to be relativistic *Weltanschauung*, collide head-on with a common-sense contrast to the aforesaid alternative: Increasing inexact truth is ascribable to mature theories in ever larger domains of an historical sequence. Thus, although "retail arguments" restrict possibly real theoretical entities to ones posited by scientists,[3] these sequential theories imply *ceteris paribus* a general

2. Devlin and Bokulich (eds.), *Kuhn's Structure of Scientific Revolutions*, §1.
3. Cf. Chen, "Experimental Individuation," §1–6.

increasing reality of theoretical entities just as an increasing reality of the entities imply an ever greater truth of the theories in terms of which those entities are understood. On this understanding, all things equal, *truth implies reality* and *reality implies truth* in the sense that an epistemic status of the theories is interrelated inextricably to the status of their ontologies (existence of the entities). Recall the entity-realism of Nancy Cartwright that, although rejecting a truth of the theories, accepts a reality of many theoretical entities. These entities would be understood necessarily in a context of theories such that the theories cannot be said to not be approximately true when the entities are said to be real.

A reality of theoretical entities is related inextricably to a realist acceptance of commensurability because, as noted eruditely by Newton-Smith, a commitment to the reality of theoretical entities most often "arises when we adopt theoretical hypotheses in giving causal accounts of observed phenomena [as with Sir Joseph John 'J. J.' Thomson's theory of electron.]"[4] The electron as a theoretical entity was included in Thomson's initial hypothesis (say H_1) and could have been excluded by another hypothesis, for instance (H_2); the latter hypothesis omitting the electron as a cause of observed scintillations in a cathode ray tube. And so if H_2 fails in its causal account of the scintillated phenomena and H_1 succeeds in not only accounting for them but also in leading to a theory and follow-up theories that were able to predict, manipulate, and even to create new phenomena, as Ian Hacking suggests, then the comparability claim that H_1 is a good or better hypothesis can be based on an existential inference; one afforded from the phenomena being real to a reality of the entity, as earlier noted in terms of the weak-realism reasoning of Cartwright. And in light of the aforesaid inference of "truth from reality," to say that an entity is real is to be able to say not only what that entity is in terms of a theory in which it is understood but also that the theory is true by virtue *inter alia* of its steadily true predictions of those scintillated phenomena.

From Comparability to Necessities that Secure Truth

While allowing for the comparability of theories is presupposed by admitting of their possible truth, this essay holds the bold thesis that there is increasing historical truth about phenomena.[5] How could phenomena

---

4. Newton-Smith, *The Rationality of Science*, 38.
5. Cf, Fuller's discussion of scientific progress per Kuhn and Feyerabend in "Is

be predicted in a systematic way by a mature theory if the theory, in a given domain, is not at least approximately true? Unless it truly reflected phenomena, how could the phenomena be predicted systematically by the theory? Thus, although the theory's falsity is *logically possible*, most scientists would ordinarily say that the theory's not being roughly true is impossible, or that it *must* be true (reflecting necessity). Its not being roughly true is an *epistemic impossibility*, and its *having* to be true an epistemic necessity of modal logic. This logic refers to an impossibility that scientists would admit of in linguistic conventions, as either a mother would laughingly assert "That's impossible" in reply to a sock being said to have vanished (going clean out of existence) in the dryer or an engineer would say that one would be joking if one insisted, "It's possible a breeze blew down a soundly designed concrete bunker." In these cases "impossible" would not usually be replaced by either "improbable" or appeals to proofs. That is, a proof by the generic well-established law *Force* $= A$ (area) $\times P$ (wind load) $\times C_d$ (drag coefficient), for instance, would not ordinarily be undertaken by engineers since, precisely, one's believing in the possibility of a breeze blowing down a reinforced concrete bunker proceeds *pari passu* with believing absurdly that the *law* is entirely false despite its systematically true predictions: Necessarily if systematically true predictions are yielded by the law, the law is roughly true.

A true law, in terms of "necessity" and "impossibility," bears on the terms *de dicto* and *de re*. "The first full use of the terms *de re* and *de dicto* is due to Thomas Aquinas," state Ezra Keshet and Florian Schwarz, "who was also the first to define the terms syntactically: A modal proposition is either *de dicto* or *de re*."[6] They say that a *de dicto* proposition is where "the whole dictum is the subject and the modal is the predicate [e.g.,] 'For Socrates to run is possible.' A modal proposition *de re* is one where the modal is interpolated in the dictum [e.g.] 'For Socrates it is possible to run.'"[7] They add, "Aquinas divides the sentence syntactically into the subject and the predicate. The subject may be a full clause (in the *de dicto* case) or a thing (in the *de re* case) . . . ."[8] And Newton-Smith notes that a "necessary truth is *de dicto* if its necessity arises from our linguistic practices."[9] These practices may bear on a proposition *qua* theory in

---

Science an Ideology," 565–72.

6. Keshet and Schwarz, "De Re/De Dicto," §1–6.
7. Ibid., emphasis.
8. Ibid., emphasis.
9. See Newton-Smith, *The Rationality of Science*, 170. See also Simchen's "The

terms of the aforesaid inference of a *mature* theory's approximate truth from its systematically true predictions. These predictions may be either (a) extraordinary predictions that include but are greater than a Newtonian domain such as those of Einstein's theory, the theory being around for about a century where its domain limit is not yet certified or (b) more modest predictions such as those made by Newton's theory over centuries. A scientist would either seem senselessly skeptical in denying that the theories have any truth at all in given domains or ordinarily say that within given domains the theories *must* at least be roughly true; making them non-trivial necessary truths *de dicto*. But where a "necessary truth is *de re* if its necessity arises from how the world *is*,"[10] claiming that how the world *is* renders the theories entirely false would beget a reasonable reply of that being impossible. And this impossibility implies the counterclaim's necessity. Hence both the necessity and impossibility in regard to assertions about the theories relate also to how reality really *is*, roughly, and are denotable *de re*. That is, what holds for the *de re* in this case holds equally for *de dicto*.

De dicto and *de re* modalities as equally describing necessity and impossibility are defended also by Scott Shalkowski. He says that if propositions refer to "entities of any sort, whether abstract or concrete, then *de dicto* modality is just a special case of *de re* modality—modality as it pertains to a thing" and so "*de re* modality undergirds the propositions we might plausibly think of as *de dicto* necessary."[11] This necessity bears, consequently, on "Necessarily if a theory yields systematically true predictions (P), the theory is roughly true (T)." The latter modality is expressible as $Nec(P \to T)$ where it is an epistemic impossibility, even if it is possible logically, that the theory is not roughly true ($\sim T$) when it makes systematically true predictions (P). This modal conditional contrasts to the truth-functional conditional $P \to T$ that admits of only a logical possibility that the theory is false when it makes the true predictions. And although the "Thomson electron" may not be a theoretical entity identical to "other electrons," which are understood in successive theories up to today, one may agree with Newton-Smith that while the theories have changed, the electron *per se* did not change. There is no change in the entity not only because everything changing excludes truth

---

Barcun Formula," 375–92.

10. Newton-Smith, *The Rationality of Science*, 170, emphasis.

11. Shalkowski, "The Ontological Ground," 687.

but also because the changing truth of theories is presupposed by their historically becoming truer as evidenced by an increasing predictability of the scintillated phenomena; establishing again that comparability is related closely to verisimilitude.

Before discussing verisimilitude, note that a comparability of theories is possible for realists, in part, because truth is not relative to varying theories, paradigms or *Weltanschauungen*, in the genre of Kuhn, Feyerabend and social constructionists, which are imposed *a priori* on an observable reality. While the realism herein allows for degrees of theory-laden language, the language does not exclude a robust realism that features these innovations: (1) Low-level observation claims that are clarified by existential phenomenology wherein there is a non-conceptual consciousness of reality (apart from theory) of which there is also an indirect awareness and (2) This self-awareness imparts a unifying, restraining and objectifying influence on language—"anything does *not* go" epistemologically and ontologically (*pace* Feyerabend); (3) The notion that reality *in itself* is disclosed by a non-conceptual consciousness is fortified by a warranted general faith in low-level observation reports on the basis, per Newton-Smith,[12] that we are largely successful in coping with the world and would not have survived were we unable to manage as such by our relatively objective low-level observations; and (4) The latter observations afford evidence for scientific theories wherein these theories are comparable by having more or less truth. So these roughly true theories do not depend on observations being circularly explicable through the languages of theories, much less paradigms with incomparable languages. The languages of theories by an aforesaid interactional relationship means that if observation is laden by theory, then theory is laden also by observation.[13] And reasoning from observed predictions to a theory's inexact truth relies on a modal logic and low-level observation. This observation is itself rooted in a theory-neutral consciousness of reality of which there is also an immediate incontrovertible awareness.

Truth of Theories Is Not Undercut by Meaning Variance

One may object that the epistemic impossibility of theories being entirely false when their predictions are systematically true, in given domains,

---

12. Newton-Smith, *The Rationality of Science*, 28.
13. Roth and Bautista, "Transcriptions," 51–76.

does not address problems of meaning variance. The latter variance is illustrated by the meaning of "cathode ray phenomenon," as noted by Newton-Smith.[14] And Newton-Smith is correct when he notes that "In spite of the great variation since Thomson's time in beliefs about electrons, we are united with him in that the things we call electrons [are] responsible for the cathode ray phenomenon . . . ."[15] A phenomenon of glowing beams that were seen by J. J. Thomson were first understood by him as "corpuscles" and later, in his initially formulating the "idea for the structure of the atom" as "negatively charged particles . . . in a sea of positive charge."[16] The charged particles do not reflect the same theoretical view as today's notion of electrons as subatomic particles that belong to the first generation of the lepton particle family and that have quantum mechanical properties of both a particle and wave.[17] Therefore, there is a variance of meaning, the objection goes, since Thomson meant something different by what he observed than what scientists mean today by what they observe. Thus these different observations would supposedly undercut the phenomenological realism, the objection may continue, because this realism assumes *invariant* observation reports by virtue of an *invariant* observational consciousness.

This consciousness may seem to be undercut by a variance of meaning because both scientists now and in the time of Thomson understand, and hence observe, the same beam differently. But appealing to this difference in what scientists "see today" and "saw yesterday" is a straw-man attack on our realism because this realism admits of a benign variance of *conceptual* low-level observational consciousness, expressed in reports, that is sufficient for certifying true predictions. The predictions do not preclude the reports being rooted in an invariant *non-conceptual* consciousness of the *same* thing at different historical times. At those times the reports would be *ceteris paribus* of a "glowing phenomenon" that, however, is better explicated, predicted and manipulated now than in the past. If either past or present phenomena were described by an observation language either entirely dependent on or determined by theories (or theoretical *Weltanschauungen*) in a way reminiscent of Feyerabend and Kuhn if not Popper, then, yes, theories would

14. Newton-Smith, *The Rationality of Science*, 174.
15. Ibid., 173–74.
16. Shuttleworth, "Cathode Ray Experiment." para. 2.
17. Cf. Curtis, *Atomic Structure and Lifetimes*, 74 and Arabatzis, "Cathode Rays," 89–92.

be incomparable. Comparisons do obtain, though, such that succeeding theories are deemed reasonably to be truer because of their increasing power to predict, manipulate, explicate as well as answer unanticipated questions about new phenomena (per Fritz Rohrlich).[18]

Observation reports of phenomena are faultily held to undergo drastic meaning changes since lower-level theory-laden observation reports are thought to be affected by higher-level languages of incomparable theories.[19] So theories would seem to determine the lower-level language, excluding theory comparisons that, however, do in fact occur. There may occur theory comparisons in that the manner of meaning advanced for observation terms, in the phenomenological realism herein, is one where there is only a mild meaning variance at lower levels of observational language.[20] And a relation of this language to the language of theory, by the aforesaid theory-observation interdependence, means also that the historical growth of mature theories, besides having a continuity of growth, are theories that are observation-laden and have a vital recourse to a virtual invariance of (or to a very gradually changing) observational language. A constancy of this language is precisely by virtue of it being grounded in an unvarying non-conceptual consciousness of phenomena of which there is an irrefutable awareness.

Given this awareness of our consciousness of a *reality* that *is* as it *is* despite our will, wish or thought, the phenomenological realism herein avoids both a Protagoras-man-is-the-measure relativism and a relativism held by Feyerabend in terms of which persons are causally determined to accept observational sentences that are subject to clashing theoretical interpretations. That is, besides a continuity in the maturing meaning of theoretical terms of major theories, say from Thomson's particle to the Bohr and present-day theories of electron, meaning variance does not suppose that theories have a truth which is relative to either opposing factions of scientists or scientists whose observation claims are causally determined by different disciplinary matrices, paradigms or sensory stimuli such that the meanings of their sentences are incommensurable. And thus we have seen how a claimed incommensurability, by relying on both a *materialism* that renders vacuous "truth" (since "truth" is

---

18. Rohrlich, "The Theory of the Electron," §1–5.

19. Cf. Newton-Smith, *The Rationality of Science*, 174, although low-level reports are rooted herein to an *unchanging* concept-less consciousness of phenomena wherein Thompson and scientists today could see the same thing but interpret it differently.

20. Ibid.

not ascribed to matter) and a *determinism* that renders incoherent our truth-claims (since contradictories can be true if the truth-condition is a causally determined reality), collides head-on with both our patent phenomenological experience of ourselves and what it makes sense to say. It is unambiguously senseless to say also that scientific theories have *not* historically become increasingly truer.

Variance vs. a Verisimilitude of Increasing *Truth*, Not Truth-likeness

If there can be no evidence for roughly true scientific theories, then there can be no historical sequence of the theories that are ever more true. And to add that there are these truer theories and thus that there is evidence for their comparable truth amounts to a *modus-tollens* argument for a much stronger verisimilitude than that proposed by Popper. In denying without a caveat that "truth" is ascribable to theories, Popper's reference to their increasing "truth-likeness" is patently empty.[21] The emptiness is, indeed, an understatement. Following my previous point that Popper's thesis of theory-dependence either presaged or was the underlying influence for Kuhn and Feyerabend's relativistic anti-realisms, Susan Haack notes that "Some critics have observed that, for all its ostensible rationalism, Popper's philosophy of science paved the way for the wildly irrationalist [relativistic] ideas that later became almost *de rigeur* among sociologists of science."[22] These senseless spins on science aside, he is still credited with formulating the first rigorous account of verisimilitude. On the one hand, however, verisimilitude was understood in terms of "true and false consequences of theories [where a theory in the sense of] proposition P is closer to the truth than Q if P entails more truths than Q, and no more false-hoods (or, fewer falsehoods, and no fewer truths)." On the other hand, this understanding allegedly undercut verisimilitude, strictly speaking in terms of truth-functional propositional logic, by implying precisely that "no false theory is closer to the truth than any other."[23]

Since the theories *qua* propositions P and Q have an epistemic significance only when their consequences are *false*, falsification being Popper's signature achievement, and they are indeterminately either false

---

21. See Schlipp (ed.), *The Philosophy of Karl Popper*, 1192–93.
22. Haack, "Just Say 'No,'" 33–54.
23. See Oddie, "Truth, Verification," 15932–37.

or true when they have true consequences, according to Popper, a better way to explain the problem more clearly herein may be by construing P and Q as conjunctive propositions. Suppose that these propositions are composed of laws, say L_{Q_1} and L_{Q_2} for Q and laws L_{P_1} and L_{P_2} for P. Here, the notion that P with any false laws is no closer to truth than can Q with any false laws, where the laws and thus the theories were falsified, is nothing more than the commonplace recognition that truth-functional propositional logic specifies that a conjunctive proposition is true if and only if every conjunct is true. That is, truth obtains for theories Q and P, per $(L_{Q_1} \wedge L_{Q_2})$ and $(L_{P_1} \wedge L_{P_2})$ respectively, where $\wedge$ denotes "and" if and only if every law is true for both theories. Yet theory P as $(L_{P_1} \wedge L_{P_2})$ where only *one law* is false and theory Q as $(L_{Q_1} \wedge L_{Q_2})$ where *both laws* are false would denote *equally false* theories. The theories are false per se despite Q having two false conjuncts and P only one. But why could not ordinary language and commonsense permit us to say that one theory is truer than another? The odd epistemic status of scientific theories when logic overrides ordinary commonsense bears heavily on problems of verisimilitude. Before examining this oddity further, consider another curiosity of conjunction.

Truth-likeness and the Inverse-Probability Thesis

In terms of conjunction's practical limitations for applied truth-functional propositional logic, logic professors might inform their students to avoid conjunctive propositions in favor of those that are disjunctive; in the context, for example, of the students graduating, having a job in marketing and being responsible for promoting ingredients on the packages of products. Suppose the product is a can of soup and they are to list its healthful benefits. A disjunctive propositions might be favored that specifies $[(A \vee B) \vee C]$, where $\vee$ denotes "or" and the letters represent simple propositions (disjuncts) about the soup's alleged benefits. The benefits might include "Either the soup will help prevent colds (A) or taste delicious (B), or it will quickly satisfy hunger (C)." Despite C being false, for instance, there would be no falsification of the entire compound proposition about the claimed benefits because the relevant rule of the truth-functional logic specifies that a disjunctive proposition is true if at least one disjunct is true. What is permitted to be true about the benefits here, however, is quite different than the conjunction $[(A \wedge B) \wedge C]$ where $\wedge$ denotes "and" and where a falsity of even one conjunct such as C falsifies the entire compound proposition. And the proposition has implications for more troubling expectations legally; the legal concerns being much graver when, for example, the subject involves toxic substances and medical claims.

This is not to say that these claims, much less the laws of science, should always be connected by disjuncts. It is to say, rather, that in some cases the suitable reasoning might be better interpreted in terms of ordinary language and what it makes sense to say (in a manner reminiscent of Wittgenstein). Wittgenstein would likely indeed say that it makes sense to say ordinarily that $[(A \vee B) \vee C]$ with two disjuncts that are true is *more true* than another proposition with only one true disjunct, although both disjunctive propositions are *equally true technically*.[24] And Wittgenstein would likely say that $[(A \wedge B) \wedge C]$ with two conjuncts that are true can be said *to be more true* than a three-conjunct proposition with only one true conjunct, although both propositions are *equally false technically*. The technicalities *alone* of logic, however, are acknowledged by most of those who have drawn skeptical anti-realist implications from Popper's position.[25] And if his position did appeal to a common-sense notion of what it makes sense to say, namely that one technically false conjunctive proposition *can* be truer than another, then he would undercut his signature falsification thesis that presumes the dubious truth-functional material implication.

This implication specifies that antecedents referring to theories with undetermined truth-values cannot be known to be true by consequents referring to true predictions since the theories may be either false or true when there are true predictions. Rather, the theories can only be known to be false by false predictions. In terms of predictions, the only knowledge we have is that theories are false. The undercutting of Popper's falsification thesis if he appeals as such to ordinary language—this language favored by Wittgenstein over rules of logic when there are these

---

24. This ordinary language approach of saying one false conjunctive proposition might be truer than another was noted to me by the late Professor James Kimble, who had expertise on Wittgenstein, at the University of Colorado at Boulder.

25. See Tichy's "On Popper's Definition," 155–60 and Miller's "Qualitative Theory," 178–88. Per Popper implying that "no false theory is closer to the truth than any other," Tichy and Miller argue: "Let G be some truth implied by P but not by Q, and let F be any falsehood implied by P. Then F&G is a falsehood implied by P, but not by Q. (If Q implied F&G then Q would also entail the second conjunct, G—contradiction.) We cannot add truths to P without adding falsehoods [or subtract] falsehoods without subtracting truths...." Oddie, "Truth, Verification," 15932–37.

sorts of conflicts, holds despite what I call Popper's *Inverse Probability Thesis* where the probability of a theory's truth is related inversely to the improbable truth of the theory's prediction: The more that a prediction is improbable, the more probable is the theory's truth when "truth" is ascribable to the prediction. This appeal to predictions, however, depends precisely on inductions whose rejection by Hume was accepted paradoxically by Popper. And the further irony of Popper appealing to the probability is captured by the title of his coauthored article "A Proof of the Impossibility of Inductive Probability."[26]

This probability notwithstanding, the theories of physics (among the alleged "hard sciences") have an historically increasing predictive power. And this power, suggests Newton-Smith, is almost universally accepted. After adding that to argue from this acceptance to the acceptance of verisimilitude is to consent to the intuitively strong premise that "If a theory T_2 is a better approximation to the truth than a theory T_1, then it is likely that T_2 will have greater predictive power than T_1."[27] Furthermore, he concedes that the premise begs for a justification since *inter alia* verisimilitude is not defined as the likelihood of observational success but rather about the success being explained. Central to the explanation, he says, is that one theory is nearer to the truth than another when it has greater content and more of the content is true (and less is false by a definition of qualified truth) wherein it does indeed follow that "if one theory has greater verisimilitude than another it is likely to have greater observational success."[28] This success is uniquely related herein to a common-sense modal logic and existential phenomenology. The latter explain both how the greater observational success is related by this logic to a truth of theories and how these theories can have observational predictions that are able to be confirmed objectively. The objectivity stems from scientists having an irrefutable and immediate *awareness of* their observational consciousness of the predicted phenomena.

---

26. Popper and Miller, "A Proof of the Impossibility," The article's Abstract reads: "Proofs of the impossibility of induction have been falling 'dead-born from the Press' ever since the first of them (in David Hume's *Treatise of Human Nature*) appeared in 1739. One of us (K.P.) has been producing them for more than 50 years. The present proof strikes us both as pretty."

27. Ibid., 196–97.

28. Ibid., 205.

A Logic for What It Makes Sense to Say

Predicted phenomena expressed as propositions to which truth is ascribable warrants a common-sense reasoning: While it is *logically possible* a theory is false when it makes systematically true predictions in a given domain, it is an *epistemic impossibility* that can be recast as "Necessarily if systematically true predictions are made by a theory in some domain (*P*), then in this domain the theory is approximately true (*T*)." Read $P \Rightarrow T$, this modality means that if *P* is true, then the truth of *T* follows necessarily and it is an epistemic impossibility for the theory to not be generally true. How could theories make systematically true predictions of phenomena when they are not reflected truly, at least roughly, by the theories?

The theories T_A and T_B could be roughly true on this view even though T_B may be more true than T_A where these theories consist of postulates, principles or laws where T_A reads $[(L_{A_1} \wedge L_{A_2}) \wedge L_{A_3}]$ and T_B reads $[(L_{B_1} \wedge L_{B_2}) \wedge L_{B_3}]$. Here, $\wedge$ denotes "and," *L* refers to a law that can be subject to particular applications; Popper noting that laws tend to be generalizations that beg for interpretive applications. The applications pertaining to a theory's laws could have several different formula for a given law. For the second law, for instance, $f = ma$ of Newtonian physics for example, there is free fall as $mg = md^2/sdt^2$ for formula F_1, the simple pendulum as $mg\mathrm{Sin}\phi = -md^2/sdt^2$ for the formula F_2 and coupled harmonic oscillators in terms of $m_1 d^2 s_1 /dt^2 + k_1 s_1 = k^2 (d + s_2 - s_1)$ for formula F_3.[29] The given law of a theory as well as the theory itself may *eo ipso* be read as a vulnerable conjunction of formulas that include the 2nd law of Newtonian Physics in terms of $(F_1 \wedge F_2 \wedge F_3)$, although this point about epistemic problems with the conjunctive nature of laws has gone unnoticed. And the applied formula bears on a verisimilitude that can be illustrated for the above mentioned theories T_A and T_B. Here, theory T_B may be more observationally successful and thus truer than theory T_A. And T_A may have either more false or doubtful laws that may include their applications and have its truth restricted to a given domain; say domain *A*, as opposed to theory T_B whose truth applies to both of the domains *A* and *B*. In this way, Einstein's theory can be said to be truer than

---

29. Neither Thomas Kuhn nor others have noticed that *formulas* as conjuncts for laws are analogous to laws as conjuncts for theories. See Kuhn's "Second Thoughts on Paradigms," Suppe's *The Structure of Scientific Theories*, 464–465 and Roberts et al (eds.), "What is the Experimental Basis?" §1–11.

Newton's theory by virtue of applying both to the Newtonian domain as well as to a domain beyond his domain where bodies approach the speed of light. And Newton's theory likewise can be said to be truer than Aristotle's theory since his theory is restricted to the terrestrial domain. And so Aristotle's physics is nested by Newton's physics, because the latter physics can predict and explicate everything that Aristotle's physics can, *and more*, and Newton's physics is nested also by Einstein's physics for these same or similar reasons.

Is It Senseless to Say That Superseded Theories Are True?

The reasons for saying that one theory nests or cradles another theory historically because it has more verisimilitude underscores the need to expand upon Newton-Smith's *pessimistic induction* because, he says, we could inductively infer that any major theory will turn out to be *false* "within, say 200 years of being propounded."[30] While we may be certain that our current theories are true, he questions if modesty does not require "us to assume that they are not so?"[31] And although Newton-Smith does not challenge the notion that today's theories are preceded strictly by falsified theories by a Popper-like position, he says that a rational realist like himself "is likely to respond by positing an interim goal . . . of getting nearer the truth" such that the "inductive argument outlined above is accepted but its sting is removed [because] that argument is compatible with maintaining that current theories, *while strictly false*, are getting nearer the truth."[32] Notwithstanding getting ever closer to truth, modal logic is ignored for inferring theories to actually be roughly true from systematically true predictions.

These predictions led me to propose a *Principle of Optimistic Induction* as opposed to his *Pessimistic Induction*. This induction aside, a problem with this truth is that Newton-Smith *accepts* also a truth-functional propositional logic. This logic is held bogusly to establish that antecedents (theories) are *known* only to be false by false consequences (predictions) and never to be true by true predictions. This renders problematic Newton-Smith's position that theories are getting nearer truth when both that truth is *unrelated logically* to observational successes of theories and

---

30. Newton-Smith, *The Rationality of Science*, 14.
31. Ibid.
32. Ibid., emphasis.

theories are known to be strictly false by false predictions. Where a prediction occurring is expressed as *P*, that is, a theory being true reads *T* and the arrow → denotes "if . . . then," *T* → *P* is a material implication which specifies that it is logically *possible* that *T* is false when *P* is true but logically *impossible* that *T* is true when *P* is false. Thus false predictions ostensibly falsify theories. But theories are inferably true, at least inexactly, in contrast to the foregoing by virtue of systematically true predictions per the epistemic modality (*P* ⇒ *T*). By this conditional, while it is logically possible that a theory is *not* roughly true (~*T*) when there are systematically true predictions by theory (*P*), there is an epistemic impossibility that ~*T*. And theories are *not said to be false* in a Popper-like way or even *limitedly successful research programs* in a Lakatos-like language when they are superseded historically by truer theories.[33] Rather, theories may be said to have a truth restricted to given domains, as a domain of Newtonian physics is limited to Planck's constant being negligible and phenomena not approaching the speed of light.

Truth As the Main Aim of Scientific Methodology

Scientific progress has thus far been articulated in terms of theories that are increasingly truer. This truth is not based on an intuitive leap from observational success to truth but rather by truth being *inferred* from success by a modal logic rooted in what it makes sense to say. In not being restricted to logical possibilities, as is truth-functional logic, this logic begets an epistemic impossibility of theories not being roughly true when they make systematically true predictions in given domains. Aside from these domains and before delving into other details of scientific method, consider truth related to an epistemic reasonableness recognized by Wittgenstein. He notes in *On Certainty* that there is a mode of impossibility whose denial is patently unreasonable.[34] In courts of law, for instance,[35] ordinary people assess a reasonable probability of statements. But claiming "someone came into the world without parents," he says, "wouldn't ever be taken into consideration." In considering "parents" to

---

33. Lakatos, *The Methodology*, 6.

34. Cf. Trundle, "St. Thomas' Modal Logic," 79–99. I argue that Wittgenstein and Heidegger, by their own poignant words, did indeed covertly embrace the world's creation.

35. This can be recast as an impossibility that someone came into the world when there were no prior biological processes. Wittgenstein, *On Certainty*, 42e, n. 335.

include technological developments, what can Wittgenstein mean other than there are no facts that would count against it to overcome doubt? While the claim that "someone came into the world without parents" is more doubtful than a false empirical assertion such as saying "someone's parents are so and so" when they were registered incorrectly, the assertion is not logically impossible. "There are cases where doubt is unreasonable, but others where it seems logically impossible" and he adds that "there seems to be no clear boundary between them."[36] The boundary between a logically impossible doubt and a doubt that is empirically unreasonable bears precisely on a certainty that, while not logically conclusive, is more reasonable than empirical truths which do not count against it. This point both captures a nature of modal truth and bears on a *more than reasonable* inference of truth from observational success.[37]

Given a sound inference from the success to a truth of theories, as hopefully established, a scientific methodology is invigorated by what ought to guide theory choice. First, the choice for a theory would be diminished *prima facie* if its observational success could not be duplicated. Insistence on duplication should not be made too hastily, however, as illustrated by the reactions to failed attempts to replicate results of cold fusion in late March 1989. "The 'discovery' of cold fusion . . . astonished the world," notes astrobiologist and geophysicist David Waltham, "since it suggested that an almost inexhaustible supply of energy could be obtained from relatively simple and cheap equipment."[38] And while Waltham admits of the mind-boggling benefits for the world of "controlled nuclear fusion, the process that powers the stars" because we don't need to "spend billions of dollars on a complex apparatus" but only "a jar of heavy water and some palladium electrodes," he both reveals a *rigid duplication methodology* that ignores how it was obstructed by politics and states disingenuously (without qualification) that "scientists failed to reproduce the findings . . . ." The failure to replicate the initial findings, in constituting a death knell to further research, reminds one of Popper's inflexible thesis of falsification. The falsification is brought to mind when Waltham laments that the findings were defended by the supporters "of cold fusion [who] stuck by their results nonetheless and explained away negative results . . . by their detractors, who, in turn, became increasingly

36. Ibid., 59e, n. 454 for the second quote.
37. Cf. Grayling, "Wittgenstein" Intro. and §IV–VII.
38. See Waltham, "Alone in the Cosmos," para. 1–26, for this and the next two quotes.

vociferous in their criticism of the original experiments." Waltham adds, in lockstep thinking without any misgivings, that "Today this is a toxic area for research. Any scientist attempting to publish a cold-fusion paper would be committing career suicide."

New Phenomena That Resist Duplication

A threat of career suicide when scientists are open-minded requires, among other things, a more *flexible duplication methodology* by the scientific community. Those in this community for whom careers override truth are reminded shamefully of their reticence by several sources. One source at the end of this topic is a report in 2016, which contradicts these careerists, by the US House Committee on Armed Services. The report states both that cold fusion is taken seriously around the world and that, "according to the Defense Intelligence Agency (DIA), if [Low-Energy nuclear Reactions *qua* Cold Fusion] works it will be a *"disruptive technology that could revolutionize energy production and storage."*[39] To begin with, then, one source was the refereed rejections of a submitted article in theoretical support of cold fusion by the Nobel-Prize Winner of Physics Julian Schwinger ("Cold Fusion: A Hypothesis") for *Physical Review Letters* in mid-1989 after claimed positive result of the fusion led to a few failed duplications. The dismissive and even "venomous" tenor of the anonymous rejections resulted in the resignation of Schwinger from the American Physical Society which published the journal,[40] his noting that "Reproducibility is often cited as a canon of science. And so it is, in *established areas*. But, early in a study of a new phenomenon that involves an ill-understood macroscopic control of a microscopic mechanism, irreproducibility is not unknown," adding that it was unknown "at the onset of microchip studies" and also "in the initial phase of the discovery of high temperature superconductivity, which, by the way, is a prime example of 'embracing the concept' without having 'to understand the mechanism.'"[41] And a further source that shows the need for a more flexible duplication is an "upbeat, enthusiastic" panel of experts that were assembled in late-1989 by the National Science Foundation's engineering division. The division maintained that the effects of cold fusion "are real"

---

39. 114th Congress *2nd Session*, H.R. Report 114–537, emphasis.
40. Rabinowitz, "In Memory," ix–x.
41. Kowalski, "Julian Schwinger," §2, emphasis.

and "cannot be explained [away] as a result of artifacts, equipment, or human errors."[42]

In addition to human errors and other typical rationalizations being unable to explain away the continuing effects of cold fusion, there were the following developments that were truly breathtaking (given the spectacular specter of both a new scientific understanding that might rival the Copernican-like impact of Einstein's physics and a virtually free, unlimited, non-toxic, and dramatic poverty-reducing global source of energy): U.S. Navy researchers at the Space & Naval Warfare Systems (SPAWAR), whose scientists had shown admirable mettle in pursuing study of the shunned cold fusion for several years, published "THERMAL AND NUCLEAR ASPECTS OF THE Pd/D2O SYSTEM" in 2002 (S. Szpak and P. A. Mosier-Boss, eds.[43]) with an imploring entreaty to their government to provide substantive funding for research on the fusion;[44] the foremost scientists Yoshiaki Arata and Yue Chang Zhang demonstrating an autonomous fusion "heater" in 2007/2008 that "generated a steady outflow flow of heat at slightly above room temperature throughout a run lasting hundreds of hours" (Arata noting this as an energy source which is "potentially more important to us than hot or 'thermonuclear' fusion and notes that . . . it does not emit any pollution at all")[45]; and, among other advances, the Italian research agency ENEA (National Agency for New Technologies, Energy and Sustainable Economic Development) published *COLD FUSION–The History of Research in Italy* (2011). This document states that, by a new process "based on theoretical considerations" that achieved a concentration threshold for observing cold-fusion phenomena in a manner which was "*extremely reproducible*," the ENEA has established a strong collaboration between itself and "some U.S. institutions (SRL Energetics, NJ, and more recently Naval Research Lab, Washington D.C.)."[46] Indeed, Dr. Frank E. Gordon, Head of the Navigation and Applied Sciences Department at San Diego's Space and Naval Warfare Systems Center, noted that the government should start funding research:

42. Anderson, "Clandestine NSF Panel," para. 2.
43. Cf. Mosier-Boss, et al, "Review of 20 Years," 173–87.
44. Chubb, "In Honor of Yoshiaki Arata," Intro. and para. 1–7.
45. Cartwright, "Cold-fusion," See para. 1–14.
46. Martellucci et al. (eds.), *COLD FUSION*, Foreword, emphasis.

As I write this Foreword [for P. A. Mosier-Boss' *Thermal and Nuclear Aspects of the Pd/D2O System* Vol. 1 (Long: 3 MB)], California is experiencing rolling blackouts due to power shortages. Conventional engineering, planned ahead, could have prevented these blackouts, but it has been *politically* expedient to ignore the inevitable. We do not know if Cold Fusion will be the answer to future energy needs, but we do know the existence of Cold Fusion phenomenon through repeated observations by scientists throughout the world. It is time that this phenomenon be investigated so that we can reap whatever benefits accrue from additional scientific understanding. It is time for the government funding organizations to invest in this research.[47]

Finally, there is a further spectacular update. A short version of the update, on the cold fusion *qua* low-energy nuclear reactions (LENR), is as follows: The US House Committee on Armed Services, in its report for the National Defense Authorization Act for Fiscal Year 2017 (H.R. 4909), stated that "The committee is aware of recent positive developments in developing low-energy nuclear reactions."[48] In light of these reactions *qua* "cold fusion" being a "*disruptive technology that could revolutionize energy*," the committee's report directs the Secretary of Defense to "provide a briefing on the military utility of recent U.S. industrial base LENR advancements to the House Committee on Armed Services by September 22, 2016."[49] Below is the full passage:

> *Low Energy Nuclear Reactions (LENR) Briefing*[:] The committee is aware of recent positive developments in developing low-energy nuclear reactions (LENR), which produce ultraclean, low-cost renewable energy that have strong national security implications. For example, according to the Defense Intelligence Agency (DIA), if LENR works it will be a "*disruptive technology that could revolutionize energy production and storage*." The committee is also aware of the Defense Advanced Research Project Agency's (DARPA) findings that other countries including China and India are moving forward with LENR programs of their own and that Japan has actually created its own investment fund to promote such technology. DIA has also assessed that Japan and Italy are leaders in the field and that Russia, China, Israel, and India are now devoting significant resources

47. Rothwell, LENR-CANR.ORG, Foreword, emphasis.
48. 114th Congress *2nd Session*, HR (Report 114–537) 87.
49. Ibid.

to LENR development. To better understand the national security implications of these developments, the committee directs the Secretary of Defense to provide a briefing on the military utility of recent U.S. industrial base LENR advancements to the House Committee on Armed Services by September 22, 2016. This briefing should examine the current state of research in the United States, how that compares to work being done internationally, and an assessment of the type of military applications where this technology could potentially be useful.[50]

Cold fusion not useful? A waste of time and tax-payer money? We may conclude that the article in *The Chronicle of Higher Education* by a scientist who warns of "career suicide" by doing research in the "toxic area" of cold fusion,[51] in light of the above developments of which he and other scientists should be in the know, does indeed suggest a cowardly conformity in both higher education and the scientific community. The article not only reminds us of Einstein's stress on imagination over knowledge but also of our having the *courage of our convictions* and ensuring that the *convictions* are not based on a self-deceptive careerism but rather on sound scientific methodology. A main part of the methodology is an allowance for pliable concepts of "duplication" that distinguish old from new and novel areas of research. Scientists should not impose rash inferences from the one to the other wherein, as a Nobel-Prize winning physicist stated, for example, a bias of the "physics community against cold fusion was based on inferences from hot fusion that are not valid in this new regime."[52]

In regard to new regimes, there are two points. First, it would miss the point to suppose that my discussion is to marshal support for cold fusion that may not prove fruitful in the long run as now conceived. My point about emerging concepts of this fusion was to provide an example of why there should be a flexible methodology for duplicating experiments or other scientific ventures. Second, the "regimes" may seem reminiscent of "normal science" resisting new paradigms (per Kuhn). But paradigms, which amount initially to incomparable conceptual frameworks that are imposed *a priori* on reality, need not be accepted to accept a respectful openness to the development of innovative theories that might either explicate, predict and manipulate new anomalous phenomena or interpret

50. Ibid., emphasis.
51. Waltham, "Alone in the Cosmos," para. 22.
52. Rabinowitz, "In Memory of Julian Schwinger," 3.

the old phenomena in novel ways such as possibly unifying weak and electromagnetic forces into the "electroweak force" or how using the Casimir force to "explain what holds an electron together."[53]

From Duplication to Novelty and New Research

We have thus far noted the need for being open to both innovative theories and experimental results that resist duplication such as cold fusion. And we have recognized also the need for a defensible notion of scientific progress via increasing theoretical truth. Consider now how the foregoing bear on a methodological norms for guiding theory choice.[54] The first norm is that new theories should be able to duplicate the observational success of current theories. On the one hand, it was mentioned that a sound methodology will enhance historically increasing scientific truth even when the methodology *tolerates* initial failures to duplicate either novel experimental results or the results of new theories. Theory toleration would hold most notably if the radically novel results would have dramatically beneficial consequences of an immediate practical nature, such as cold fusion would have. The toleration would hold also when the new theories would have revolutionary theoretical consequences for the scientific enterprise such as the extraordinary explanatory and predictive powers of the physics of Einstein; he and his heirs making the seemingly bizarre predictions that space is expanding from a Big Bang, that spacetime is related inextricably to black holes where time stops and space has an energy that pulls apart the universe.[55] These theoretical and practical consequences can overlap, of course, rendering more vital an initial, even protracted, toleration of either quasi-duplication or non-duplication as part of the methodology. While the methodology should still specify that a failure to duplicate the observational success of a current theory by a new theory will count against the new theory, says Newton-Smith,[56] this theory should be entertained despite its duplicative drawbacks if the

---

53. Ibid.

54. These methodological norms are both indebted to and modify some of those noted by Newton-Smith in *The Rationality of Science*, 226–32. The methodological norms of simplicity and a metaphysical compatibility of theories are not included because of a modal logic herein that may in some cases supersede his metaphysics and other discussions.

55. See U.S. Government, NASA, "Expanding Universe Shapes," para. 7–8.

56. Cf. Newton-Smith, *The Rationality of Science*, 228.

theory has a high degree of success in atypical areas where the present theory fails. And although failure should not necessarily result in abandoning the present theory *in toto* for the new one, neither should the new one be accepted as either truer or an alternative until, by testing, modification and further evidence, the success of the current theory is duplicated unequivocally by the new theory.

If this theory both duplicates the success of a current theory and either has more accurate predictions or expands the predictive domain such as Einstein's theory did over Newton's, then the new theory may replace a current theory. This theory's replacement as such follows from the robust realism herein in which science should seek explanatory theories that are ever truer about how reality really *is*. And reality being reflected by these truer theories is related inextricably to their predictive observational success. This success, which strictly implies truth, is precluded when all observation is theory-laden and there is no existential phenomenological account of how consciousness has a *theory-independent non-conceptual touchstone* with physical reality. Reality that is observed non-conceptually apart from theory, as an overlooked presupposition of a realist methodology, bears also on a second methodological norm. This norm is that theory choice, as Newton-Smith says, should strongly tend to favor theories that lend themselves to guiding research.[57] The research is enhanced by theories that, having allegorical components that are imaginative, kindle many other innovative notions.[58] These notions are addressed by Amy Kind and Peter Kung in *Knowledge through Imagination*. They say that "Blending perspectives from philosophy of mind, cognitive science, epistemology, aesthetics, and ethics . . . sheds new light on the epistemic role of imagination."[59] The notion by Einstein that imagination is more important than knowledge, as discussed above in terms of existential phenomenology, brings to mind precisely a guidance prescribed by Newton-Smith. Here, theories should have a fertility induced by imaginative metaphorical components "as in the early days of the ideal gas theory" in which gases "were thought to be like collections of small hard balls colliding in space."[60] He adds that collisions in space, as this metaphor, begets "exploration of the similarities and dissimilarities with

---

57. Ibid., 227.
58. Ibid.
59. See Kind and Kungs's *Knowledge through Imagination*, description.
60. Newton-Smith, *The Rationality of Science*, 228.

the phenomenon to which it has been likened," the fertility illustrated as well by Planck's quantum of action for explaining "the distribution of radiation given off by a black body"[61]; and evoking the possibility "of applying the idea of the quantum to other unexplained phenomena."[62]

The phenomena can be considered creatively by a quantum of action that, says Arthur Young, "has the measure formula ML^2/T" where "If action comes in wholes which cannot be further reduced, then action is the whole of which the three parameters, mass, length, and time, are parts!"[63] Accordingly, it is "proper to think of action as the whole, and mass, length and time as its fragmentation," noting "other measure formulae which are compounded of M, L, and T; for example, energy is ML^2/T^2 ($E = MC^2$, Einstein's formula, is a special case; it gives the amount of energy available from a given mass." And leading to further philosophical points, he adds, "In this case, $L/T = C$, the velocity of light). But energy does not come in whole quanta whereas action does; so the whole which by division produces M, L, and T must be action (the quantum of action)."

> We are touching here on [philosophical] profundities.... Recall that science excludes *purpose* from its formulations, and that for science the three parameters, mass, length, and time suffice. I believe the rejection of *purpose* and the omission of the fourth parameter, action, are one and the same. If we were presented with only the parts of a machine, we could not deduce its purpose; one must see the machine in operation to discover the purpose. Purpose is not physical and action (in the sense of the quantum of action) is not observable; we can observe a change of state due to action but not action itself; so, too, we can observe the result of purpose but not the purpose. These clues point to the dependence of purpose on wholeness. They also expose the *fallacy of reductionism* in that reduction of the universe to mass, length, and time no more proves the nonexistence of purpose than [reducing] a machine to its elements proves that a machine has no purpose and is "nothing but" its parts.[64]

---

61. Ibid.

62. Ibid.

63. See Young, "The Quantum of Action," 12, for this and the next three quotes in this paragraph.

64. Ibid., emphasis.

This parts-versus-whole analysis on behalf of *accepting* a "purpose," which is not oxymoronically determined, and *rejecting* reductionism is a reminder that the very notion of "novel ideas" is incoherent apart from our direct consciousness of phenomena being both itself unreducible to a measurable phenomenon and that of which we are implicitly aware. If there were not this awareness of consciousness relating itself to a phenomenon *in one way*, say by a received view, then consciousness could not relate itself *in a different way* by novel ideas. The ideas are not explainable by the following: today's typical theories in terms of sensory stimuli that causally determine ideas (*pace* Feyerabend and his heirs); by many philosophers of neuroscience or neuroscientists who predictively say that "new research suggests that [free will] might be nothing more than a trick the brain plays on itself";[65] and by early modern theories in terms of a mind related only conceptually to reality (*pace* Descartes' rationalism). Rather, reality is comprehended as it really *is* by virtue of a non-conceptual consciousness that is infused into a conceptual consciousness of which there is an indirect awareness.

This awareness *of* our direct consciousness of phenomena explains how both the *conceptualizations* and the *phenomena in themselves* are that of which we are indirectly aware so that they can be compared, i.e., the comparisons being possible since our conceptual observational consciousness always includes a non-conceptual consciousness of the *phenomena themselves*. And an indirect awareness our observational consciousness, in being an implicit awareness of our freedom to see or not see something as well as to imagine it in different ways, is why our awareness is *free from* univocal relationships to physical reality. While reality being imagined in different ways permits, as Newton-Smith says, novel ideas and theories "with association ideas for further development," the development may not be "ultimately successful" since indicators of success and the theories are troubled by a fallible induction[66]; an induction that, I may add, influenced Popper to reject science proceeding upward from reality to universal truth, thus seeming to threaten the methodological norms herein. But Hume's notion that induction is justifiable on which the threat is based is criticized convincingly by Stephen Körner who notes that Hume's assertion that only fools would deny induction implies that a cogent induction *is* itself a justification that need not be jus-

---

65. See Bear, "What Neuroscience Says," subtitle.
66. Newton-Smith, *The Rationality of Science*, 227.

tified: Hume is not warranted in replacing justification with a justifiable justification in which there can be no justification since every justification must be justifiable; indicating that induction as a justification, while not itself justifiable, is neither wrong nor a reason for skepticism.[67]

These points against both skepticism and Popper's anti-realism influenced by Hume, boost a realism for reasoning from experience to theory and are augmented by other methodological norms for theory choice. Reinforcing this norm is Catherine Legg who maintains, "Much mainstream *analytic epistemology* is built around a *sceptical treatment of modality* which descends from Hume."[68]

From Research and Success to Internal Inconsistency

Recall that the previous methodological norms for guiding theory choice were both that new theories should duplicate observational successes of extant theories and that theories have metaphorical elements that fuel future research. The third norm, noted by Newton-Smith, is that research and testing should result in a new theory's sustained success in a given domain.[69] We add that the domain's scope of phenomena should *ceteris paribus* be equal to or greater than the greatest domain of a current theory, such as relativistic physics including the scope of classical physics. That being said, the longer that the new theory is successful is *directly proportional* to a greater chance that the theory will inspire imaginative ideas as well as have increased applications to phenomena.[70]

Phenomena in the neo-Kantian philosophy of science à la Kuhn and Feyerabend, it should be noted, cannot include a notion of "observational success" and thus of "scientific progress," which is part of our phenomenological realism. This realism admits of successful predictions, related logically to roughly true theories, and excludes theory/paradigm-dependent observation reports. Rather, the reports, while variously theory-laden, can be roughly true. But the truth of observation reports, for the neo-Kantian philosophy science, depends *a priori* on possibly contradictory theories, paradigms or worldviews. These worldviews bring to mind

---

67. See Körner, *Experience and Theory*, 190–94.
68. See Legg, "Things Unreasonably Compulsory," abstract.
69. Cf. Newton-Smith, *The Rationality of Science*, 227.
70. Ibid. See my prior discussion of imagination, per the history of science, explicated by existential phenomenology.

Kuhn's distinction of an unknowable *world in itself* from a world grasped by paradigms. The paradigms beget an epistemic neo-Kantian *relativism* whereby Kuhn embraces a multiplicity of phenomenal worlds, versus a noumenal world, that depend on possibly contradictory conceptual paradigms *qua* Weltanschauen (worldviews).[71]

Yes, the worldviews and anarchical theories held respectively by Kuhn and Feyerabend have immediate roots in Sir Karl Popper. That said, the two relativists are rooted more historically in Kant's *a-priori categorial interpretations* of reality since they replace that by neo-Kantian *a-priori interpretations by theories (paradigms)*. While these theories (paradigms) allegedly interpret observation reports and even our sensations, they are themselves based on convoluted metaphysical theories that collide head-on with the sensations and reality of which we are incontrovertibly conscious. In appealing to our own immediate experience of ourselves, we can be directly conscious of our sensations but they are not confused with our consciousness of external things. In being indirectly aware *of* our direct observational consciousness, a "consciousness of this or that thing-in-the-world [can be encountered]," states Sartre, but not our "visual or tactile sense."[72] And besides these senses, one may add, we are *not* conscious of reality being interpreted automatically by Kantian mental categories, paradigms, or theories.

Using possibly contradictory theories, paradigms, etc., to either determine the truth-values of observation reports or be the contexts in which they are understood, for neo-Kantian philosophers of science, proceeded hand-in-hand infamously with the thesis of theory-dependent observation. This illogical stance on observation, in turn, resulted in severe harm to society: relativism, political correctness, and skepticism. "We are not dealing here ... with skepticism" says Sartre about a phenomenology of knowledge, or "with relativism."[73] The relativistic-skeptical-cynical misadventures of both the twentieth and twenty-first century are avoided by a version herein of his existential phenomenology. Based on a theory-free and concept-neutral consciousness of reality of which we are aware (conscious), the phenomenology provides an ontological basis for the epistemology of rational realists who include Newton-Smith. Newton-Smith refers to a fourth methodological norm for new theories,

---

71. Cf. Hoyningen-Huene, *Reconstructing Scientific Revolutions*, 60–61.
72. Sartre, *Being and Nothingness*, 316.
73. Ibid., 218.

namely that they should both explain and support current theories that are successful; as the successful laws of thermodynamics were explained by statistical mechanics.[74]

While this mechanics illustrates the methodological norm of explaining and supporting extant major theories, the norm follows in a broader way from the ideal of an historical growth of theories that are ever truer in reflecting roughly what reality is really like. This likeness of reality reflected by increasingly truer theories (verisimilitude) cannot be considered intelligibly apart from the theories increasing explanatory power. The norm not only explains the efforts to either unify general relativity with quantum mechanics or construe them as consistent (if not mutually supportive) but also underscores that prescribing that new theories underpin and explain previous ones has resulted in boosting scientific progress.[75]

The idea of progress herein, though, differs from that of Popper and Newton-Smith. In contrast to Newton-Smith, this essay restricts the growing truth of superseded theories to *domains* and does not refer to them as falsified as does his "pessimistic induction."[76] His induction fails to consider that past major theories being entirely false is an *epistemic impossibility* if they yield systematically true predictions in the domains. The domains as such are equally omitted by Popper. And so my position rejects Popper's falsification thesis and his pursuit of increasing truth-likeness as a mere aim. The aim reflects a vacuous realism due to his likening reality to the bottom of a swamp that is never reached by lowered pillars (theories), underscoring his thesis of theory-dependent observation and its oddly overlooked influence on Kuhn and Feyerabend's relativism, if not the success-seeking, but truth-ignoring/guessing, pragmatic positions of Richard Rorty, Larry Laudan, and Imre Lakatos. In regard to Lakatos on the matter, "all we can do is 'hopefully guess' that the historical succession of scientific theories is leading us closer to the truth."[77] While making profound contributions, they have disregarded how success is related logically to truth.

The fifth methodological norm mandates that new scientific theories be able to at least adjust to failures or, better, succeed in responding

---

74. Newton-Smith, *The Rationality of Science*, 228.
75. Ibid.
76. Ibid., 14.
77. Allan, "Imre Lakatos," §3.3 para. 13.

to them, says Newton-Smith.[78] Failures as well as successes will tend to typify new theories that may nonetheless become part of an historical sequence of theories that are ever truer. The lack of a few true predictions, among a new theory's mostly successful or impressive predictions, may initially be disregarded and eventually explained by auxiliary hypotheses. The hypotheses notwithstanding, competition among new theories, or even these with extant theories, may be assessed by favoring those that can cope with failures with fewer hypotheses or modifications.

The minimal modifications agree with the idea that systematic failures may accompany systematic successes, as noted by Newton-Smith. Newton's theory was favored, for example, despite *repeated* failures where Planck's constant counted or bodies approach the speed of light, because of the theory's *steady* success with classical phenomena. Phenomena that are predicted presuppose causal regularities, reflecting *continuity* as a primary feature of Nature. As noted by Compton in *Phenomenology in America*,[79] continuity denotes an evolving behavior intrinsic to the nature of things of which we are both conceptually and non-conceptually conscious, as explicated by our existential phenomenology. This phenomenology precludes a theory-dependent observation, which is *not* averted by a rational realism of Newton-Smith; as salient as his insights are. And the phenomenology explains both our unassailable encounter with *being*, fortifying a classical realism of *being as existing*, and why we are warranted in expecting the future to behave as the past in regard to Nature. Besides Nature as *Being* having causation intrinsic to it, as per Etienne Gilson, Gilson echoes our realism of encountering *being as existing*, rejecting its roots in Cartesian thought:

> If modern idealism has nothing more than that to oppose to medieval realism, then I venture to say that it no longer has any conception of what a genuine realism is. Undoubtedly, the unfortunate habit we have acquired since Descartes of proceeding always from thought to things, leads us to interpret the *adequatio rei et intellectus* as if it involved a comparison between the representation of a thing and this mere phantom, which is all that the thing outside all representation can be for us.[80]

---

78. Cf. Newton-Smith, *The Rationality of Science*, 228.

79. Compton, "Natural Science," 91. Again, as insightful and pioneering as was Compton's insight (to which I am indebted) "aspects" of reality are not noted by him to be *non-conceptually seen*.

80. Gilson, *The Spirit of Medieval Philosophy*, 90. The words *Adequatio rei et*

Our relating methodological norms to both Etienne Gilson and existential phenomenology, which fortifies a classical realism of *being as existing*, leads to the sixth methodological norm: A new theory is accepted *ceteris paribus* only if the theory is internally consistent in terms of the theory's laws being true without contradiction as a consequence.[81] With a caveat that the need to avoid this consequence has exceptions which are oddly omitted in the literature as noted below, the consequence of contradiction otherwise is that *any* sentence denoted by q can follow validly. The validity is typified by arguments such as $p \: / \: {\sim} p \: // \: q$ where q is a conclusion inferred from the contradictory premises p and ${\sim}p$. Thus if there are contradictory sentences in a new theory, the theory cannot be true in a realist sense because, as Irving Copi says,[82] any sentence would follow literally. The literal sentences would include "no events have causes," whose contrary is presupposed for the intelligibility of scientific inquiry, when they instantiate the conclusion q. In regard to q, Newton-Smith stresses also that consistency is demanded *a priori*. For, for him, where q is an arbitrary sentence in a new theory that is inconsistent, $p \land {\sim} p$ obtains where $\land$ signifies "and" and p is inferable by Simplification. And from p can be inferred by Addition $p \lor q$ where $\lor$ reads "or" such that when p is true, q can be either true or false. However, from $p \land {\sim} p$, there is inferable as well ${\sim}p$ such that, taken with $p \lor q$, the truth or falsity of q is equally entailed. Accordingly, "once we admit of an inconsistency... we have to admit everything."[83]

Is this so, however? Is everything permitted if theories contain an inconsistency or contradiction, bringing to mind covertly that everything is permitted if there is no God (as warned famously by Dostoevsky)? In speaking of the supposed menace of contradiction, the logician Peter Geach, awarded the *papal medal pro ecclesia et pontifice* for fidelity to divine revelation, noted that "A demand for a strict proof of non-contradiction is... often unreasonable—even, as recent logical researches have shown, in pure mathematics."[84]

Aside from mathematics, consider contradictions in quantum mechanics where wavelength is inversely proportional to velocity because it

---

intellectus may mean "the intellect (of the knower) must be adequate to the thing (known)."

81. Cf. Marcus, *Modalities*, 133.
82. Copi, *Symbolic Logic*, 63.
83. Newton-Smith, *The Rationality of Science*, 229.
84. Geach, *God and the Soul*, 107.

decreases as velocity increases of a particle, per the particle-wave equation $\lambda = h/p = h/mv$ where λ is wavelength, h is Planck's constant and $p = mv =$ the magnitude of a moving particle's momentum. This means, says physicist Saul Youssef, that light *is* and *is not* a particle (wave) and, in later research by others, the contradiction holds experimentally "at all times."[85] Where "W" denotes light is a wave and "$\sim W$" otherwise, the *received view* states that contradiction results in the argument either that $W / \sim W // S$, where S denotes any sentence, or that any sentence S is inferable from $W \wedge \sim W$. But should not contradiction be rejected only *a priori* and not *a posteriori* as inferred from experimental setups?

Inferences *from* the setups (reality) *to* light being both a wave (λ) and non-wave ($\sim\lambda$) does not violate *a priori* the Principle of Non-contradiction. And so the inferences do not entail any sentence S or q that follows from contradiction. The critiques of contradiction by Copi, Newton-Smith and others, as profound as these philosophers are, are purely logical (validity focused) and disregard both *empirical* considerations of contradiction and *successful* laws such as the de Broglie equation that systematically predict phenomena. The phenomena being successfully predicted as such are related logically to the equation's truth by a common-sense modal reasoning. This specifies that while it is logically possible that the equation is false when the predictions are systematically true, it is an epistemic impossibility. How can de Broglie's equation be used to systematically predict, manipulate and explicate phenomena when the phenomena are not reflected truly by the equation, at least approximately? This question suggests that we must consider if contradictions, inconsistencies, and paradoxes arise *a priori* because, say, of inadvertent meanings of terms that can be reinterpreted, or if the reinterpretation is inappropriate; as was the inappropriate reinterpretation of waves as "waves of propensities," by Popper, when the contradictions were appropriately inferred *a posteriori* from evidence-based experiments.[86]

In sum, the aforesaid norms foster a robust realism wherein what reality is really like is reflected progressively by mature historical scientific

---

85. See Youssef's "Is Quantum Mechanics an Exotic Probability Theory?" 904, for one context of the contradiction. And see Flores, McDonald and Knoesel's "Paradox in Wave-Particle Duality," 295–305, for the wave/particle contradiction obtaining for *every* context.

86. See Trundle, "Aristotle *Versus* Van Til and Łukasiewicz," 323–44. See also Popper who relates contradictions (whether *a posteriori* or *a priori*) to relativism in *Quantum Theory and the Schism in Physics*, 142.

theories that are ever truer (verisimilitude). Verisimilar truth contrasts to an incommensurability whose proponents hold that major theoretical changes exclude theory comparisons owing to radical meaning variance. The variance was denied by a reminder that while Thomson meant something else by what he observed in a cathode-ray tube than what we mean, our realism begets a benign *variance* of low-level observation reports. These do not avert their basis in an *invariant* non-conceptual consciousness of the *same* thing at other historical times. Despite these times, the reports are of a glowing phenomenon that is better predicted and explicated now, raising the specter precisely of verisimilitude. It has a second challenge of theories achieving approximate truth. This truth is viable by recalling that, while it is logically possible that theories are false if they steadily make true predictions, it is an epistemic impossibility. The impossibility bears on a third challenge of theories being allegedly falsified.

The falsification proposed by Popper is bogus not only by virtue of an epistemic modal logic relating observational success to truth, where a *truth of theories is retained but restricted to domains,* but also since the domains of truth increase from Aristotle and his heirs to Newton to Einstein's physics where the latter physics includes Newton's domain and it that of Aristotle and his heirs. Finally, a fourth challenge was to establish that culture plays only an ancillary role in skewing observation, much less incurs an epistemic relativism. This is because we have a theory-neutral consciousness of reality, of which we are aware, that provides an objective, unifying, and restraining influence on formulating theories. And although theories as worldviews led to a truth of observation reports being relative to different conceptual frameworks, observation is actually rooted in a sheer consciousness of phenomena of which we are aware. Also, an awareness of our conceptualized consciousness of phenomena permits the comparison of a *phenomenon in itself* to its *conceptualization.* And while conceptualizations can be theory-laden, *theory* is also *observation-laden* with an ontological origin in a pure consciousness of reality. How reality really is, in this existential phenomenology, appeals to an integrity of our immediate and incontrovertible experience of ourselves and is the very footing for reasoning from reality to theory as well as for explaining how theories can be true about reality. Consider now how reality, as held scientifically, is related logically to a naturalistic ethics, politics, art, and theology despite divisive dogmas of modern philosophy.

7

From Scientific Truth to Truths of Theology, Ethics, Art, and Politics

Having shown that there is scientific truth, by overcoming knotty epistemological problems, we will seek to show that ethics, art, and politics have truths informed by truths of science. Let us begin by noting that these sciences are related logically to natural theology by a true causal principle.[1] For this principle both strictly implies a first cause of the universe(s), which involves natural theology, and is presupposed by scientific inquiry. To say this inquiry presupposes the causal principle is not controversial. The controversy enters by seeking to show that the principle is certifiably true and strictly implies a first cause. This cause as an inferable supreme norm is shown also to have created our psycho-biological nature as it *ought* to be. So with no naturalistic fallacy, scientific truths about our nature imply a naturalistic ethics that informs truths of a politics that is the *institutionalization of ethics*. Given that modern secular ethics is divorced from our nature to avoid a naturalistic fallacy, which has induced political ideologies to reshape our nature with pathological consequences, there is more at stake than may be supposed. Vital to a supposition in this essay is that commonsense modal inferences are grounded in our phenomenological experience.

---

1. Cf. Trundle, "A Thomistic Integration of Truth," 721–38.

Our Phenomenological Experience of Causality

There are many philosophers of science, in the positivist-analytic tradition, who want to deny that the causal principle is either directly referenced by today's science or presupposed by scientific inquiry. For, following Kant, the principle as a truth-functional claim that "all events are caused" is *synthetics-a priori* and thus purportedly a senseless/meaningless metaphysical pseudo-statement because it is not either empirically or logically true. This lack of truth results in a K-K Thesis (how do we *know* we *know*?) because its presupposition by scientific inquiry undercuts the inquiry's alleged truths. These truths presuppose what is *not* known to be true, namely the causal principle. Or as Frederick Suppe superbly puts it, "If skepticism is to be avoided, the exploitation of . . . 'causal' regularities in obtaining *a posterior* knowledge must not require *prior* knowledge of those regularities."[2] These regularities, however, are conceded covertly by physicist San Liang, for example. Liang states that "The *principle of nil causality* that reads, an event is not causal to another if the evolution of the latter is independent of the former . . . turns out to be a proven theorem [in this article]."[3] So in the essay herein it is both novel and significant to reasonably establish not only that the causal principle has an unusually strong truth, as a non-truth-functional modality of modal logic, but also that this principle is known to refer to a really existing phenomenon ("the very being of the cause"[4]) in virtue of our consciousness of *being* of which we are unassailably aware. This awareness is undeniably consistent with a medieval conception of causality, as described by Etienne Gilson:

> If, then, we would arrive at an exact understanding of the medieval conception of causality we must ascend to this very act of existence, for it is clear that if being is act, the causal act must necessarily be rooted in very being of the cause. This relation is expressed in the technical distinction . . . but very clear in the upshot, between *first* act and *second* act. The first act is the being of the thing, of that which is called being in virtue of the very act of existing exerted: *ens dicitur ab actu assendi*: the second act is the causal operation of this being, the intrinsic or extrinsic manifestation of its first actuality by the effects it produces within or

---

2. Suppe, "Afterword," 722, emphasis.
3. Cf. Liang, "Information Flow," Abstract.
4. Gilson, *Spirit of Medieval Philosophy*, 89.

without itself. That is why causal action, which is nothing but an aspect of the actuality of the being as such, finally resolves itself into a transmission or communication of being: *influxum quemdam ad esse causati*.[5]

In regard to the words "Hoc vera nomen causa importat *influxum quemdam ad esse causati*," Gilson says "if we conceive existing as an act, we shall see it in that primal act by which a being which first exists in itself, equally exists outside itself in its effects."[6] That effects qua events occurring without causes is deemed physically impossible, in the modal logic herein, underscores that causal action is "an aspect of the actuality of the being." And this being *in itself* is precisely that of which we are non-conceptually conscious; a consciousness that is infused into our conceptual consciousness, ultimately expressed by the causal principle. Thus, this principle is grounded in our conscious of phenomena as both they really are *in themselves* without concepts and they are conceptually interpreted. This phenomenological relationship to really existing things *in themselves* is a reminder that this essay is not just another Thomistic essentialism that ignores existential elements of realism.

The realism herein might appear to be challenged by Piotr Jaroszyński who notes that "Much of what is called Thomism is a kind of essentialism [that emphasizes] concepts rather than real existence, and takes its starting point in logic rather than in existence."[7] The existential phenomenology in this essay, however, does *not* start in logic but rather exactly in existence. And yet, at one go, this existentialism is not only consistent with essentialism but is also related to it by the causal principle's truth. This truth integrates the truths of science, natural theology, ethics, art, and politics; political science *as a science* presupposing the causal principle and, as a study also of political *rights and responsibilities*, presupposing free will. Free will as well as the causal principle's truth have their phenomenological footing in our incontrovertible immediate self-conscious experience that finds expression in certain propositions. In terms of the proposition "It is physically impossible for *s* to be immersed in aqua regia when *s* does not dissolve," where "*s*" denotes gold, Ruth Barcan Marcus notes that an object would either "have ceased to exist"

---

5. Ibid., 89–90.
6. Gilson, *Thomism: The Philosophy of Thomas Aquinas*, 210
7. Jaroszyński, "A Brief Overview of Lublin Thomism," para. 3.

or "have changed into something else" if it ceased to have the property.[8] Even more primary than this property, though, is a *continuity* of evolving coordinated change because if this change were to cease, then *s* and any other phenomenon would likewise cease being subject to any other scientific inquiry.

The inquiry presupposes a continuity of interconnected change that is intrinsic to the phenomena of which scientists are conscious, without concepts, which are conceptualized as causal connections. And the connections are expressed by a causal principle whose truth is rooted in ordinary language. Consider this language after recalling that the principle's truth is vital for any robust realism whose aim is to obtain truth in ethics, art, politics and science. Sadly, science is largely held today, even by notable realists such as Frederick Suppe, to be the "paradigm knowledge-yielding enterprise." Suppe states both that *how* this enterprise "goes about achieving knowledge" indicates "the nature of knowledge" and that "to an overwhelming degree the history of epistemology (and metaphysics) *is* the history of the philosophy of science [if not the history of science itself]" even if "histories of philosophy give scant attention to this fact."[9] This fact is countered by another: In thus far lacking any certifiable truth because of problems granted even by Suppe, such as the above K-K Thesis, the scientific venture proceeds *a fortiori* with "truth" excluded from ethics, art, and politics that, for Aristotle, include studying causes of the "good," good government and beauty.

Causality, Concurrent with Free Will, as a Modality

Bertrand Russell's assertion that "The law of causation ... has often been held to be *a priori*, a *necessity* of thought, a category without which science would not be possible"[10] brings to mind Kant's relegation of free

---

8. Marcus, *Modalities*, 69. The proposition about this physical impossibility is my formulation, used to illustrate and extend one possible understanding of the point made by Ruth Barcan Marcus. The formulation connects essentialism to existential phenomenology.

9. See Suppe, *The Structure of Scientific Theories*, 716–17, where the history of philosophy *is* the history of science. On his realism: "In its final version, theories are construed realistically as describing systems of non-observables which relate in *incompletely* specifiable ways to their observable manifestations." See "Introduction,"7, emphasis.

10. Russell, *Our Knowledge*, 179.

will to a mere possible reality (*noumenon*). Its *noumenal* status was deemed necessary because Kant (and his heirs today) have a naïve notion of causality. In laboring under the misunderstanding that causality is inconsistent with free will, this will is rejected as a reality for the sake of science that presupposes the causal principle; also misunderstood as an unknowably metaphysical *synthetic-a priori* judgment "all events are caused." There being causes for beauty and the "good," however, reflect the Greek term *aitia* that is more liberal epistemologically than today's Atomist-like materialistic idea of cause. For it includes causes that are voluntary (Aristotle's *Metaphysics* A.3 ff) that, admitting of free will and purpose, preclude reductionisms that are now rife such as the aforesaid neuroscience and cognitive philosophies. But by (1) replacing a *philosophical view* of causal determinism that reigns today, in which free will is denied, with a *methodological view* where the determinism is accepted for the limited purposes of scientific inquiry and (2) grasping the inquiry's presupposed causal principle via modal logic, many modern problems are resolved. These problems include a K-K Thesis of "how we know we know": Knowledge yielded by scientific inquiry presupposes a causal principle whose truth is not known. Its not being known undercuts the supposed scientific knowledge. This setback of the "not known nullifying the known" is overcome by existential phenomenology and a common-sense modal reasoning. The reasoning for realism starts in our consciousness of reality and shows that the sciences are related logically to ethics, art, and politics by a first cause.

The first cause is strictly implied by a causal principle in which all events have either exactly or inexactly measurable causes. Before noting how the first cause is strictly implied by the causal principle, consider the principle as a modality of modal logic. This logic avoids Kant's critique that the causal principle cannot be known to be true because it is *synthetic a priori*; *synthetic* meaning that the different concepts "events" and "causes" preclude the principle's analytic truth and *a priori* signifying that the principle, as per Russell above, is presupposed prior to scientific inquiry so that the inquiry cannot result in its empirical truth. The latter truth is actually weaker than that ascribable to the principle, however, since by modal logic the principle can be shown to border empirical and logically necessary truth, rendering its truth extraordinarily strong. This strength blurs a sharp divide between invincible logical certainty and uncertain empirical contingency, taken dogmatically today as *analytic* and *synthetic* judgments (where subject and predicate concepts are the same in the former judgment but different in the latter). Long before modern philosophy, this strong sort of truth was known by, among others, St. Augustine and St. Thomas, who noted impossibilities and necessities that were not analytic but were instead founded on our unassailable experience.[11]

Modal Scientific Reasoning and the Causal Principle

One kind of experienced-based reasoning, which yields a strong sort of truth, can be understood as a modality or modal conditional. This conditional contrasts to a weaker, and often overly restrictive, material conditional $p \rightarrow q$. The latter conditional dominates modern truth-functional propositional logic. In this logic p and q are most frequently factual or empirically contingent statements where the arrow $\rightarrow$ reads "if . . . then" and $\sim q$ is logically possible when p. That is, where "logically possible" means that something is conceivable, it is not only conceivable but also reasonable to believe that p may be true when q is false. In terms of a weak material conditional such as "If my faltering car engine stops, then the car is out of gas," for example, its being out of gas may be false when it is true that the engine stops; its stopping, say, because of either a faulty carburetor (pre-1990s) or a defective fuel-injection system.

A stronger modal conditional, however, may stipulate that it is *physically impossible* that $\sim q$ when p. There are diverse conditionals suggested by scientists. Scientists specify a law of thermodynamics wherein "it is *impossible* to construct . . . a periodically functioning machine that would do more work than energy supplied to it from outside."[12] This may be expressed "*Necessarily* if a periodically functioning machine has no outside energy source, then work does not exceed its internal energy." Or compare a modal conditional to the weak truth-functional material conditional "If antibiotics are administered for an infection, the infection will be healed" where it is both physically and logically possible that the infection will not be healed despite the antibiotics by, say, an insufficient dose.

---

11. See Trundle, *Medieval Modal Logic*, in general, and Trundle, "St. Augustine's Epistemology," 187–205.

12. Cf. Yavorsky and Seleznev, *Physics*, 165; a rare and succinct summary of the history of physics.

This dose notwithstanding, consider the modality "*Necessarily* if antibiotics are applied to bacteria, then the bacteria will mutate." Given the mutating nature intrinsic to the nature of bacteria in response to antibiotics, it is irrefutably irrational to allow for a possibility that there were no mutations when there were the antibiotic stimuli. This stimuli as a cause of resistant mutations, whose non-occurrence is logically conceivable but not believable, is illustrated by microbiologist Stuart Levy, M.D., for whom new antibacterial drugs should be used very judiciously because it is "*not possible* that resistance won't occur."[13] The non-occurrence not being possible may be because the "resistance happens naturally, due to underlying biology. The rapid replication rates of bacteria, viruses, parasites and fungi mean their turnover is high" so that "they are able to quickly evolve past a problem they encounter . . . ."[14] But these reasons do not obviate the occurrences being strictly implied by applications of antibiotics. The strict implication can be expressed by the following: "p strictly implies q" if and only if "p therefore q" is a valid inference. That is, the modality *necessarily* $(p \rightarrow q)$ must be true necessarily without being trivial.

This non-triviality can be expressed as $p \Rightarrow q$ where $\sim q$ is physically (but not logically) impossible when p. In this manner, as expanded on shortly, experience bore reciprocally on theology and science because science presupposes the impossibility of events occurring without causes in terms of which the world as an event or phenomenon does itself beg necessarily for a first cause "to which," Thomas says famously, "everyone gives the name God."[15] Before rebutting the bogus but common criticism that this God as a first cause must itself be caused if everything is caused, we need to note that this first cause may be regarded as being strictly implied by the causal principle. But the principle is also presupposed by scientific inquiry for the inquiry's intelligibility. And given this requirement for intelligibility, it is unintelligible as well to *accept* scientific theories afforded by the inquiry and to *deny* the first cause. The first cause is not only consistent with science and scientific theories but related logically as well to the theories. The theories presuppose a causal principle that posits an impossibility of events having no causes. This can be recast as the necessity "Necessarily if there is no event ($\sim E$), there is no cause ($\sim C$)," where

13. Levy, "Drugs," No. 338.
14. Senthilingam, "5 Things You Need to Know," §3, para. 2.
15. Aquinas, *Summa Theologiae* i, 2, 3.

this modality is expressed $\sim C \Rightarrow \sim E$ and where $\Rightarrow$ means "Necessarily if ... then." Since this necessity means that $\sim E$ follows necessarily from $\sim C$ in the sense that it is *physically impossible* that there *is* an event (E) when there is no cause ($\sim C$), even if it is *logically possible*, the truth of a denial of both the first cause and causal principle can be regarded as conceivable but as patently irrational and unbelievable.

The unbelievable brings to mind Wittgenstein's insight about a man coming into the world without parents. The notion that without parents it is impossible for persons to come into the world, given our reproductive system, is as "certain as anything I could produce in evidence for it."[16] Reproductive technologies do not avert the point because there would still be prior biological processes for capturing both the necessity of there being causes and our regarding a denial as irrational. The irrationality of denying a cause when there is an event is captured also by humor, as when either a mother laughingly declares "That's impossible!" when her child says cookies just appeared in his hand out of nothing or as an auto mechanic would be taken as joking if he told you that your car ceased to work for no reason. Indeed, these examples are evocative not only of a false metaphysics but also of "metaphysical impossibilities,"[17] as noted by W. H. Walsh before modal logic was more widely known.[18] In this way Wittgenstein exclaims in Norman Malcolm's *Memoir* that "Experiential propositions do not all have the same logical status," in referring to some "we *know* . . . to be true" but can imagine turning "out to be false" and yet others where "there are no circumstances in which we should say it could turn "out to be false."[19] The falsity of a proposition being impossible brings to mind a reformulation of Wittgenstein's example as "It is impossible for a person to come into the world when there are no parents" where this can be recast as the modality "Necessarily if there are no parents, a person does not come into the world"; where the consequent cannot be false when the antecedent is true, so the modality is necessarily true.

---

16. Wittgenstein, *On Certainty*, 33e (#250), 42e (#335) and 59e (#454).

17. Walsh, "True and False in Metaphysics," 269–82.

18. Years after Walsh's *Metaphysics: An Exposition and Defense of a Controversial Branch of Philosophy*, Rev. Msgr. Antonio Livi, PhD, Emeritus Dean of Philosophy, Pontificia Universita Lateranense, founded the pioneering *Sensus Communis: Annuario di Logica Aletica*. Some of its contributors may have understood many of Walsh's metaphysical sentences as alethic modalities.

19. See recollections of Malcolm, *Ludwig Wittgenstein*, 73.

This non-trivial necessary truth, as previously noted, lies in epistemological strength between an empirically contingent truth and a truth that is trivially analytic. Accordingly, my view is not on either side of a divide that Schönbaumsfeld says are two extreme opposite camps. One camp, regarding what she calls "hedge propositions," is "a 'quasi-epistemic' reading [that downplays] the radical nature of Wittgenstein's proposal by assimilating his thought to more mainstream epistemological views."[20] My view, though, is scarcely mainstream. The mainstream ignores a modal-logic view of impossibilities and necessities that bear on doubt and certainty. And my view does not downplay, either, a non-mainstream radical nature of Wittgenstein's proposal. The downplayed proposal is a "non-epistemic, 'quasi-pragmatic' conception [that] goes too far in the opposite direction by equating 'hinge propositions' with a type of 'animal' certainty . . . ."[21] The certain non-trivial necessary truth in this essay, however, is not reducible either to an unrefined animal certainty. My certainty, based on modal logic, does bear on both a causal principle and its strict implication of a first cause.

The Causal Principle Strictly Implying a First Cause

The analysis thus far has posited the physical impossibility of events having no causes by a causal principle presupposed by science. Despite sciences such as physics not always referring directly to causes, causal regularities from present to future *states* of physical systems, as described theoretically, are presupposed by the theories. In short, the theories presuppose a causal principle with a strong sort of truth that borders truth that is empirically contingent and logically necessary. And without the trivial necessity, the principle strictly implies a first cause of the world that Thomas names "God."[22]

God as a first cause excludes the phenomenon of a causal series into the past *ad infinitum* that, having no cause, would not be subject to science and be scientifically *unlike* all the caused phenomena of which it is composed. With no fallacy of composition any more than inferring

---

20. Schönbaumsfeld, "'Hinge Propositions,'" 165–81.

21. Ibid.

22. See the Scottish Qualifications Authority, *2016 Religious and Philosophical Studies*, 6. This Authority addresses, among other things, the controversy over "whether Aquinas's Cosmological Arguments only prove a first cause of the universe and not of God."

that something can no more come from nothing than the things composing it, the series does indeed beg for an uncaused first efficient cause ("if there be no first cause among efficient causes, there will be no ultimate, nor any intermediate cause," says Thomas, "which is plainly false"[23]). Further, the falsity of there being the causal series without a first cause agrees with Thomas that "By faith alone do we hold . . . the world did not always exist."[24] For whether its existence "always was" (per a recent quantum-corrected Raychaudhuri equation) or whether the world exists with finite time as revealed scripturally and accepted by faith (compatible with the Big-Bang Theory), its existence either way begs for a first cause.[25] This cause is rooted in the modal conditional: "Necessarily if there is no first cause, there is no causal series a part of which we experience" that, taken with "there is the series a part of which we experience," entails that "there is a first cause." Besides this cause having no cause because of its purely voluntary nature (the nature of second causes requiring other second causes since they are corporeal *and* voluntary), voluntary causes as such preclude the incoherence of both denying free will and accepting a deterministic materialism which typifies neuroscience philosophy and relativistic *Weltanschauungen* analyses. The first cause is *prima facie*, in the minimum, a freely choosing, purposive, providential agency.

This providential agency of natural theology is not identical to the God of omniscience and omnipotence of supernatural theology. The former theological agency, however, serves to explain the origin of the cosmos. The first-cause agency, for example, may have caused either a protonic-sized singularity with maximum disorder (entropy), which fluctuated into our ordered universe, or a series of previous universes that arose from and collapsed into singularities. Certainly, the explanation of a first-cause agency is preferable to a counter explanation by one religious skeptic, astronomer Victor Stenger, who both denies free will and holds that all of reality is explicable naturalistically (*scientistically*). This *scientistic* self-refuting naturalism results in a deterministic materialism that renders incoherent his own truth-claims because "truth" is not ascribable to material things. Stenger is nonetheless undaunted by the

---

23. Aquinas, *Summa Theologiae*, i, 2, 3.

24. Ibid. I.Q. 46. In Baird, *Medieval and Renaissance* Philosophy, 337. I am indebted to Professor Peter Redpath for correctly construing "always existing" as "everlasting temporal existence."

25. See Ali and Das, "Cosmology," 276–79. See also the article by Farag and Das at arXiv: 1404.3093[gr-qc].

incoherence, claiming as true that the primordial maximally disordered singularity that fluctuated into order was caused by "natural processes of [autonomous] self-organization and even . . . a kind of Darwinian natural selection among . . . possibilities."[26]

These and other possibilities tend to be regarded merely as what is logically possible or, less often, in terms of modal logic. This logic is often restricted to arcane philosophical issues or, if applied more mundanely, to be confined within the parameters of present-day philosophical dogmas influenced by empiricist, rationalistic, neo-Kantian, positivist, analytic, or post-modern traditions. These avoid any ethics related to our psycho-biological nature, lest the dreaded naturalistic fallacy be committed. So these traditions divorce ethics from science and it from theology; colliding head-on with an Aristotelian-Thomism for which the truths of science, natural theology, ethics, art, and politics are related logically. This logical interrelation reflects a robust realism that is equally unlike the trendy "interdisciplinary" or "transdisciplinary" spins on knowledge. The spins are proselytized by so-called "strategic plans" in academia that, notes Karen Kelsky in *The Chronicle of Higher Education*, is "corporate-speak" foisted on faculty and students by wannabe-CEO "administrators marching in lockstep toward neoliberal oblivion under their new corporate overlords on the Board of Trustees."[27]

These trustees, adds Hunter Rawlings (President of the Association of American Universities) focus shortsightedly on what universities can do "economically [and] for preparing kids for jobs, but not much . . . on their research role, and what you might call their broader educational role."[28] In their practical bottom-line roles,[29] these corporate-oriented trustees are insensible to a liberal arts pedagogy or, worse, pander for entrepreneurial reasons to epistemic relativisms that include a politically correct feminism and multi-culturalism, which echo an episodic silliness over the centuries. "For centuries," Peter Redpath reminds us, "classical philosophical realism" firmly "united the disciplines of higher education in an integrated pursuit of truth."[30] Truth is interrelated logically in

26. Stenger, "The Face of Chaos," 13–14.

27. Kelsky, "The Professor Is In," See also Trundle's critique of a religio-ideological capitalism in America in "America's Religion," 3–20. This article was in an issue of a journal sponsored by the US Department of State.

28. Rawlings, "Public Colleges," para. 4.

29. Cf. also Schick, "Up Close," para. 1–13

30. Redpath's pedagogical insight in "Understanding," 703–20.

this essay by virtue of politics and art being inferred from truths of a naturalistic ethics and the ethics inferred from truths of science, science's morally relevant status inferred from a natural theology. All these logical integrations, which academe studiously ignore, are rooted in our phenomenological experience of reality.

If the reality we experience as such is a second-cause series that is related logically to a first cause, then this cause is inferable by second-cause persons. And these persons in Thomistic thought, in terms of *natural theology*, are both natural causes and self-conscious voluntary agencies that bear on a *supernatural theology* in which we are related analogically to the God of Scripture. The Scripture bears on the distinction of supernatural from natural theology by revealing a straw-man fallacy committed by creationists and evolutionists when they think all theology is supernatural. The supernatural aside, evolution is consistent with a first cause that could causally create either a single singularity that fluctuates into physical systems, which evolve into systems that are biological and psycho-biological, or a series of collapsing universes and fluctuating singularities; or even a multiplicity of concurrent universes (cosmos). Consider a novel defense of Thomas' first cause and how this cause logically interrelates the truths of theology, ethics, art, and science.

A First Cause Challenged by Modern Truth-Functional Logic

Is a first-cause creator validly inferred, is science inconsistent with a first cause? In regard to this cause being unscientific, Sten Ebbesen states that St. Thomas "would allow no genuine conflicts between scientific propositions and articles of faith; apparent conflicts arise from flaws in the scientific argumentation; in principle a unified system of knowledge must be possible."[31] Before considering the neglect of modal logic in favor of a truth-functional mathematical logic, which cannot suitably symbolize many terms such as "cause," let us briefly recall that the central scientific belief contrary to a first cause is the Big-Bang Theory. This theory typically lends itself to the notion that the origin of our universe resulted from a tiny singularity's post-fluctuating evolution into physical systems and these systems into ones that support both biological and psycho-biological organisms.[32] The organisms and evolving systems, far

---

31. Ebbesen, "The Paris Arts Faculty," 286.
32. Cf. Barnesmoore, "Conscious vs Mechanical Evolution," 105–15.

from precluding a purposive first cause creator, however, actually serve to explain teleologically how there could be a Darwinian self-organization that some prominent scientists advance.[33] And the advanced teleology does *not* have a self-refuting deterministic-materialistic metaphysics that, as earlier discussed, is a metaphysics that is truly senseless because it renders incoherent its proponent's own truth-claims. The claims that a first cause is invalidly inferred, in any event, brings us back to the issue of a more formal proof. In the late 1960s, the distinguished Catholic logician Peter Geach held that Thomas' first three *ways*, which included the argument for a first cause, were "intended to be logically conclusive and may . . . be so."[34]

This support by Geach for Thomas' reasoning was shocking to those familiar with logic textbooks at that time. The textbooks can now be understood to have committed both the straw-man fallacy and the fallacy of ignorance when, by ignorance of modalities and the meaning of efficient causality, a first-cause proof was distorted by a truth-functional mathematical logic. The latter logic was used to mock the argument.[35] Characteristically, starting with the premise "For every x there is a single thing y such that x relates C to y" ("Everything which occurs has a cause"), the invalid conclusion is said to be "There is one y such that for every x, x relates C to y" ("There is a first cause of everything"). This alleged analogous argument is ostensibly evident also by the argument that "Everyone loves someone so there is someone whom everyone loves." Here, the notoriously ambiguous meaning of "love" is as overlooked as the misread "cause" in the other reasoning. Later, however, another mode of reasoning was used effectively on Thomas' second-way argument for a first cause that was presaged by Geach.[36]

Geach remarked that formal logicians are "so predominately mathematical that they have quite neglected causal propositions which . . . are not needed in mathematical reasoning."[37] And Arthur Gibson says sarcastically in this vein, "we can derive [C. I.] Lewis's [modal] logic from [Bertrand] Russell's (and thus choose to ignore the latter's lifelong neglect

---

33. Trundle, "Quantum Fluctuation," 269–81.

34. Geach, *God and the Soul*, 77: this, decades before modal arguments.

35. Cf. Salmon's *Introduction to Logic*, 317, 356.

36. Besides Trundle's "Thomas' 2nd Way," 145–68 whose import for integrated truth is extended here, see Koons, "A New Look," 193–211.

37. See Geach, *God and the Soul*, 76–78.

of modal logic), even though some ingenuity is required."[38] The studious disregard of modal logic by mainstream logicians, such as the iconic Bertrand Russell, resulted in truth-functional mathematical reasoning governing the meaning of "follows necessarily" but, in often being too restrictive and insensitive to nuances of language, shows how *empty* is the claim "that we know enough about the logic of causal propositions to see that there can be no causal deductive proof of God's existence," says Geach; adding "It may even be rational . . . to accept some such proof as valid before a satisfactory logical analysis has been worked out; mathematical proofs were valid and rationally acceptable long before logicians could give a rigorous account of them."[39]

The optimism about a sound first-cause proof, expressed by Geach, was warranted not merely by Thomas using *modal* terms in drawing inferences from an experienced world. Also Geach's optimism is appropriate since many scholars such as the medievalist logician Ernest Moody observed that "Aristotle's *De Interpretatione* and *Analytica Posteriora* [exhibit] acute discussions of logical questions, especially those pertaining to modal arguments."[40] And after noting Thomas' modal terms "Bene sequitur, si consequences est impossibile, quod antecedents sit impossibile" (Well, if a conclusion is impossible, the antecedent is impossible), per *Metaphysica* 9, 3, 1810, Joseph Clark, S.J., notes "evidence that Thomas knew . . . theorems of a calculus of modal statements."[41] These are in Thomas' second-way, its referring to "an order of efficient causes" such that "there is no case known [where] a thing is found to be the efficient cause of itself, which is impossible."[42] This impossibility is a physical one, not one that is logical.

The New Logic Averts a *Leap of Faith* and Interrelates Truth

Before examining the modal nature of inferring a first cause, it needs to be said that the first cause as "God" used in Thomas' proof is, strictly, the God of Nature of *natural theology*. This theology, however, is partly included in the *supernatural theology* of the Scriptures because God

---

38. Gibson, "Ockham's World and Future," 336.
39. Ibid., 85. This point brings to mind Plato, before Aristotle's analytics.
40. Moody, *Studies in Medieval Philosophy*, 376.
41. Clark, *Conventional Logic*, 52.
42. Aquinas, *Summa Theologiae* i, 2, 3.

proclaims Himself to be the cause of the world, from Genesis to Job; justifying Thomas' reference to the revealed God. The God of supernatural theology overlaps with natural theology, which *as in* a Venn Diagram, is in the center with philosophy on the right side. That is, Protestantism traditionally omits natural theology and this theology *bridges* philosophy and supernatural theology. This excludes Søren Kierkegaard's "leap of faith" from an alleged philosophical rationality to an irrational paradox of supernatural theology where Christ is both man and not-man—with the caveat that accepting a paradox or contradiction *a posteriori*, if either its inference is sound or it is accepted by faith (when it is revealed and/or makes sense of Scripture), does not lead to self-contradiction. It is not irrational as is its acceptance *a priori* that does result in self-contradiction.[43] Faith in the revealed God is reasonable by virtue of a *bridge* of natural theology.[44] This theology, which avoids Kierkegaard's leap of faith, illustrates a Thomistic continuity of reasoning to supernatural theology that begins (below) with our non-conceptual phenomenological experience:

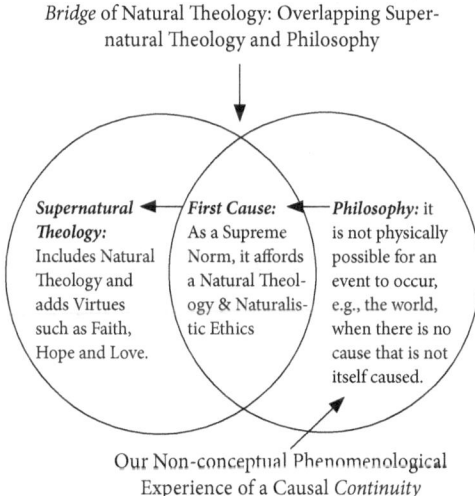

Kierkegaard's "Leap of Faith" (*from a Philosophical Rationality to an Irrational Religion*) is Averted by a *Bridge* of Natural Theology

---

43. Trundle, "Aristotle Vs Van Til and Łukasiewicz," 323–44. For example, light inferred *a posteriori* as both a wave and non-wave by experimental setups does not admit *a priori* of contradictory truth.

44. Cf. Trundle, *Integrated Truth*, 124.

The natural theology of a first cause also logically interrelates the truths of science, natural theology, a naturalistic ethics, art, and politics. The point of politics, precisely, is or should be to *fulfill our psycho-biological nature*, socially as well as politically. The politics proposed herein, consequently, is not said in a cliché manner to be "democracy." In addition to other non-democracies prescribed by Aristotle, he says that when *polities* go awry, they develop into depreciatory *democracies*. Many so-called democracies or republics are actually furtive oligarchies that foster *anything but* fulfilling our psycho-biological nature (think of America's toxic for-profit-big-pharma-lobby-centered healthcare fiasco).[45] The word "oligarchy" may seem an exaggeration to those inured to thinking of "oligarchs as despotic rulers who [are] incompatible with democracies like the United States."[46] But the United States, says Jeffrey Green who is a scholar on oligarchies, is an "'oligarchy' where a tiny and extremely wealthy slice of the population was able to use its vastly superior economic position to promote a ... politics that served first and foremost itself."[47] This unpatriotic, even treasonous, self-serving oligarchy that conservative icon William F. Buckley scorned as an "Anarcho-Totalitarianism,"[48] does not rule directly. Rather they use "their fortunes to produce political results that favored their interests."[49] In response to these interests, Noam Chomsky viably disparages the oligarchical psychopathic society:[50]

> Well there is a huge propaganda effort that we are all aware of to try to turn people into psychopaths who don't care about anyone but themselves.[51] That's not new actually. They [aka

---

45. Cf. Berwick, MD, "The Toxic Politics of Health Care," 1921–22: "More than $2.7 trillion changes hands in health care. No one who gets paid now will happily accept less. Vast [toxic] financial interests create lobbying interests, who populate the corridors of Capitol Hill and CMS."

46. Mayer, *Dark Money*, 18.

47. Ibid. See also Green, *The Shadow of Unfairness: A Plebeian Theory of Democracy*.

48. Mayer, *Dark Money*, 5. Some challenge whether Buckley or the John M. Olin Professor of Jurisprudence and Public Policy at Fordham University, Ernest van den Haag, who wrote for Buckley's *National Review*, first used the words.

49. Ibid., 18.

50. Kall, "Chomsky Talks about Psychopaths and Sociopaths," emphasis.

51. See Voigt's review "Bad Bosses: The Psycho-path to Success?" A psychopathy diagnostic PCL-R (check-list) bears on CEOs who may be "charismatic charmers on first meeting, emoting confidence that is rooted in deception. [But they] lie without remorse, steal credit for accomplishments ... transfer blame for their mistakes ... and are easily bored ... They are prone to take risks without concern for the ramifications."

disordered "moral idiots"]⁵² go back a hundred and fifty years, the early days of industrialization in the United States. Working people were bitterly condemning the industrial system that was being imposed, the way it was taking away their freedom, and one of the things they condemned is what they called the new spirit of the age—"Gain wealth forgetting all but self"—exactly what you're describing. That's a hundred and fifty years ago and ever since then there have been enormous efforts to drive these sociopathic attitudes into people's heads. There are extreme cases like the Ayn Rand cult [*à la* Rep. Paul Ryan]⁵³ where it's kind of like, open but yeah we should be psychopaths . . . it's very authoritarian. But a lot of it is based on the same principles. "Why should I pay taxes to send somebody else's kids to school or why should I support the disabled widow across town, her social security is her problem, not mine." That's pathological. In fact there's an interesting book that just came out, . . . *The Sociopathic Society*, . . . describing accurately the development of these [sociopathic] things.

These "things" may be construed as Wall Street regulating the US Congress rather than Congress regulating Wall Street, the words "Wall Street" generally denoting rabid corporate abuse. In the past few decades, echoing Peggy Noonan's alarm,⁵⁴ Wall Street as such virtually either owned most campaigning U.S. congressmen and presidents or they had to be billionaires themselves with covert connections to, and ideological sympathies with Wall Street. Its ignominious power raises the specter of America needing a Wall-Street-*free* public funding for campaigning candidates in order to counter the vicious oligarchical cycle of corruption.

The corruption is bad because, by its devastating impact on the social safety net for the preponderance of citizens, it causes injurious worry, impedes work, weakens families and thus wreaks havoc on our wellbeing: It harms our psycho-biological nature that should be *nurtured*. *Nurturers* should not, as with the sophistical relativists, seek to determine our nature. Our *nature* could be nurtured by several political forms of state, not just so-called democracies, which institutionalize a naturalistic ethics.

---

52. "Moral idiots" was a pre-twentieth-century name for psychopaths.

53. Cf. Chait, "7 Ways Paul Ryan Revealed His Love for Ayn Rand": Ayn Rand's virtue of selfishness is "'sorely needed right now'" because Rand, for Ryan, "'did a fantastic job of explaining the morality of capitalism . . .'"

54. See Noonan's critique of current capitalism, *John Paul the Great: Remembering a Spiritual* Father, 111.

The ethics, which is empirically *evidence based*, fulfills our psycho-biological nature by inferences from the natural and human sciences; or, as often said, medicine and its allied sciences.

Returning to these sciences is now proper, their presupposing a causal principle. The principle, as an impossibility that there are events when there are no causes, can be re-formulated as the modal conditional "necessarily if there are no causes, then there are no events": as either $Nec\ (\sim\!C \to \sim\!E)$ or $\sim\!C \Rightarrow \sim\!E$. These conditionals for the causal principle, epistemologically, have an unusually strong truth. The nature of the truth was earlier compared to Wittgenstein's analyses of propositions that border empirically contingent and logically necessary truth. Given that the borderline truth $\sim\!C \Rightarrow \sim\!E$ strictly implies a first cause (F) by virtue of the universe's creation being an event, where the event was the creation of second causes (S), there ensues the conditional $\sim\!F \Rightarrow \sim\!S$. It is a premise for the proof of F via an analogue of the *modus-tollens* sequent $\sim\!F \Rightarrow \sim\!S,\ S \vdash F$, expanded on below. What entity other than a provable *first cause* could serve as an ultimate norm of the "good"? As a provable supreme norm (any other ostensible norms being its creation), this cause created our psycho-biological nature as it ought to be. Since our nature *is* as it *ought to be*, there is no commitment of the naturalistic fallacy. This fallacy, in other words, is avoided because we are not reasoning from a merely factual "is" to an "ought," *pace* Hume or G. E. Moore. Rather, we are reasoning from an implicit "ought" to an "ought" which is explicit. The aforesaid logical interrelation of fields of study—whereby political truths are inferred from truths of a naturalistic ethics, ethical and artistic truths from truths in the sciences, and science's presupposition of a causal principle strictly implies a first cause—is shown in the following schema.[55] The schema starts with scientific inquiry:

---

55. See Trundle, *A Theology of Science*, 183, 184.

TRUTHS OF THEOLOGY, ETHICS, ART, AND POLITICS 183

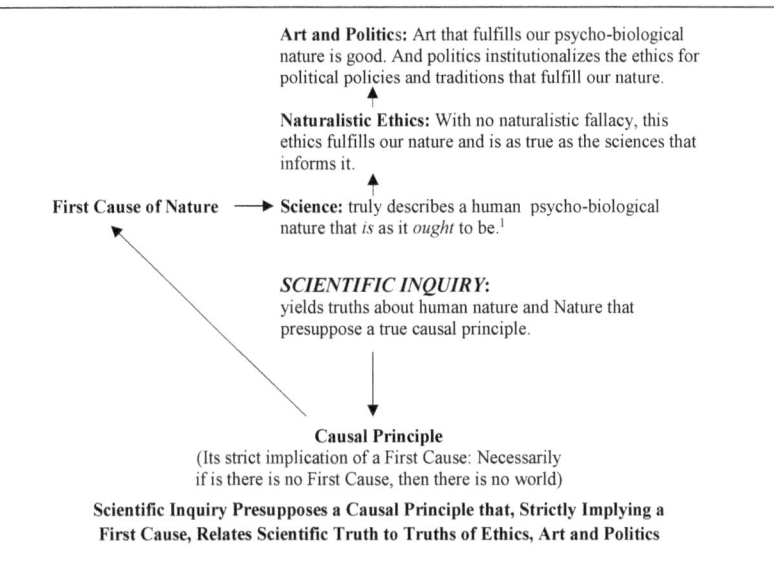

---

1. Consider this God (Cause) as an axiological condition for our nature *being* as it *ought to be*: Things are ranked as more or less good. Unless this good is false or meaningless, there must be a real standard of perfection to render coherent the hierarchy since something is ranked higher only if it is closer to the standard. And unless there is a Being to be that standard (who would be less than perfect if our nature was not created as it ought to be), even saying that one scientific theory is good or better than another would be meaningless or impossible. Intriguingly, Dostoevsky is brought to mind: Without God all things are permissible. See Peter Kreeft, "First Cause Argument," http://www.peterkreeft.com/topics/first-cause, 2005.

Below is a more ample schema that bears on our pre-conceptual consciousness of things *in themselves*; providing an ontological basis for truths that are strictly implied by virtue of a simple modal logic: inferring a causal principle's truth via ($\sim C \Rightarrow \sim E$); the truths of scientific theories inferred from observed success; a first cause from the causal principle so that science and natural theology are related logically. This logic echoes Thomas' proof of a first cause that, as an inferable supreme norm, created our psycho-biological nature as it *ought* to be. The *is-ought* collapse affords a naturalistic ethics inferred from scientific descriptions of our nature with no *naturalistic fallacy*. So there no fallacy in inferring from this ethics truths about art and politics that also fulfill our nature. Our nature unites truths in science, ethics, art, and a political *institutionalization of ethics* even if ethics is enriched by supernatural virtues that fulfill us more. Ethics, art, politics, science, and a natural theology, which overlaps with supernatural theology, are interrelated logically:

184 CONSCIOUSNESS AND BEING

<table>
<tr><td></td><td>Ethics should be institutionalized politically for policies and laws that fulfill our nature.
↑</td></tr>
<tr><td>Our psycho-biological nature, as described by science, *is* as it ought to be.
↑</td><td>With no naturalistic fallacy, a naturalistic ethics is as true as the sciences that inform it and from which are inferred also truths of art and politics that fulfill our psycho-biological nature.</td></tr>
<tr><td>A first cause, strictly implied by the causal principle, is inferably a supreme norm. Without this norm, a naturalistic fallacy is committed in holding that fulfilling our psycho-biological nature ought to be based on how our nature is.
↑</td><td>**SCIENTIFIC INQUIRY**
This inquiry presupposes that awareness of reality, without concepts, is infused into our conceptual observation. If observation concepts are related to theoretical concepts, then *pari passu* the concepts of theory are related to observed reality. And reality is in fact predicted, manipulated and explicated by theory. Taken with a theory and rules of logical deducibility, theory-laden observation descriptions of a physical system may imply predictions of the system's future states. These states are related to</td></tr>
<tr><td>By a consciousness of reality and what it makes sense to say, phenomena are related causally as expressed by a causal principle: It is physically impossible for there to be an event when there is no cause.</td><td>present states by causal regularities. So besides these regularities being presupposed by a causal principle, they bear on predictive reasoning; a reasoning expressed thus: A theory cannot be entirely false in a given domain when it makes steadily true predictions of phenomena. Unless the phenomena are reflected truly by the theory, at least inexactly, how could the theory systematically predict the phenomena?</td></tr>
</table>

Scientific Inquiry Presupposes a Causal Principle that, Strictly Implying a First Cause, Relates Scientific Truth to Truths of Ethics, Art and Politics

Interrelated Truth Inferred by Sound Modal Reasoning

While soundness presupposes validity, validity does not imply soundness. To say that an argument is sound is to say it is valid but to say it is valid is not necessarily to say it is sound. Soundness specifies both that the premises are true and that a true conclusion follows by logical necessity from the premises. So the premises by entailing the conclusion, whether or not the premises are true, expresses the weaker notion of validity. And thus validity alone is clearly not sought by Thomas in proving a first cause. The stronger soundness is unmistakably sought by the opening words of Thomas, which are not hypothetical or indifferent to what is experienced: "In the world of sense we find there is an order of efficient causes [with] no case known (neither is it, indeed, possible) in which a thing is found to be the efficient cause of itself . . . ."[56] An efficient cause, for Aristotle, is said by some scholars to be the cause only of *becoming* (*forming* matter but not causing matter's existence) in contrast to Thomas for whom the efficient cause *causes being* (giving *being* an existential import for a later Thomistic existentialism). But this efficient cause is said by other scholars to reflect Thomas' own words that "Aristotle . . . proves in *Metaph*. 2 that that which is maximally true and

56. Aquinas, *Summa Theologiae*, 2, 3.

maximally a being [*maxime ens*] is the cause of being [*causa essendi*] for all existents [*existentibus*]," concluding that "Thomas reads in Aristotle the very doctrine of creation which he himself presents in such a text as the Fourth Way."[57]

Either way, minimally, the first cause is a purposive, freely choosing, intelligent, if not all-knowing, agency who in this very sense is *analogical* to second-cause persons. Thus, although persons have causes inter alia because they have bodies that require the reproductive activity of parents, which is *unlike* the incorporeal uncaused first cause, persons are *like* the first cause because they are intelligent with a purposive free will despite this will having as its cause their bodies as necessary conditions (*aitia*). With a reminder that these causal conditions (*aitia*) for our free will illustrate a more liberal notion of causality than that imagined by the aforesaid modern mathematical logicians who sought to discredit deductive proofs of a first-cause, such as Bertrand Russell, there is an evident implication that this cause as the efficient causal creator of the existence of second causes must be present continually for these causes to continually *be*. That said, the *being* of second causes, in being dependent on the first cause, finds expression in an argument by Thomas that starts with the experienced world:

> In the world of sense [sense experience] we find there is an order of efficient causes. There is no case known (neither is it, indeed, possible) in which a thing is found to be the efficient cause of itself, which is impossible. Now in efficient causes it is not possible to go on to infinity, . . . if there be no first cause among efficient causes, there will be no ultimate, nor any intermediate cause . . . , which is plainly false. Therefore it is necessary to admit a first efficient cause, to which everyone gives the name God.[58]

Let me discuss this argument for God in terms of modal logic after examining by way of truth-functional propositional logic. The latter logic would, of course, posit a *modus-tollens* form of the argument as "If ~p,

---

57. One might contrast Kreeft's *A Summa* (232 fn. 59) where he says Thomas gives "a new existential meaning to efficient causality . . . as Gilson has shown (cf. *Being and some Philosophers*)," in regard to Thomas' *Summa Theologiae* I, 104, 1, to the disagreeing position of Dewan, as articulated in his "Aristotle as a Source for St. Thomas's Doctrine of esse."

58. Aquinas, *Summa Theologiae* i, 2, 3. The God of Nature is related aptly to the supernatural one.

then ~*q* and *q*, therefore *p*" (If there is no uncaused first cause, then there are no second causes and there are second causes, so there is a first cause). With a reminder that a material implication *p* → *q* allows for proposition *q* not being implied by *p* and that this conditional may be too epistemologically weak to capture their relationship, consider how a relationship of strict implication can be gleaned from the above argument. In keeping for now with the truth-functional logic, let ~*F* denote "There is no first cause" and let ~*S* represent "There is no second-cause series a part of which is experienced." When these causes are understood in terms of the material conditional ~*F* → ~*S*, the conditional is true if *as a matter of fact* it is not the case that ~*F* is true when ~*S* is false.

Now consider why the above contrasts to modal logic. Given a factual or empirically contingent nature of the conditional ~*F* → ~*S*, it is logically possible that *S* when ~*F*. Thus on this version of the reasoning, "(~*F* → ~*S*) and *S*, therefore *F*," the argument is merely *valid* but not *sound*. For although *F* follows validly from the premises, the premise ~*F* → ~*S* is not known to be true because *S* when ~*F* is logically possible. The restriction to logical possibilities, impossibilities and necessities reflects the modern truth-functional logic. This is not the logic, though, that was evidently intended by Thomas. For when Thomas states both that in the "causes it is not possible to go on to infinity" and that "it is necessary" to admit of a first cause, he intends prima facie both that ~*S* is inferred *necessarily* from ~*F* and that a denial of the inference is impossible.

Reasoning to a First Cause and the Causal Principle

It is *impossible*, in other words, that *S* when ~*F*. And so ~*F* → ~*S* is true necessarily and can be read "*Necessarily* ~*F* → ~*S*." The truth of this conditional is not empirically contingent because of the necessity and the necessity is not logically trivial (analytic) because ~*S* and ~*F* have different meanings. In both meaning different things and not being contingent, the conditional is not either *analytic* or *synthetic* in the Kantian tradition. This tradition includes the logical positivists and their successors, such as the analytic (linguistic) philosophers, who would tend to relegate the conditional to either meaningless metaphysical gibberish or a patently senseless pseudo-statement. An alternative to the latter, where an epistemologically strong truth is ascribable to the premise, is now considered. Consider an alternative that, consistent with Thomas' language, explicitly admits of words such as "not possible." While it is possible logically that S when ~F, ~F renders it patently impossible that S in light of the nature of experienced things. The impossibility can be recast as "Necessarily if ~F, then ~S"? Given that S, where ⇒ reads "necessarily if . . . then" and ⊦ symbolizes a valid inference, there is an evidently *sound* analogue of a *modus-tollens* sequent:

$$\sim F \Rightarrow \sim S, S \vdash F$$

Since F is inferred validly from the premises and premise S is true empirically ("there are second causes"), a soundness of the sequent will center on a truth of the other premise ~F ⇒ ~S. To say that the latter is true is to say *positively* that the cosmos must have a cause like any other phenomenon subject to scientific inquiry for the inquiry's intelligibility. And the cause is not itself caused on pain of an infinite regress of causes where there would be no cause of the cosmos and it would not be subject to scientific inquiry, resulting precisely in the inference to the first cause as being purely voluntary. Also, to say the conditional is true is to say *negatively* that the premise has a denial that, although conceivable, is not believable. The disbelief is explicable by a *reductio ad absurdum* where a denial of the premise ~F ⇒ ~S results in various absurdities: In having no uncaused first cause, the cosmos would absurdly be unlike all the other phenomena that *compose* it that are subject to a scientific inquiry which presupposes that they have causes (recalling that no fallacy of composition is committed any more than inferring from phenomena having mass to mass being ascribed to the cosmos); the cosmos would absurdly have caused itself; or would absurdly have materialized out of nothing. Thus, notes T. R. V. Murti, a *reductio* may not establish a position except in subjects such as mathematics, where "we so completely possess the field *in concreto* that the alternatives are narrowed down to two," and by denying one the other is proved. And we agree that the subject of a first cause is not such a field in *concreto* completely possessed epistemologically. But there is no reliance on proving that there exists a first cause only by absurdities which ensue from denying the premise.[59]

---

59. Western logic often both imposes reason (*a priori*) on reality and ignores, especially, limitations of the *reduction ad absurdum*. For this quote see T. R. V. Murti's *The Central Philosophy of Buddhism*, 131, 132. The latter work underscores that reality need not conform to principles of logic. See also Trundle's *Camus' Answer: "No" to the Western Pharisees Who Impose Reason on Reality* as well as Trundle's "Aristotle *Versus* Van Til and Łukasiewicz," 323–44.

Thus a truth of the premise $\sim F \Rightarrow \sim S$ is more than reasonably established not only by its denial (S when $\sim F$) leading to absurdities such as the cosmos coming from nothing, which both excludes an origin of the cosmos from scientific inquiry, but also by the cosmos having a first cause strictly implied by a causal principle: Construed as a modality where uncaused events are physically impossible, the principle's falsity is *more* of an epistemic impossibility than a falsity of the thermodynamic laws, whose denials are said to be impossible by the scientific community, which *presuppose* the causal principle. Indeed, this stronger status of the principle reveals both that there are degrees of epistemic strength of impossibilities (and necessities) and that the causal principle has a relatively strong strict implication of a first cause; a calculus for calibrating the relative strengths being deferred herein to future developments by other logicians.

Finally, the first cause is related logically to astronomical and other scientific inquiries since these inquiries presuppose a causal principle that strictly implies the first cause; an infinity of causes without an uncaused cause otherwise ensuing. An express purpose of astronomy, after all, "is the study of the *origins*, physics, and evolution of planets, stars, galaxies, and *the universe as a whole*."[60] The import of the cosmos having a natural cause, such as a Big-Bang singularity or some other phenomenon, which beg finally for a first cause, is critiqued by Quentin Smith. Smith does not argue against a first cause by denying that scientific inquiry presupposes the causal principle. Rather he argues, "Since definitions of causality often make explicit or implicit *reference* to laws, it is natural to suppose that, if there is only one completely lawless thing [a Big-Bang singularity], this thing will also be the only thing exempt from causality."[61] But definitions of causality do not make reference to the laws. Rather, the laws make "reference to" (actually presuppose) a causal principle; again, not the principle "to" the laws.

Laws are the fruits of scientific inquiries which presuppose the causal principle for their intelligibility. For otherwise the inquiries would be undercut by assuming that either events can occur for no reason or some events have no causes, one's never knowing which events are or are not caused. And causal regularities are presupposed by laws, as well,

---

60. See astronomy as that which *inter alia* is an inquiry that investigates the cause or origin of the universe as discussed, for example, at Ohio State University, per their website http://astronomy.osu.edu/, 8 July 2014.

61. The answer is "No." See Quentin Smith, "Can Everything Come?," 6, emphasis.

for the intelligibility of predicted future states of a physical system being related to that system's present states. But the causal principle does not either imply or presuppose any theory or law. And while today there may be no known lawful "states" of a singularity since it is devoid of anything known to *current* theories, it is reasonable to believe that these theories will be superseded by future theories that *do* specify lawful states of a singularity. And the Big-Bang singularity even in terms of a present-day theory was, of course, a potential phenomenon of energy (E) correlated to the universe's mass (m) by $E = mc^2$, the celebrated equation.[62]

This equation's applicability to the Big-Bang singularity does itself render inclusive scientific inquiry and the causal principle to studies of the singularity. So while it is logically possible that the phenomenon of the singularity is not subject to scientific inquiry, this possibility is unreasonable to suppose. And future inquiries that are unreasonable to omit, *presuppose* a physical impossibility that the singularity as a phenomenon came from nothing, arose out of nowhere, or caused itself. The presupposition need not be a "truth" that is defended metaphysically, as suggested by Smith. Rather than his proposal, a presupposition of there being causes for phenomena subject to scientific inquiry is defendable by modal logic.[63]

The Principle's Denial and Dreaded Naturalistic Fallacy

Consider how inferences from the first cause to a naturalistic ethics, based on our psycho-biological nature, does not lead the ethics to commit a naturalistic fallacy after reviewing how this fallacy both resulted from

---

62. An inductively reasonable pessimism about the *total* truth of extant theories warrants doubt about their arrant applicability to phenomena since every past major (mature) theory was superseded by another mature theory that addressed phenomena that had not been acknowledged. *Cf.* Newton-Smith's *The Rationality of Science*, 14, where he discusses pessimistic induction, although I disagree with him that superseded mature theories are falsified since their truth can be restricted to given domains.

63. One may say, says Smith, that it is "logically possible for everything to come to be without a cause [but that it is] (metaphysically) impossible." His parenthetical reference to metaphysics suggests that one may hold that both the denial of a first cause is "metaphysically false" and the affirmation is "metaphysically true"; puzzling in regard to truth-values, however since metaphysics after Kant is *synthetic a priori*: *A priori* since metaphysics is prior to experience and not empirically true; *synthetic*, so it cannot be logically true. In post-positivist thought, the metaphysics is senseless. See Smith, "Can Everything Come to Be Without a Cause?" 3.

denying a first cause and rendered impotent modern ethics.[64] A review of this ethics reminds us of the value of proving a first cause. The cause was dismissed tragically by our culture largely because of a Humean-Kantian-positivist tradition, although there were others such as G. E. Moore; claiming "that a naturalistic fallacy is committed by any attempt to prove a claim about ethics by appealing to a definition in terms of natural properties (which is the basis for the doctrine of Ethical Naturalism)."[65] That the Humean-Kantian-positivist tradition rejects even scientific theories having any known truth, much more "sciences" of art and ethics that, from an Aristotelian-Thomistic view, study causes of beauty and good.[66]

A central problem with the good, or anything else related to causality, even causes understood liberally in terms of *aitia*, stems not only from Hume's denial of any "necessary connexion" between causes and effects but also from the Kantian K-K problem of "Knowing we Know." In terms of this predicament, scientific knowledge presupposes knowing the truth of a causal principle whose truth cannot be known because it is *synthetic-a priori*. Recall that the principle's *a priori* status precluded knowing its empirical truth and that its truth analytically is excluded by its being *synthetic*. So the *synthetic-a priori* causal principle, which is metaphysical, is not known to be either empirically or logically true (although the principle's analytic truth would make it useless because trivial). The lack of any non-trivial truth of the principle undercut the purported truths that ensue from scientific inquiries, with ruinous epistemic results for physics and for less mathematically rigorous inquiries such as ethics. Worsening these results was the consummate denial, because of inapt epistemic commitments, of any certifiable moral truth by the Humean-Kantian-positivist tradition. This tradition, while ironically taking physics to be the ideal knowledge-yielding enterprise, contributed to a catastrophic twentieth century that is dubbed the most murderous century in human history.[67]

This horrific history aside, the backseat of ethics to science was presaged by Hume. Having formulated what came to be named the

64. Cf. Trundle, "A First Cause and the Causal Principle," 107–35, which deals with modern ethics.

65. Mastin, "Ethical Non-Naturalism."

66. Trundle, "Value and Scientific Theory," 85–100. This article argues that scientific theories are related logically to values and norms of the "good."

67. See Trundle, *From Physics to Politics*, 119–54, for how ethics as well as science was politicized. See also Levinson, "A Century Awash in Blood—Spotlight Genocide."

"naturalistic fallacy," in which moral *prescriptions* are not inferable from *descriptions* of our nature, Hume said that "The great advantage of the mathematical sciences above the moral consists in this, that the ideas of the former, being sensible, are always clear and determinate . . . ."[68] The influence of Hume is augmented by others, as noted by Lorraine Daston. Daston states the following:

> [Since] at least the nineteenth century, powerful voices—John Stuart Mill, Thomas Henry Huxley, Émile Zola—have insisted that there are no values in nature. Nature simply *is*; it takes a human act of imposition or projection to transmute that "is" into an "ought." On this view, there is no legitimate inference that can be drawn from how things happen to be (equated with natural regularities) to how things should be (equated with human norms), from the facts of the natural to the values of the moral order. To try to draw such inferences is to commit what has come to be called the "naturalistic fallacy"—a kind of covert smuggling operation in which cultural values are transferred to nature and nature's authority is then called upon [circularly] to buttress those very same values.[69]

This alleged circularity in regard to values notwithstanding, the question ensues about the more famous critique by Hume of how determinate ideas of the mathematical sciences can be advanced, given his sweeping skepticism? The skepticism undermines his disingenuous praise of science since: (1) the so-called determinate ideas of the mathematical sciences, if they were "legitimate ideas," would be derived from sensations that are bifurcated from an external reality whose very existence is unknowable; (2) the causal principle is not known to be true despite its presupposition for intelligible scientific inquiries; (3) given Hume's rejection of induction and disregard of any other reasoning, there can be no valid inferences to universal empirical propositions; and (4) transposing the propositions into theoretical laws or theories would be precluded because they are not traceable directly to sensations; with the official consequence, for Hume's radical empiricism, that any scientific law or theory would have to be relegated to the status of an unknowable metaphysics (illusory or imaginary "associations of ideas").

This pioneering skepticism is related to a modern secular ethics that was devised *intentionally* to be irrelevant to fulfilling our psycho-biological

68. Hume, "Of the Idea." Hume did not name that fallacy as such.
69. See Daston, "The Naturalistic Fallacy," 579–87.

nature in order to avoid the naturalistic fallacy. In arrogantly appealing to only the "empirical" and "rational," modern ethics not only lost all credibility but also, in a way reminiscent of Hilary Putnam's point that a seemingly abstract philosophy can have a profoundly pejorative effect on society,[70] resulted in one notorious crisis after another in Western culture (some non-Western cultures fairing relatively well by not suffering fascist and communist ideologies). These crises range from ubiquitous mass shootings in schools and an intolerant political correctness to the drug, abortion, and divorce epidemics. These social pathologies, which remind us that even good people tend to be influenced badly in bad cultures, were the fallout from the West's dominant secular ethical theories of consequentialism and deontology. Whereas deontology appeals naively to our reason for doing the right thing for its own sake (despite denials of the reasons resulting in no self-contradiction), consequentialism appeals to empirically certifiable consequences of the *morally desirable* (where the desirable is conflated infamously with what *in fact is desired*). The obvious irrationality of modern ethics returns us to the causal principle that, when it is a true modality, binds science to ethics by virtue of a first cause.

No Fallacy Because Our Nature *Is* as It *Ought to Be*

No anachronism is committed by noting that the trivial analytic and contingent truth espoused by Hume have grave limitations that are suggested by Aristotle who discovered modal logic; the logic then developed until the time of St. Thomas as noted by Fr. Joseph Clark, revived in the twentieth century by C. I. Lewis and developed by others from W. V. O. Quine to Ruth Barcan Marcus.[71] One result is that a strong sort of truth is ascribable to the causal principle because although it is *logically possible* for events to have no causes, it is *physically impossible* where this impossibility can be recast as a non-trivial necessity: "Necessarily if there is no cause ($\sim C$), there is no event ($\sim E$)" where this is *not* denoted as the truth-functional $\sim C \rightarrow \sim E$ but rather as the *alethic modality* $\sim C \Rightarrow \sim E$. And an *epistemic modality*, expressing a non-trivial necessary truth, may permit reasoning from systematically true predictions of a theory to its truth. This truth is profoundly important since it avoids restrictions to

---

70. Cf. Putnam, "Philosophers and Human Understanding," 100.
71. Clark, *Conventional* Logic, 53.

falsified theories that, per Popper, rely on truth-functional conditionals. By conditionals that are modal, the restrictions are overcome. Overcome also are limitations to a weak material implication. A strong *strict implication* permits inferring a first cause from the causal principle whose truth revives modalities related to Thomas' proof of Nature's God. Denying this God as a first cause excludes astronomical inquiries because, as noted earlier, the inquiries ultimately presuppose a first cause for their very intelligibility. An infinite regress of causes has the anomalous consequent *inter alia* of either there being no cause of the cosmos or the cosmos causing itself (its absurdly being a phenomenon unlike all other phenomena subject to science that depend on causes).

With a reminder that the first cause is consistent with the Big-Bang theory and evolution (whether or not they are modified significantly or even superseded scientifically in the future per the aforesaid principle of *pessimistic induction*), this cause as the causal creator of our psycho-biological nature and Nature, on which scientific inquiry depends ultimately for its intelligibility, is an intelligibility that bears also on this creator's status as a supreme axiological norm. As this norm, the creator is presupposed for the ranking of things as more or less good by virtue of that norm. For norms other than a first cause (and this cause via the proof is more than reasonably established) cannot in principle be perfect because everything depends on the first cause. *Without* this cause, one thing cannot be said to be objectively good or better than another. Even the mathematical sciences, so celebrated by Hume over moral studies of the "good," could not be meaningfully compared in terms of one scientific theory being good or better than another unless there was the provable first cause as *the* Good.[72] And this Good means that our psycho-biological nature is the basis for a naturalistic ethics. For our nature, in *being* as it *ought to be* by virtue of a first cause of natural theology (reflecting a supernatural theology where God says His creations are good) affords inferences to how our nature should be fulfilled; this, by virtue of how it is. Inferences to ethical prescriptions come from, precisely, scientific descriptions of our nature.[73]

---

72. Cf. Trundle, "Value and Scientific Theory," 85–100.
73. Cf. Peter Kreeft, "First Cause," para. 1–13.

Our Psycho-biological Fulfillment by the Family

In this scientific ethics, an "ought" is not inferred invalidly solely from how our nature *is*. And the *is-cannot-imply-ought* naturalistic fallacy, of inferring how our nature *should* be fulfilled from how it merely *is*, is not committed since our nature is as it ought to be. In our ethics, something that fulfills our psycho-biological nature, from marriage and family to art, architecture, music, fashion, and food, permits objectively true claims that they are good. In regard to the good, norms derived from psychology are rooted in biology.[74] Our biological functions induce a conscious will to live, for example, which is natural psychologically and is unlike suicide that *ceteris paribus* is unnatural; though the unnaturalness is qualified by the Roman Catholic Church that recognizes the possibility that a person's psycho-biological suffering or potential suffering in certain contexts can reduce, if not exclude, the sin of suicide.[75] But the degree to which our nature is ignored by modern ethics is revealed by how much persons today are provoked by other medical findings. These findings support traditional families that consist of male and female marriages that were defended by the architects of a naturalistic ethics. Whereas Aristotle held that families are established by Nature for the natural affection of men and women as well as between generations for the stability of children (*Politics* 1252), St. Thomas adds that society is perfected by matrimony since it nurtures self-sacrifice and sacrificial Love (*Summa Theologiae iii*, 65).

Sacrificial Love, over the ages, has proven to be the foundation of the family (an analogical church). And although Aristotle and Thomas lived long before today's science, this science increasingly supports their ethics. And although the ethics applies to biological differences of men and women that make a difference in societal aspirations that *should* be fostered, a wanton denial of gender differences is now entrenched; not by science but rather by a political correctness, where something can be "correct" but factually false, where truth about gender is not informed by science but is absurdly relative *a priori* to different cultures because "truth" is allegedly a mere cultural construct. The constructionist

---

74. This discussion of the family is based on my article with Michael Vossmeyer, M.D., "Sex Revolution," 129–48.

75. Cardinal Ratzinger and the Interdiscasterial Commission, *Catechism of the Catholic Church*, 2282. See also *Catechism of the Catholic Church*. It states that "Grave psychological disturbances, anguish, or grave fear of hardship, suffering, or torture can diminish the responsibility of the one committing suicide."

ideologies, maintain former women's-studies pioneers Noretta Koertge and Daphne Patai, begot a naïve and deadly BIODENIAL for men as well as women that continues to flout psycho-biological facts.[76]

One fact is that the steroidal hormone $C_{19}H_{28}O_2$, which is produced in the male's testes, bears biologically on a *Physical Possibility Principle* (of modal logic): Generally, it is immoral to demand of persons that they do what is impossible for them to do. Regarding men in the context here, it is immoral to expect that they should do what is contrary to their psycho-biological nature. Despite the nature-versus-nurture debate where morphometric analyses show that homosexual behavior has genetic causes *versus* the behavior itself causing structural changes in the brain,[77] it is as physically impossible for most men to not seek heterosexual unions as for them to be no more aggressive than women. While men's responsibility for their behavior is not entirely erased by hormonal effects, the effects mean also that society is responsible for nurturing stable behavioral outlets. These outlets include marriage and work-place meritocracies in order to fulfill the male's sexually active and competitive nature.[78] And this natural fulfillment is as socially desirable for women as it is for men. Besides marriage reducing "the risk of mental disorders for both men and women,"[79] for example, both women and children are largely victims of the male's DSM-IV Disorders; disorders that include pedophilic exploitations of children are diagnosed more than twice as often in men and are related to single-parent families in which male children have a fifty percent increase in risk of various psycho-social impairments.[80]

And the impairments and disorders do not include violent crimes such as rape that, while often construed ideologically by feminists as a mere exercise of male power (that studiously ignores biology), cannot be disassociated from either biological urges of men or unmarried mothers who are three times more likely to be assaulted than married

---

76. Patai and Koertge, *Professing Feminism*, 138.

77. Cf. Venosa, "The Environmental and Biological Factors," para. 1–9.

78. Vossmeyer, M.D., adds *inter alia* that traditional marriage may preserve a gene pool for sexual unions that promote genetic diversity, minimize inbreeding and provide a stability for offspring. But one gender could predominate whereby monogamy is untenable. I note, however, that imbalances tend to be caused not by Nature but rather by cultural meddling. Cf. Hesketh, "Abnormal Sex Ratios," 13271–75.

79. Blackshaw et al., "Teaching on Gender," 1–3.

80. Jellinek et al., "Use of the Pediatric Symptom Checklist," 254–60.

mothers.[81] Also, a sexual unresponsiveness of young married women can be induced by political ideologies, such as a radical feminism, that undermine marriage as well as by various biological dysfunctions.[82] For example, ideological attacks on marriage were expressed in feminist Jessie Bernard's *The Future of Marriage* (1972), fueling a false belief that it oppressed women, and in the iconic film *The Stepford Wives* (1975). This latter invites wives to rebel against their robotic roles as sex slaves. Besides patronizing women, this politically correct gender feminism is rooted in an incoherent relativism where how male and female natures are is relative to different cultures, and where their psycho-biological natures play no role. Researchers at the Markkula Center for Applied Ethics address a confusion of relativists who disregard entirely our psycho-biological nature in favor of nurture:

> Most ethicists reject the theory of ethical relativism. Some claim that while the moral practices of societies may differ, the fundamental moral principles underlying these practices do not. For example, in some societies, killing one's parents after they reached a certain age was common practice, stemming from the belief that people were better off in the afterlife if they entered it while still physically active. . . . While such a practice would be condemned in our society, we would agree with these societies on the underlying moral principle—the duty to care for parents. Societies, then, may differ in their application of fundamental moral principles but agree on the principles.[83]

Indeed, in contrast to a feminist gender relativism that ignores our psycho-biological nature, nature as well as nurture are stressed by Aristotle. He aptly notes that wives are by *nature*, but not always by *nurture*, respectful of sexual differences from their husbands. And the feminist ideology of wives being sex slaves collides head-on with former US Attorney-General Robert F. Kennedy's wife, Ethel Kennedy, for whom "ministering to her husband was . . . self-fulfillment. It did not result in any manifest repression of an irrepressible personality."[84] The point is that theory, much more politically correct ideology, needs the test of lived experience. An experienced reality should inform our beliefs. Our beliefs, especially ones that are ideological, should not be imposed *a priori* on

81. Fagin and Johnson, "Marriage: Safest Place," 1.
82. Gyelvan, *Professional Guide*, 1001.
83. Velasquez et al, "Ethical Relativism," para. 4.
84. Schlesinger, *Robert Kennedy*, 96.

our behavior. In short, besides psycho-biological dysfunctions, political ideology can contribute to extramarital sex and sexually transmitted diseases that infect not only wives but unborn children;[85] children and parents having a beneficial symbiosis. While the symbiosis is not separated phylogenetically,[86] it is largely downplayed politically for women. Women's best childbearing age conflicts with agendas that promote their careers, on a *traditional male norm*, at a time when marriage is biologically preferable (a famous feminist saying "*Some of us are becoming the men we wanted to marry*").[87]

Marriage is not just about the fact, although it is significant, that men beget children and women bear them. Bearing multiple children at an early age, breast-feeding, and also being faithful in marriage reduce the risks of cervical and breast cancers; breast-cancer risk dropping 7% per child and 4% more for each year of breastfeeding, with low incidence where the average woman has multiple breastfed children. And Harvard Medical School's Dr. Susan Hankinson admits that marital postponements pose serious risks of breast cancer, despite sympathy with unmarried working women. And Dr. Patricia Novak notes that cervical cancer is caused by the genital herpes virus linked to extramarital sex.[88] Ironically, in the Netherlands where a court of law sought to prosecute the Roman Catholic Pope for "hate speech" after he criticized extramarital unions,[89] Norwegian medical oncologists in the *Journal of Epidemiology* found that unmarried women had an increased Overall Risk for ovarian, uterus, brain, and hematological cancers (or = 1.13, 95% confidence interval [ci] 1.05, 1.21). And risk of cervical and thyroid cancer was lower for married

---

85. See Gholipour, "Hidden STD Epidemic," para. 1–17: STDs in the us include "chlamydia, gonorrhea, hepatitis B virus (HBV), genital herpes, hiv, human papillomavirus (HPV), syphilis and trichomoniasis" with about 50.5 million of these stds in men and 59.5 million in women. "Each year, new cases of STDs cost nearly $16 billion in direct medical costs." 50% of these "occur in young people, ages 15–24," although this group is only a quarter of those who have had sex.

86. Cf. Dimijian, M.D., "Evolving Together," 217–26.

87. Quoting Gloria Steinem, Schaef adds "We wanted to make it in a man's world. . . . It is time to stop and see what has happened to us in the process." The process is worsened by medical journals that, cowed by political correctness, contribute to confusing male and female norms. See Schaef, *Meditations*, 1–8 emphasis, as well as Glueck and Cihak, "Medical Journal," 1–2.

88. See the Collaborative Group, "Breast Cancer and Breastfeeding," 187; Hankinson et al, *Healthy Women*, 95; and Novak, *Mosby's Medical*, 328.

89. See Brinkman, "Sex, Lies," para. 11, 38.

women, while unmarried women had a greater 26% risk of dying. "The increased death rate for unmarried women was seen for cancer of the cervix, lung, and thyroid."[90] And women who have children after their mid-thirties in order to establish professional careers (though careers do not exclude early marriage) is related to birth defects and difficulties of conception; marital postponements being a subject that resulted in serious alarm from extensive news coverage. In an interview by medical doctors, for example, Nancy Weil admitted:

> "Hey, I can do my career and have children later." . . . At 42, Weil met her soul mate and decided it was time. For two years, they've been trying, first naturally, now with fertility drugs. A year ago she conceived, then miscarried. Last month alone, she spent $3,300 on injections. "If you ever told me I'd be having this kind of difficulty, I would have laughed in your face. . . . I exercise, I eat well, I keep better work hours, but I'm really not in control of . . . my little eggs. It's devastating. It's a terrible sense of failure."[91]

Early conception in marriage without divorce, which depresses the immune system, is supported by this scientific ethics. It is not merely the sex drive, need for natural affection, and optimal childbearing age of women that support early conception and marriage. Marriage is fortified also by a virtual *physical impossibility* that its postponement will not increase abortion, out-of-wedlock birth and sexual diseases that are already of epidemic proportions. And in reply to no-fault divorces favored by feminists, Linda Waite and Maggie Gallagher note that the goodness of "marriage is visible even on the *biological level*"—Dr. Janice Kiecolt-Glaser and her colleagues finding that marriage "improves immune function" and divorce "depressed it, even years after the divorce occurred."[92] Research establishes also that extending domestic benefits to cohabiting couples sends a message that "scientists now know to be dangerously false" because "cohabiting couples are less sexually faithful, lead less settled lives, are less likely to have children, are more likely to be violent, make less money, and are less happy—and less committed—than married couples."[93] This does not mean that women should abstain

---

90. See Kvikstad et al., "Cancer Risk," 1826–27.
91. Kalb, "Should You?" 40.
92. See Waite and Gallagher, *The Case for Marriage*, 668–78, emphasis.
93. Ibid. Yet unmarried couples are becoming the so-called "new normal."

from careers but rather that careers should be enabled by a societal dynamics that coincides with psycho-biological realities. Instead of only urging women to "break glass ceilings" that is alone invariably exalted, for example, virtues of motherhood should be publicly praised and made compatible with transitions from rearing children to the workplace. Gender expectations in the workplace, much more in the military, should be based on scientific findings and not on a social-political ideology that experiments with our lives.

From the Family to Scientific Truth that Informs Art and Politics

The traditional family and marriage, as good institutions since they fulfill our psycho-biological nature, are augmented by art, music, and architecture.[94] Thus, example, there is a well-known Mozart Effect whose healthful benefits are affirmed repeatedly in medical journals such as the *Journal of the Royal Society of Medicine*. Noting that patients with comas and epilepticus were healed by the music of Mozart, John Hughes, M.D., refers to a "periodicity in the power of Mozart's music, seen also with J. S. Bach . . . ," adding that "periodicity is key" to improving "brain and bodily functions."[95] The improved functions, furthermore, are amplified by Pietro Modesti, M.D., Ph.D. Modesti states that rhythmically homogeneous music comparable to Bach, such as "classical, Celtic and Indian," do indeed "have an anti-hypertensive effect."[96] And Vincent de Luise, M.D., observes that "There is not just a *Mozart effect*; there is also a '*J. C. Bach effect*', and likely, an '*effect*' by other composers . . . whose melodic themes happen to 'align' with the periodicities of neuronal network activity"; enlarging on the point by noting that "types of music with specific rhythms and periodicity, create an arousal effect, and it is this arousal that creates temporary enhancement in cognitive capacity."[97] Finally, because these beneficial effects are so enhanced by music, we may reasonably infer that other modes of art (likened to forms of *frozen music*) can also be good by fulfilling our psycho-biological nature; starting with architecture

---

94. This discussion on art, architecture, music and fashion draws on Trundle, "Women's Fashion," 2–21.

95. Hughes, "The Mozart Effect," 316.

96. Modesti et al., "Daily Sessions," Abstract, emphasis.

97. Luise, M.D., "Mozart's Effect," §VII 3–4.

that enhances our health. Healthful effects, say many architects, consist in "informing design, leading to cutting-edge projects such as residences for seniors with dementia in which a *building itself is part of the treatment*."[98]

This treatment for fulfilling our psycho-biological nature by well-crafted architecture is reinforced by Breeze Glazer, Perkins Will and Robin Glazer of *The Creative Center: Arts in Healthcare*. They hold that "The relationship between the built environment and health has long been understood, but only recently prioritized, as a key consideration for both healthcare providers and designers."[99] And they observe both that "When the nature of healthcare delivery is considered, we immediately think of . . . the practitioners, doctors, nurses, and other medical professionals"[100] and that "Within the last several decades an emergence of research connecting health and design has led to a greater acceptance of additional means to improving health."[101] Finally, in emphasizing that "integrating environmental qualities into the design of a healthcare building in order to positively impact patient recovery has become widely accepted,"[102] they explicitly link architecture to healthful art:

> With that in mind, the next frontier may be the role of art in the healing process. Just as with healthcare design, this idea is supported by a growing body of research [per "Visual Art in Hospitals," *JR Soc Med*. 103.12 (2010) 490–99] that reveals the physiologic processes taking place when a person is in contact with different forms of art. Some of these processes are related to the release of endorphins that can function as stress and pain relievers for the human body. Evidence-based artwork is the outcome of the analysis . . . of art, such as landscape scenes, on patients and staff in healthcare environments. Hospitals and healthcare institutions have shown an understanding of the value of placing evidence-based artwork in their lobbies, hallways, grounds, and patient-care rooms.[103]

---

98. Anthes, "Building Around the Mind," 34, emphasis.

99. Glazer et al, "Designing for Health," para. 1. See also Editor, "winners Announced for the European Healthcare Design Awards 2016," *Architects For Health*. These architects held a conference on healthcare-design architecture at the Royal College of Physicians, London, 11–14 June 2017.

100. Glazer et al, "Designing for Health," para. 1.

101. Ibid.

102. Ibid.

103. Ibid., para. 2.

After noting the indisputable relation of art to architecture, Glazer, Will and Glazer relate the art existentially (viscerally) to artists who suffered injuries. They ask, "Who could better understand what will be visually impactful for these individuals than artists who are, or have been, patients themselves?"[104] They quote two artists about art and their own health. "'I live to paint. After my injury, art became my therapy in both a psychological and physical sense. I stretch and move my hands and body in needed movements while I enjoy the act of creation,'"[105] confirms artist Cliff Enright. And artist Aleta Yarrow says, "Painting transition in landscape is a metaphor for the possibility of swift and positive change. Through art, I define myself as human, not as one who suffers. Art is [thus] hope."[106]

This hope and the goodness of art and architecture are true universally in terms of fulfilling our psycho-biological nature. For this nature is as universal as primary worldwide medical-school teachings. The teachings are not true in one culture and false in another, any more than the related healthful art is good in one culture and not in another (as held by relativistic social constructionists). The case against these constructionists stems from the fact that the good is grounded in our common psycho-biological nature as human beings. At the same time, a given person's fulfillment may be obstructed by *nurture* inasmuch as persons, although having free choice of will, may lack the relevant cultivated taste; Aristotle suggesting famously that the cultivation supposes a modest degree of material wellbeing in order to free persons from being consumed by endeavors to escape poverty. Furthermore, persons may be socialized or conditioned to bad art and architecture, or to almost anything else that is undesirable. Undesirable amounts of sugar, by analogy, can condition persons to eschew nutritious foods that fulfill their psycho-biological nature (which are thus called good).

The good bears also on beautiful fashions that may be included in the domain of art, revealing again how a naturalistic ethics and science are related logically. Accordingly, fashion as art is not a mere imaginative concoction whose goodness is relative to different cultures. Rather than cultures capriciously and conflictingly determining which art is beautiful, beautiful fashion is founded on the human being's body and

---

104. Ibid., para. 10.
105. Ibid.
106. Ibid.

bodily forms. And this fashion is that, as well, which fulfills our psychobiological nature in terms of Aristotle's insight that "The chief forms of beauty are order and symmetry and definitiveness" which the "mathematical sciences demonstrate in a special degree" (*Poetics* 1078b). Also, Aristotle's empirical approach to ethics, which bears on our bodily and intellectual well-being, is amplified aptly by Thomas who refers to Aristotle when he asserts that "happiness consists, according to the Philosopher (*Ethics* i, 13) in *an operation according to perfect virtue*; and it is clear that man can be hindered, by indisposition of the body, from every operation of virtue."[107] This virtue in the more exact sciences, as said by Thomas, involves both the *form* of a natural substance and its *matter* since "otherwise there would be no difference between definitions of physics and mathematics."[108]

And relations of mathematics to virtue, bearing on the body and its form, foreshadows scientific research in the international medical journal *The Lancet* to *Proceedings of the Royal Society B*, where fashion as a mode of art is related to both the beauty of a female *body* to men and the male's *body* to women. Women also find beautiful a male's bodily form, despite women having less acute attractions than men to bodily mathematical ratios and the ratios' aesthetic effects on women increasing or decreasing due to genetic or paternal traits[109] (e.g., a male's affinity for children that sustains a "long-term attractiveness").[110] In short, natural attractions between men and women, because of physical beauty and beautiful fashions that *highlight the body*, are illustrated by many sources: From the Scriptures where the erotic sandals of Judith enraptures an Israeli enemy[111] to the psychological phenomenon of females in high heels being an intercultural fetish item of beauty (that accentuate sensual appearances of leg-muscle tone). The latter phenomena bear on interrelated truths in ethics and science because the phenomena relate aesthetically to bodily ratios and so forth, studied by biology, psychology and medicine.[112] These ratios and other aesthetic phenomena bear on a

---

107. Aquinas, *Summa Theologiae* i–ii, 4, 6.
108. Aquinqs, Ch. 2, *On Being and Essence*. 37.
109. Maisey et al., "Characteristics," 1500.
110. Roney et al., "Reading Men's Faces," §4, Discussion 12.
111. Church, Book of Judith. *New American Bible*, 10:4.
112. See Scorolli et al., "Relative prevalence," 432–37, and J. Dawson et al., "An Investigation of Risk Factors," 823–30, that deny an alleged harmfulness of high heels.

beauty that, by virtue of fulfilling our psycho-biological nature, can be regarded as objectively good.

Good fashion that is sensual for both men and women, wherein the erotic is related to beautiful art, involves art that enhances our moral and intellectual ascension to Beauty *itself*, according to Plato's *Republic*. Here, Beauty is part of the ultimate triune Form that includes the One and Good and which, interestingly, is beheld by the philosopher who has a synoptic vision of the *interrelation of all knowledge*. And in the case of Aristotle, sensually alluring fashions, despite the modest public dress of most Greek women (who even so wore cosmetics to attract men),[113] would better attract men without which formations of families by marriage would be unnaturally impeded. And largely unnoticed is Thomas' avowal that *only* "those women who have no husband nor wish to have one," and only women in conditions "inconsistent with marriage, cannot without sin desire to give lustful pleasure to those men who see them . . . ."[114] Kelly Ross says of erogenous beauty that the "*horative*, as part of ethics, is what is good for human life."[115] Since both the quality of human life and our health are enormously benefited by beautiful art, we are reminded that art is not a trivial endeavor but rather has serious ethical import. This fact is often dismissed in consumerist societies whose citizens are obsessed by material things. In my own county, when neither it nor our country were in a recession, a law suit was filed against the county libraries, which had free displays of art and performances of music, to prevent them from using tax funding. The law suit was filed by local self-avowed "Tea Partiers," who considered libraries to be unnecessary expenses. Interestingly, the Tea Party is related to the previously discussed corporate oligarchs, "funded by corporate billionaires, like the Koch brothers"[116] who "for decades poured money, often with little public disclosure, into influencing how Americans thought and voted."[117]

---

113. Kluth, "Hairstyles and Cosmetics," §10 Cosmetics.
114. Aquinas, "Adornment of Women?" II-II. Q. CLXIX. Art. II.
115. Ross, "The Erotic," para. 26.
116. Mayer, *Dark Money*, 168.
117. Ibid., 4.

Politics Informed by Truths of Ethics and Science

A first cause, strictly implied by a modal-logic reading of the causal principle, affords evidence-based inferences *upward a posteriori* from science to a naturalistic ethics, to art and politics. Politics has as its main mission the institutionalization of an ethics that is as certifiably true as the truths in medicine and its allied sciences that inform that ethics.[118] Not using ethics to infer political principles, to avoid a naturalistic fallacy, resulted in core political ideologies (Marxism, National Socialism), which are not evidence-based, that pervert politics by reasoning *downward a priori* from politically correct norms to science; producing a relativism that is pathological. Pathological disorders have arisen that should alarm any medical community that professes the Hippocratic Oath. This Oath, as suggested by Peter Redpath, was undercut by the Enlightenment's covert "utopian socialism," proselytized today as "real social science" by "scientific socialists"; although, notes Redpath, there may be some good modes of socialism.[119] Socialism, capitalism, and any other "-ism" per the point herein cause the very evils they eschew when they are treated ideologically as if they are absolutely and exclusively true. This illusory truth is not based on evidence, even evidence over the ages that is fortified by present-day medical research. The research establishes, among other things, that the traditional family of male and female parents and their children is a singularly good institution by virtue of both its benefit to society and the degree to which it fulfills our psycho-biological nature.

Our psycho-biological nature as the empirical basis for evidence is frequently avoided by spinning inconvenient facts, bringing to mind medical journalist Miranda Hitti. Ignoring research that contradicts Hitti, by the U.S. Division of Vital Statistics at the Advanced Data Centers for Disease Control,[120] she says disingenuously that married people who are healthier may not "mean that marriage improves health" but rather that "healthier people get married and stay married."[121] This pedantry, indeed sophism, is similar to those who downplay medical findings because they do not represent causes but mere correlations. But besides the *lack of any correlations* that favor their own ethics—an inevitable result of the false fact-value divide of modern ethics, the correlations if not causes,

---

118. This analysis modifies my book, *A Theology of Science*, 171–78.
119. Redpath, "Globalization," 143.
120. See Bramlett and Mosher, "First Marriage," No. 323.
121. Miranda, "The Health Perks," §2.

are strong and based on major perennial international studies as well as numerous medical research approaches.

And the many research approaches and studies reveal that the so-called "mere correlations" *can* frequently be understood causally, as breast-feeding is known to cause a suppression of carcinogenic ovarian estrogen levels in the breast because of a subdual of menstrual cycles that produce those levels. Also, the correlations do not lend themselves to a false-cause fallacy wherein, say, one infers that Jones should stop brushing his teeth because he got cavities! The traditional views highlight an ignored mode of reasoning: It is an epistemic impossibility that traditions such as the family do not truly fulfill our psycho-biological nature if they are *not* abandoned over the ages (millennia); the ideology touted as Marxism being abandoned in a mere matter of decades, despite its despotic control of the media and propaganda. Also, the aforesaid modal reasoning, about the impossibility of traditions not being abandoned when they fulfill our psycho-biological nature, resembles both inferences in science and lessons learned painfully from political tyranny.

The main reason why most tyrannical nations were defeated in the twentieth century—the bloodiest century in human history according to researcher Jean-Louis Panné (historian and secretary to *Comintern's* Boris Souvarin who was later a leading Sovietologist and anti-communist), is that communists and their fellow travelers sought to mold our psycho-biological nature to fit ideology rather than to fit their ideology to our nature. Indeed, admitting of facts about our nature conflicts with the very nature of political ideology, including ideology as a social constructionist worldview that is advanced by politically correct feminists.[122] This feminism and other ideologies fail, or will fail, precisely because they suppress evidence-based truths and facts. Facts are understood illogically as a mere function of molding reality *a priori*, to create facts, as opposed to being inferred *a posteriori* from what is the case. *A posteriori* inferences should be rejected, according to the ludicrous thinking, of the politically correct pioneering feminist Kathryn Payne Parsons. Parsons maintains that our malleable nature ought to be shaped and possibly reshaped *a priori*, in possibly contradictory ways, by Kuhn-like conceptual paradigms. The

---

122. See Koertge and Patai, *Professing Feminism*, 135, 136. Having pioneered the development of women's studies, their position that "politically correct feminism" is a blind ideology carries much weight; a weight noted, I recall, by the renowned philosopher of logic Susan Hack several years ago in the journal *Signs*. See Hack's critique of the feminism in "Epistemological Reflections," 31–43.

paradigms are not merely that by which we see the world, says Parsons, but also that which shape "facts of the human world."[123] And it is not only the human world that is affected. Scientific theories that neglect the facts, likewise, are abandoned because these theories do not succeed in the explication, prediction, and manipulation of phenomena.

These points about phenomena are unified by Popper's successor at the London School of Economics, Imre Lakatos. Lakatos noted that Einstein's physics flourished by extraordinary predictions such as there being different measurements between two stars at night and day, whereas Marxism was abandoned intellectually as well as in practice because of its failed productivity and false predictions.[124] If scientific theories do not reflect facts, or how reality really *is* (approximately) in a given domain, then they are abandoned. And they are not abandoned if facts or reality are addressed successfully. Successful theories are analogous to societal traditions over the ages such as marriage; unless, that is, marriage and the other traditions are repressed ideologically. One reason to repress marriage is that the health-inducing love between biologically related family members threatens pathological loyalties to tyrants and fatal fidelities to evidence-ignoring ideologies (including both anti-progressive and progressive globalist ends). Ends of thwarting an ethics informed by science are more subtly advanced by ideologues who abuse medical findings. Sally Lehrman, of the National Diversity Chair for the Society of Professional Journalists, argues *for* a sexual promiscuity that threatens a naturalistic ethics. "The latest anthropological research shows that female infidelity is good for the family . . . ,"[125] she says incredulously. In order to reject a naturalistic ethics, such as that of Aristotle and Thomas, she appeals to research wherein men's sperm evolved to attack other sperm which would not occur if we were naturally monogamous.[126] But to say that this monogamy is unnatural because otherwise there is no reason for that phenomenon is as silly as saying that there would be no reason for cavities if dental hygiene were natural: The hygiene is unnatural and should be stopped for the sake of our oral and general health?

---

123. Parsons, "Nietzsche," 186. Panné et al., *The Black Book*, 4. The latter reports that nearly 100 million died, mostly women and children, not counting mass murders by the Nazi Gestapo modelled on the Soviet NKVD.

124. Lakatos, *The Methodology* I, 5, 6. Lakatos, who superseded Popper, also disavowed *any kind* of realism.

125 Lehrman, "The Virtues," subtitle.

126. Ibid. Cf. para. 1-23.

In regard to general health, medical research establishes that, besides weakening marriage by ensuing socio-economic calamities that cost at least "$112 billion annually,"[127] sexual promiscuity causes unparalleled psycho-biological pathologies. The pathologies caused by promiscuity has led to a revival of syphilis that causes new neurological and psychiatric syndromes.[128] And besides the syndromes, promiscuity correlates to escalating anal cancers in the West that reveals how pathological cultures spread disease. Disease is cultivated singularly by evidence-ignoring *ideological* agenda of some progressives.[129] These points illustrate how disingenuous notions of the "natural" miss the point of a naturalistic ethics: *fulfilling* our psycho-biological nature by prescribing things such as marriage, having children, hygiene and sheer physical survival. Precisely, a survival of the very critics who belittle this ethics is at risk.

The risk is now institutionalized by those with vested interests in tolerating, if not positively promoting, the pathologies; from unethical lawyers and social workers to the child support industry. Given that these events result markedly from ideological influences of Western society, which range from progressivist to politically correct and corporate oligarchical ideologies, it is clear that this society has been ill served by ideologies rooted in modern secular philosophy. The heart of the conundrum is that this philosophy led to skepticism since it abandoned a realism of objective truth, much more truths of medicine and the other sciences that inform a true naturalistic ethics. This ethics is of vital concern globally, bearing on a *common psycho-biological nature of the human race* for which physicians are uniquely poised to contribute. A natural theology, which is shareable by the three major monotheistic religions, may seem arcane and to make no immediate reference to science. But we have nothing to lose and everything to gain by reconsidering how natural theology, along with religion too, may reclaim a normative significance of the medical profession and its allied sciences.

While multiple sciences inform a naturalistic ethics on the goodness of marriage, as previously discussed, marriage takes on the status of a holy sacrament in religion. On the one hand, the U.S. Conference of Catholic Bishops states that "Marriage is not . . . the effect of chance or the product of evolution of unconscious natural forces" but rather

---

127. Schramm, "Counting the Cost," *The Natural Family*, para. 2.
128. Hankovic et al., "Dementia Paralytica," 135–38.
129. See, for example, Singh's "Regulation," 63–74.

marriage is "the wise institution of the Creator to realize in mankind His design of love." (*Humanae Vitae*, no. 8).[130] "Marriage is a blessing," add the Bishops, "that God gave men and women for the good of humanity," not just for themselves, and that so "essential is this blessing that Christ redeemed and elevated it to become one of the seven sacraments. In doing so, Christ restored the original blessing of marriage in its fullness." And the fullness of marriage is contrasted to the sexual revolution whose revolt against traditional marriage led to societal pathologies. The Bishops note, "The wounds that the sexual revolution inflicted on our culture are deep." The revolution stresses "selfishness" and "encourages people to treat each other like objects that can be used and tossed away." Due to the revolution, "Divorce, broken hearts, and broken families are becoming the norm. The sexual revolution has brought no long-term happiness, just a cheap imitation, at a very high cost."

The high cost of the sexual revolution since the 1960s, reminds us that science should inform a naturalistic ethics and the ethics a politics whose *raison d'être* is to institutionalize the fulfillment of our psycho-biological nature.[131] And it is established that marriage and the traditional family, in particular, fulfill our psycho-biological nature; providing the most intimate form of friendship, safe sexual relations, preventing disease, and propagating as well as educating future generations. These generations in turn reciprocally protect, provide, and care for their extended family and parents. Parents who live together cooperatively, with a natural vested interest in their biological offspring, are the best assurance that the offspring will not, as children of divorced parents, "perform more poorly in reading, spelling, and math [and be] more likely to repeat a grade and to have higher drop-out rates and lower rates of college graduation."[132] But these facts fall on hardened hearts and closed minds of those in higher education who, while uniquely poised for a healthful influence, proselytize politically correct policies that *at best* draw no moral distinction of traditional from nontraditional families and *at worst* ideologically extol nontraditional families;[133] this, despite a crisis of American students who have among the *lowest* scores in science and

---

130. Secretariat, U.S. Conf. of Catholic Bishops, para. 17–19. Quotes below from the same source.

131. Cf. Trundle and Vossmeyer, "Sex Revolution," 129–48.

132. Fagan and Rector, "The Effects," No. 1373. Fagan has testified before Congress on marriage and family.

133. See Taylor, "Get Politics," para. 1–12.

math,[134] but the *highest* self-esteem of the advanced nations. Inevitably, ubiquitous remedial studies have been established at virtually all public colleges and universities.

In summary, solace may be taken from Aristotle and Thomas, whose wisdom evokes a long-term optimism. The optimism ensues, according to Thomas, because of "the fact that virtue, as the Philosopher says in Book Two of the *Ethics* [6, 1106a 15–19], is what makes its possessor good and renders his operation good."[135] This good that makes us happy (*eudaimonia*), Thomas adds, impels us to pursue "the perfect happiness" which cannot be satisfied except by "an innate desire whereby from effects [we are] moved to seek causes."[136] And this desire for causes is not satisfied, Thomas concludes, until we have "arrived at the *first cause, which is God*."[137] God, who created human nature, will win over evil. Thus, although great evil is caused by the institutionalizations of heinous ideologies, no conditioning process can sustain behavioral norms that do not fulfill our nature. Even the less malignant societies that do not try to recreate our psycho-biological nature, but fail to nurture it, will eventually be dissolved. The words of Aristotle and Thomas ring down the vista of time, warning that the unavoidable dissolution of these societies will stem from our physical, mental and spiritual dysfunction. There will ensue a loss of common civility, social cohesion and mutual pursuits of truth required to sustain even our oppressors, their toadies and the opportunists who exploit societal disarray for their own gain. While most citizens will be dismayed by the indecent gain and sophistry, Nature will inevitably reap her revenge by the failure and disgrace of the citizen's tormentors.

The tormentors fail to notice that a bittersweet optimism for the future, of those they oppress, consists in political institutions having to either cultivate an ethics that fulfills the psycho-biological nature of its citizens or undercut their happiness and productivity. And the productivity cannot be forcibly motivated. "You cannot motivate people through the Gulag—like in the Soviet Union,"[138] any more than the motivation

---

134. For the continuing crisis and disregard of the family, despite massive federal funding, see Dragoset et al, "School Improvement Grants." Cf. chs. 1–8.

135. Aquinas, "Question 1: On the Virtues."

136. Ibid.

137. Ibid, emphasis. Thomas' reference to reasoning *from effects to causes*, and to a first cause, shows that this cause is central to modern science.

138. Smolchenko, "Putin Dismisses Concerns," para. 22.

can be sustained by either corporate, oligarchical, or other pathological ideologies that are contrary to our psycho-biological nature. Our nature's fulfillment is the foundation for a survival of all social-political institutions. The latter must institutionalize the life-inducing naturalistic ethics that both avoids the naturalistic fallacy and is *as* certifiably true *as* are the truths of science that inform the ethics.

In Sum: Science Is Related Logically to Natural Theology, Ethics, Art, and Politics

Scientific inquiry yields truths about both our psycho-biological nature and Nature; thus the laborious attempt herein to defend scientific truths. These truths about both our nature and Nature, defended in this essay by both a phenomenology of our concept-free consciousness of reality and an elementary common-sense modal reasoning, presuppose a causal principle. In regard to this principle or others like it (either expressed by causes from the material to the formal or presupposed logically) as understood going back to the ancient and medieval periods, John Marenbon notes that "Whereas medieval philosophy has usually had a place in philosophy courses in continental Europe, up until the [1950s,] it was almost entirely ignored by English-speaking analytical philosophers" who worked in the "tradition of Frege and Russell. Then a number of pioneers—medievalists who had taught themselves logic, such as Ernest Moody; logicians with medieval interests, such as Peter Geach and Arthur Prior—began to point out the notable parallels between modern and medieval logic."[139] The purported parallels between these logics notwithstanding, Moody and Geach were unique by virtue of their attention, respectively, to modal logic and support for the sound deductions of St. Thomas' proofs of Nature's God.

Among the similar proofs of this God such those of an unmoved mover and necessary being, the proof of this God as a first cause is central to the controversial causal principle. For this principle is presupposed by science (as the sciences are understood today) and today's science is still related logically to natural theology because, as an alethic modality with an unusually strong epistemic truth, the principle has a non-trivial necessary truth and strictly implies a first-cause creator of natural theology. This theology holds that the world, in not having the cause, would have

---

139. Marenbon, "Introduction," 5.

needed to have absurdly either caused itself or come from nothing. As the first cause of *everything*, via proofs of modal logic in accord with St. Thomas, we can more than reasonably say that the first cause *qua* God is the supreme norm for the good, virtue, and perfection. Other norms are either not proved logically or created and imperfect (my looking forward to more rigorous proofs than mine of a first cause *qua* God.)[140]

While God *qua* first cause as the creator of the "world" may be a world that is imperfect, our psycho-biological nature was still created by that normative first cause. And this cause is nevertheless begged for by diverse cosmologies such as the Big-Bang theory and the more recent and rival alternative of the quantum-corrected Raychaudhuri equation, although even more recent research finds that this equation may be problematic.[141] This problematic equation aside, the sciences in general do not obviate either a first cause or this cause being a supreme norm. Given this norm, the sciences both describe a psycho-biological nature of persons that *is* as it *ought to be* and inform a naturalistic ethics. This ethics, where the "good" is what fulfills our psycho-biological nature and "bad" whatever obstructs that fulfillment, is an *evidence-based* ethics that is as objectively true as the truths in science that inform it.

Indeed, an increasingly true (verisimilar) science proceeds *pari passu* with a verisimilar naturalistic ethics and art. That is, given that this art and ethics are increasingly informed historically by ever truer scientific and medical findings, in a manner reminiscent of verisimilitude in science, the ethics and art are ever more effective in prescribing truths about the goodness *qua* healthfulness of things that fulfill our psycho-biological nature.[142] These increasing truths that fulfill our nature bear

---

140. Consider the first cause causing our nature *to be* as it *ought to be*: Things are ranked variously as good. Unless claims about the good are senseless, there must be a real standard of perfection to render coherent the hierarchy since something is ranked higher only if it is closer to the standard. Unless this standard has Being (that would be less than perfect if our nature was not created as it *ought* to be), even saying that one scientific theory is better than another would be senseless. See Kreeft, "First Cause," para. 1–13.

141. See Lashin and Dou, "On the Correctness," Abstract. They observe that "We find that the whole procedure is full of problematic points, on both physical relevancy and mathematical correctness." They add, "In particular, we illustrate the problems associated with the technical derivation of QRE [Quantum Raychaudhuri Equation], as well as its invalid physical implications. Thus, all claims concerning the inevitability of focusing and the formation of conjugate points, including the singularity evading, are, to us, not valid."

142. This point about increasing ethical truth proceeding *pari passu* with increasing

palpably not only on ethics and art but also on architecture, marriage, family and the other things that also inform politics. Politically, Étienne Gilson presaged my aforesaid critique of corporate oligarchs and their government enablers who abused democracy. While Gilson recognized that "democracy with its promise of political liberty had been generally successful in the civilized countries,"[143] he equally recognized that "political equality has not brought social and economic equality" and that "while many have political liberty they have not economic liberty; some have and enjoy much greater power than others in virtue of their economic status."[144] The intensification of this status favoring the wealthy and powerful, which nowadays so imperils the vast majority of citizens in many of the so-called democracies and republics, underscores that a central point of politics is the institutionalization of *evidence-based* (certifiably healthful) political policies. The policies, ranging from taxes and corporate behavior to education and healthcare, should increasingly fulfill of our psycho-biological nature, not impede our nature by evidence-flouting political ideologies. This holds irregardless of whether these ideologies are liberalism, conservatism, capitalism, socialism, progressivism, communism or any other "ism". Each of these "isms" has been treated faultily as an absolutely and exclusively true worldview.[145]

---

scientific truth goes beyond my discussion of an objectively true naturalistic ethics, which is inferred from scientific truth, in my book *Integrated Truth*.

143. FitzGerald, "Maritain and Gilson," 64.
144. Ibid. 64, 65. Étienne Gilson on democracy, 1947.
145. Cf. Trundle, "America's Religion," 4–6.

Bibliography

114th Congress *2nd Session*, House of Representatives. Report 114–537, National Authorization Act for Fiscal Year 2017. Committee on Armed Services House of Representatives on H.R. 4090 together with Additional Views, 4 May 2016, p. 87.

Agwan, Abdul Rashid. "Egyptian Scientist Amhed Farag Ali Bangs Up the 'Big Bang' Theory." *Muslim Mirror*, 18 Jan 2015. http:// muslimmirror.com/eng/egyptian-scientist-ahmed-farag-ali-bangs-up-the-big-bang-theory.

Alexander Aulfig, "Paradigm and Incommensurability—Two Central Concepts of Postmodern and Gender Constructivism." 27 Mar 2016. http://alexander-ulfig. de/2016/03/27/paradigma-und-inkommensurabilitaet-zwei-zentrale-begriffe-der-postmoderne-und-des-genderkonstruktivismus/.

Ali, Ahmed Farag, and Saurya Das. "Cosmology from Quantum Potential." *Physics Letters B*. Vol. 741 (4 Feb 2015) 276–79. DOI: 10.1016/j.physletb. 2014.12.057.

Allan, Leslie. "Imre Lakatos and a Theory of Rationality." 2016. http://www.rationalrealm.com/downloads/philosophy/ImreLakatosTheoryRationality.pdf.

Allen, Sophie R. "What's the Point in Scientific Realism If We Don't Know What's Really There?" *Royal Institute of Philosophy Supplement* 82.61 (2007) 97–123.

Anderson, G. C. "Clandestine NSF Panel Warms to Cold Fusion." *The Scientist* No. 10721, 13 Nov 1989. http://www.the-scientist.com/?articles.view/articleNo/10721/title/ Clandestine-NSF-Panel-Warms-To-Cold-Fusion/.

Andreas, Holger. "Theoretical Terms in Science." In *Stanford Encyclopedia of Philosophy*, edited by E. N. Zalta. 2013. http://plato.stanford.edu/archives/sum2013/entries/ theoretical-terms-science/.

Ankey, Rachel A., and Sabina Leonelli. "Repertoires: A Post-Kuhnian Perspective on Scientific Change and Collaborative Research." *Studies in History and Philosophy of Science Part A* 60 (Dec 2016) 18–28. http://www.sciencedirect. com/science/ article/pii/S0039368116300449.

Anthes, Emily. "Building around the Mind." *Scientific American Mind*, April/ May 2009, 33–37. 15 April 2009. http://www.emilyanthes.com/data/uploads/ neuroarchitecture.pdf.

Aquinas, St. Thomas. "On Being and Essence." In *Selected Writings of St. Thomas Aquinas*, edited and translated by R. P. Goodwin, 30–49. New York: Macmillan, 1965.

———. "On the Virtues in General." In *Selected Writings of St. Thomas Aquinas*, edited and translated by R. P. Goodwin, 100–101. New York: Macmillan, 1965.

———. *Summa Theologiae* I.Q. 86. In *Medieval and Renaissance Philosophy*, Vol. 2, edited by Forrest E. Baird, 366–67. 6th ed. New York: Prentice Hall, 2011.

———. "Summa Theologiae." In *A Summa of the Summa*, edited by Peter Kreeft, 232–33. San Francisco: Ignatius, 1990.

———. "Whether the Adornment of Women Is Devoid of Mortal Sin?" In *Summa Theologiae* II–CLXIX-II. http://www.fisheaters.com/modestyinsumma.

Arabatzis, Theodore. "Can a Historian of Science Be a Scientific Realist?" *Philosophy of Science* 68.3 (2001).

———. "Cathode Rays." In *Compendium of Quantum Physics*, edited by D. Greenberger et al., 89–92 New York: Springer, 2009.

Aristotle. *History of Animals*. In *The Complete Works of Aristotle*, vol. 1, edited by Jonathan Barnes. Princeton, NJ: Princeton University Press, 1984.

———. *Metaphysics*. In *The Complete Works of Aristotle*, vol. 2, edited by Jonathan Barnes. Princeton, NJ: Princeton University Press, 1984.

———. *Nichomachean Ethics*. In *The Complete Works of Aristotle*, vol. 2, edited by Jonathan Barnes. Princeton, NJ: Princeton University Press, 1984.

———. *Physics*. In *The Complete Works of Aristotle*, vol. 1, edited by Jonathan Barnes. Princeton, NJ: Princeton University Press, 1984.

———. *Posterior Analytics*. In *The Complete Works of Aristotle*, vol. 1, edited by Jonathan Barnes. Princeton, NJ: Princeton University Press, 1984.

———. *Prior Analytics*. In *The Complete Works of Aristotle*, vol. 1, edited by Jonathan Barnes. Princeton, NJ: Princeton University Press, 1984.

Asma, Stephen T. "The Enigma of Chinese Medicine." *The New York Times*, 28 Sept 2013. http://opinionator.blogs.nytimes.com/2013/09/28/the-enigma-of-chinese-medicine/?

Augustine. *The City of God*. Translated by G. Walsh, S.J., D. Zema, S.J., G. Monhan, O.S.U. and D. Horan. New York: Doubleday, 1958.

———. *Confessions*. Translated by R. S. Pine-Coffin. New York: Penguin, 1984.

———. *Contra Academicos* iii, xi, 26. In *Ancient Christian Writers*, translated and annotated by John J. O'meara, 35–151. New York: Paulist, 1951.

———. *On Christian Doctrine*. Translated by D. W. Robertson, Jr. New York: Macmillan, 1988.

———. *On Free Choice of the Will*. Translated by A. S. Benjamin and L. H. Hackstaff. New York: Macmillan, 1985.

Aulfig, Alexander. "Paradigm and Incommensurability—Two Central Concepts of Postmodern and Gender Constructivism." 27 Mar 2016. http://alexander-ulfig.de/2016/03/27/paradigma-und-inkommensurabilitaet-zwei-zentrale-begriffe-der-postmoderne-und-des-genderkonstruktivismus/.

Aune, Bruce. Review of Dretske's *Seeing and Knowing*. *The Philosophical Review* 80.3 (1971) 383–88. http://www.jstor.org/.

Baggini, Julian. "Daniel Dennett: 'You can make Aristotle look like a flaming idiot.'" *The Guardian*. 22 May 2013. http://www.theguardian.com/science/2013/may/22/daniel-dennett-aristotle-flaming-idiot.

———. "Interview with Hilary Putnam." *The Philosopher's Magazine*. Issue 15. http://www.philosophers.co.uk/archive/putnam_interviewed.

Baird, F. E. *Medieval & Renaissance Philosophy*. Vol. 2. 6th ed. New York: Prentice Hall, 2011.

Barnes, Hazel. *An Existentialist Ethics*. Chicago: University of Chicago Press, 1978.

———. "Response to Margaret Simons." *Philosophy Today* 42 (1998) 29–34. http://www.questis.com/library/journal/1P3-42640570/response-to-margaret-simons.

Barsoum, Nader. "Fabrication of Dual-Axis Solar Tracking Controller Project." *Intelligent Control & Automation* 2 (2011) 57–68.
Bauchspies, W. K., J. P. Van Bendegem, and S. Restivo. "The Sociology and Philosophy of Mathematics Revisited." In *Proceedings of the 3rd International Mathematics, Education & Society Conference*, edited by P. Valero and O. Skovsmose, 1–3. Copenhagen: CRLM, 2002. http:// mes3.learning.aau.dk/ Symposia_Agora/ Bauchspies_et_al.pdf.
Baumeister, Roy, and K. D. Vohs. "Determinsm Is Not Just Causality: Is the Future Set in Stone?" *Psychology Today* (2009). https://www.psychologytoday.com/blog/cultural-animal/200906/ determinism-is-not-just-causality.
Bear, Adam. "What Neuroscience Says about Free Will." *Scientific American*, 28 April 2016. https://blogs.scientificamerican.com/mind-guest-blog/what-neuroscience-says-about-free-will/.
Bear, Adam, and Joshua Knobe. "What Do People Find Incompatible with Causal Determinism?" *Cognitive Science* 40.8 (2015) 2025–49. https://doi.org/10.1111/cogs.12314.
Begley, Sharon. "Trump Is Dangerous, Mental Health Experts Claim in a New Book. Are They Right?" STAT, 29 Sept 2017. https://www.statnews.com/2017/09/29/trump-mental-health-book/.
Berezow, Alex. "Falsification: Was Karl Popper Wrong about Science?" *American Council on Science and Health*, 19 Aug 2016. http://acsh.org/news/2016/08/19/falsification-was-karl-popper-wrong-about-science.
Berwick, Donald. "The Toxic Politics of Health Care." *The Journal of the American Medical Association* 310.18 (2013) 1921–22.
Besson, Corine. "Logical Knowledge and Ordinary Reasoning." *Philosophical Studies* 158.1 (2012) 59–82.
Beziau, Jean-Yves, and Katarzyna Gan-Krzywoszyńska. "Handbook of the World Congress on the Square of Opposition IV." Pontifical Lateran University, Vatican, May 5–9, 2014. https://www.square-of-opposition.org/start4.html.
Billauer, Barbara P. "Admissibility of Scientific Evidence under Daubert: The Fatal Flaws of 'Falsifiability' and 'Falsification.'" (10 Dec 2015) https://papers.ssrn.com/sol3/papers.cfm?abstract_id=2701737.1–77.
Bird, Alexander. "Kuhn and the Historiography of Science." (1980) https://seis.bristol.ac.uk/~plajb/research/papers/Kuhn_Historiography_of_Science.pdf, 1–16.
Blood, Casey. "No Support for Scientific Materialism in Physics." *Understanding Quantum Physics and Its Implications*. 1 May 2014. http://implications-of-quantum-physics.com/index.html.
———. "Our Physical World, The Spiritual Art of Personality, and The Mystical Society of the Future." http://dwij.org/forum/future_link/future8_blood.html, 2003.
Bokulich, Peter. Review of Kent W. Stanley, *The Evidence for the Top Quark: Objectivity and Bias in Collaborative Experimentation*. Cambridge University Press, 2004. *The Notre Dame Philosophical Review*, 16 Aug 2005. http://ndpr.nd.edu/review.
Boland, Don. "Phenomenology and Philosophy." Sept 2001. *Universitas*, Center for Thomistic Studies, No. 9. http://www.cts.org.au/2001/phenomenology.htm.
Bøndergaard, Tofte, and Linda Fønss. "Dretske's Last Interview." Tanken University of Copenhagen, online at *Leiter Reports*. http://leiterreports.typepad.com/blog/2013/11/dretskes-last-interview.html.

Bramlett, M. D. and W. D. Mosher. Division of Vital Statistics. "First Marriage Dissolution, Divorce, and Remarriage: United States." *Advance Data, Centers for Disease Control*, No. 323, 31 May 2001.

Brinkman, Susan. "Sex, Lies, and Videotape." The National Liberty Council. *NLJ Online*. Dec 2000/Jan 2001. CatholicCulture.org. http://www.catholicculture.org/culture/library/view.cfm?recnum=6793.

Brown, Curtis. "Notes on Van Fraassen's Constructive Empiricism." http://www.trinity.edu/cbrown/science/realism.html.

Brown, Frederick. "The Last Days of Jean-Paul Sartre: A review of La Cérémonie des adieux by Simone de Beauvoir." *The New Criterion* 1.1 (1982) 70. http://www.newcriterion.com/articles.cfm/The-last-days-of-Jean-Paul-Sartre-6523.

Cannon, Betty. "Hazel E. Barnes 1915–2008: A Farewell to America's Foremost Sartre Scholar." *Journal of the Society for Existential Analysis* 19.2 (2008) 90–103. http://www.biomedsearch.com/article/Hazel-E-Barnes-1915-2008/191214764.

Carr, Fr. Henry. "The Function of the Phantasm in St. Thomas Aquinas." In *Philosophical Essays Presented to John Watson*, edited by John Watson, 179–219. Toronto: University of St. Michael's College, University of Toronto, 1922. http://www.arcliive.org/details/functionofpliantaOOcarruoft.

Cartwright, Jon. "Cold-fusion Demonstration: An Update." *Physics World—Member Magazine of the Institute of Physics*, 16 June 2008. http://blog.physicsworld.com/2008/06/16/coldfusion-demonstration-an-up-1/.

Cartwright, Nancy. "When Explanation Leads to Inference." *Philosophical Topics* 13.1 (1982) 111–21.

Cartwright, Nancy, and Jeremy Hardie. *Evidence-Based Policy: A Practical Guide to Doing It Better*. New York: Oxford University Press, 2012.

Caston, Victor. "Aristotle on Consciousness." *Mind* 111.444 (2002) 752–815.

Catalano, Joseph. *A Commentary on Jean-Paul Sartre's "Being and Nothingness."* Chicago: University of Chicago Press, 1985.

Chalmers, David. *The Conscious Mind: In Search of a Theory of Conscious Experience*. Oxford: Oxford University Press, 1997.

Charlton, Bruce. "Science is fundamentally self-regulated by the integrity of individual scientists: therefore young scientists must develop their personal qualities, as well as learning their subject." *The Winnower*. 2016. https://thewinnower.com/papers/4999-science-is-fundamentally-self-regulated-by-the-integrity-of-individual-scientists-therefore-young-scientists-must-develop-their-personal-qualities-as-well-as-learning-their-subject?review_it=true.

Chen, Ruet-Lin. "Experimental Individuation and Retail Arguments." 3–5 Nov 2016 at the PSA meeting. http://philsci.org/images/psa2016-program.pdf.

Chubb, T. A. "In Honor of Yoshiaki Arata." ICCF-14 Inter. Conference on Condensed Matter Nuclear Science, 2008, Washington DC. http://www.scribd.com/doc/39624711/Yoshiaki-Arata-Paper-on-Cold-Fusion.

Ckakravartty, Anjan. Review of Evandro Agazzi and Massimo Pauri, eds., *The Reality of the Unobservable: Observability, Unobservability and Their Impact on the Issue of Scientific Realism*. *British Journal for the Philosophy of Science* 54 (2003) 359–63.

Clark, Joseph, S.J. *Conventional Logic and Modern Logic*. Preface by W. V. Quine. MD: Woodstock College Press. Issued by the American Catholic Philosophical Association, Washington DC, 1952.

Clewis, Robert. "Review of *The Sublime and Its Teleology: Kant—German Idealism—Phenomenology*, edited by Donald Loose (Brill, 2011)." Kant Studies Online. 2014. http://www.kantstudiesonline.net/.

Compton, John. "Natural Science and the Experience of Nature." *Phenomenology in America*, edited by James Edie, 89–94. Chicago: Quadrangle, 1967.

———. "Reinventing the Philosophy of Nature." *The Review of Metaphysics* 33.1 (1979) 3–28. http://www.u.arizona.edu/~aversa/scholastic/pdf.

Congressional Report, 114th Congress 2nd Session, House of Representatives, Report 114-537, National Authorization Act for Fiscal Year 2017, Committee on Armed Services House of Representatives on H.R. 4090 together with Additional Views, May 4, 2016, p. 87.

Cooper, Anderson. "Neuroscientist Studying Brain Scans Discovers He Has the Brain of a Psychopath." *Anderson Cooper 360 Degrees*. 10 Jan 2014. http://transcripts.cnn.com/ TRANSCRIPTS/1401/10/acd.01.html.

Copi, Irving. *Symbolic Logic*. Toronto: Macmillan, 1972.

Curtis, Lorenzo. *Atomic Structure and Lifetimes: A Conceptual Approach*. New York: Cambridge University Press, 2003.

Craig, William Lane. "The Death of Victor Stenger." *Reasonable Faith*. 28 Sept 2014. http://www.reasonablefaith.org/the-death-of-victor-stenger.

Daston, Lorraine "The Naturalistic Fallacy Is Modern." *Isis: A Journal of the History of Science Society* 105.3 (2014) 579–87. http://www.journals.uchicago.edu/doi/pdfplus/10.1086/678173.

Dawson, J. et al. "An Investigation of Risk Factors for Symptomatic Osteoarthritis of the Knee in Women Using a Life Course Approach." *Journal of Epidemiology & Community Health* 57.10 (2003) 823–30.

De Vaus, D. "Marriage and Mental Health." *Family Matters* No. 62 (2002). AIS abstract.

Devaga, Chauncey. "Harvard Psychiatrist Lance Dodes: Donald Trump Is a 'Sociopath' and a 'Very Sick Individual.'" *Salon*, 12 Sept 2017. https://www.salon.com/2017/09/12/harvard-psychiatrist-lance-dodes-donald-trump-is-a-sociopath-and-a-very-sick-individual/.

Devlin, W., and A. Bokulich, eds. *Kuhn's Structure of Scientific Revolutions—50 Years On, Boston Studies in the Philosophy and History of Science* 311 (2015) DOI 10.1007/978-3-319-13383-6_1. http://www.springer.com/us/book/.

Dewan, Lawrence, O.P. "Aristotle as a Source for St. Thomas's Doctrine of Esse." Jacques Maritain Center: Thomistic Institute. http://maritain.nd.edu/jmc/ti00/ dewan.htm, cited 3 July 2014.

Díez, José, and Pablo Lorenzano. "Are Natural Selection Explanatory Models a priori?" *Biology& Philosophy* 30.6 (2015) 786–809.

Dimijian, Greg, M.D. "Evolving Together." *Baylor University Medical Center Proceedings* 13 (Oct 2000) 217–26.

Dion, Sonia Maria. "Pierre Duhem & the Inconsistency between Instrumentalism and Natural Classification." *Studies in History and Philosophy of Science Part A* 44.1 (2013) 12–19.

Dixon, Keith. "Is Cultural Relativism Self-refuting?" *British Journal of Sociology* 28.1 (1977)   75–88.   http://www.jstor.org/stable/589709?seq=1#page_scan_tab_contents.

Dragoset, Lisa, et al. "School Improvement Grants." 2017. US Ed Department: American Institute for Research and Institute of Education Sciences, https://ies.ed.gov/ncee/pubs/20174013/pdf.

Dretske, Fred I. *Seeing and Knowing*. Chicago: University of Chicago Press, 1988.

Ebbesen, Sten. "The Paris Arts Faculty: Siger of Brabant, Boethius of Dacia, Radulphus Brito." *Routledge History of Philosophy Vol. III—Medieval Philosophy*, edited by John Marenbon, 269–90. New York: Routledge, 1998.

Editor. "Winners Announced for the European Healthcare Design Awards 2016." *Architects For Health*. 2016. http://europeanhealthcarede;sign2017.salus.global/conference-show/european-healthcare-design-2016.

Editorial Staff. "Did Helen Gurley Brown Leave the World a Better Place for Women?" *Boomer Magazine*, August 2012. https://www.facebook.com/BoomerMag.

Editorial Staff. "Metaphysics." *Philosophy to Go: Where Science Meets Philosophy*. 2011. http://www.philosophytogo.org/wordpress/?

Efremov, A. V., K. Goeke, and P. V. Pobylitsa. "Glucon and Qurak Distributions in Large Nc QCD: Theory Versus Phenomenology." *Physics Letters B* 488.2 (2000) 183–86.

Egnor, Michael. "Materialist Neuroscience and the 'Hard Problem' of Consciousness." *Evolution News & Views*. 2008. http://www.evoltionnews.org/2008/01/materialist_neuroscience_and_t004723.

Einstein, Albert. "Reply to Critics." In *Albert Einstein: Philosopher-Scientist*, edited by Paul Schilpp, 673–79. New York: Tuber, 1951.

Embree, Lester. "The Phenomenological Derivation of Oughts and Shalls from Ises or Why It Is Right to Take the Stairs." http://www.lesterembree.net/stairmaster.htm.

Estany, Anna. "The Thesis of Theory-Laden Observation in Light of Cognitive Psychology." *Philosophy of Science* 68.2 (2001) 203–17.

Fagan, Patrick, and Robert Rector. "The Effects of Divorce on America." *Backgrounder on Family and Marriage* No. 1373, 5 June 2000.

Fagin, Patrick, and K. Johnson. "Marriage: Safest Place for Women and Children." *Policy, Research and Analysis—Heritage Foundation* No. 1535 (2002). Washington DC 2002.

FitzGerald, Desmond. "Maritain and Gilson on the Challenge of Democracy." *Reassessing the Liberal State: Reading Maritain's Man and the State*, edited by Timothy Fuller and John Hittinger. Washington DC: American Maritain Association Publications, 2001.

Fleckinstein, Dana. "A Theological Style: Dulles and Guarino . . . Loyal, Receptive Yet Rigorous, Modest, Detached." http://fleckinstein.blogspot.com/2016/06/a-theological-style-dulles-and.html.

Frisch, Mathias. "Laws of Physics." *European Review* 22 (2014) S33–S49. http://faculty.philosophy.umd.edu/mfrisch/papers/laws.

Frisch, Mathias, et al. "Sexually Transmitted Infection as a Cause of Anal Cancer." *New England Journal of Medicine* 337 (1997) 1350–58.

Frunza, Sandu, and Mihaela Frunza, eds. *Religion, Culture & Ideology in America*. SCIRI and Academic Society for the Research of Religions & Ideologies. Bucharest: Tritonic Group Editorial, 2012.

Fuller, Steve. "Discussion Notes: Is There Philosophical Life after Kuhn?" *Philosophy of Science* 68.4 (2001) 565–72.

Gattei, Stefano. *Karl Popper's Philosophy of Science: Rationality without Foundations.* New York: Routledge, 2008. http://ndpr.nd.edu/news/24108-karl-popper-s-philosophy-of-science-rationality-without-foundations/.

Geach, Peter. *God and the Soul.* New York: Schocken, 1969.

Ghaemi, Nassir, MD. "Profiles of the Past: R. D. Laing." *Mental Health*, 16 Apr 2013. http://boards.medscape.com/forums/?128.

Ghijsen, Harmen. Review of John Searle, *Seeing Things as They Are: A Theory of Perception* (New York: Oxford University Press, 2015). *Disputatio* 8.42 (2016) 125–31. http://www.disputatio.letras.ulisboa.pt/wp-content/uploads/2016/05/Ghijsen_Seeing-Things-as-They-Are-by-Searle.pdf.

Gholipour, Bhar. "Hidden STD Epidemic." *Live Science*, 6 Oct 2014. http://www.livescience.com/48100-sexually-transmitted-infections-50states-map.html.

Giancoli, Douglas C. *Physics: Principles with Applications.* 7th ed. Boston: Addison-Wesley, 2013.

Giang, Vivian. "7 Signs You're Working with a Psychopath." *Business Insider*, 6 Nov 2013. http://www.businessinsider.com/signs-that-youre-dealing-wth-a-psychopath-2013-11.

Gibson, Arthur. "Ockham's World and Future." In *Routledge History of Philosophy, Vol. III—Medieval Philosophy*, edited by John Marenbon, 329–67. New York: Routledge, 1998.

Gilson, Étienne. *The Spirit of Medieval Philosophy.* Gifford Lectures 1931–32. Translated by A. H. C. Downes. New York: Scribner's Sons, 1940.

Glazer, Breeze, Perkins Will, and Robin Glazer. The Creative Center: Arts in Healthcare. "Designing for Health." *Healthcare*. 2016. http://www.contractdesign.com/practice/healthcare/Beyond-the-Building-Leveraging-Art-to-Improve-Health-Outcomes-37644.shtml.

Gligorov, Nada. "Determinism and Advances in Neuroscience." *Virtual Mentor, American Medical Association* 14.6 (2012) 489–93.

Glueck, M. A. (M.D.) and R. J. Cihak, M.D. "Medical Journal Suffers Times Syndrome." *NewsMax.com.* 19 Aug 2003.

Grayling, A. C. "Wittgenstein on Scepticism and Certainty—page 2." http://www.acgrayling.com/wittgenstein-on-scepticism-and-certainty-page-2.

Green, Jeffrey. *The Shadow of Unfairness: A Plebeian Theory of Democracy.* New York: Oxford University Press, 2016.

Green, Michael. "Tutorial—Existential Import." http://www.wwnorton.com/college/phil/logic3/ch8/import.htm.

Greene, Joshua. "Home Page." 8 Feb 2014. http://www.wjh.harvard.edu/~jgreene/.

Gueguen, John. "St. Edith Stein on Phenomenology and Scholasticism." 18 July 2003. From "A Study of "Husserl and Aquinas: A Comparison." 1929. In *Collected Works of Edith Stein*, Vol. 8, edited by L. Gelber and Michael Linssen, OCD, 1–63. Washington, DC: Institute of Carmelite Studies, 2000.

Gyelvan, M. (Clinical ed.). *Professional Guide to Diseases.* Philadelphia: Reed Elsevier, 2001.

Hack, Susan. "Disentangling *Daubert*: An Epistemological Study in Theory and Practice." *The Journal of Philosophy, Science & Law* 5.1 (2005) 25–36. http://jpsl.org/archives/disentangling-daubert-epistemological-study-theory-and-practice/.

———. "Epistemological Reflections of an Old Feminist." *Reason Papers* 18 (1993) 31–43. https://re;asonpapers. com/pdf/18/rp_18_3.pdf.

———. "Just Say 'No' to Logical Negativism." In *Karl Raimund Popper: Une épistémologie sans visage et sans rivage,* edited by Marcel Nguimbi, *Cahiers Epistemo-Logiques* 4.1 (2016) 33–54. *University of Miami Legal Studies Research Paper* No. 16–31. Available at SSRN: https://ssrn.com/abstract=2808254.

Hacking, Ian. "Experimentalism and Scientific Realism." *Philosophical Topics* 13.1 (1982) 71–87.

Hallberg, Margareta. "Gender and Philosophy of Science: The Case of Mary Hesse." *Studies in History and Philosophy of Science Part A* 43.2 (2012) 333–40.

Halvorson, Hans. "What Scientific Theories Could Not Be." *Philosophy of Science* 79.2 (2012) 183–206.

Hankinson, S., A. Colditz, J. Manson, F. Speizer, and J. Manson. *Healthy Women, Healthy Lives: A Harvard Medical School Book.* New York, Simon & Schuster, 2002.

Hankovic, N., M. Ivkovic, D. Sokie, A. Llanovic, S. Milovanovic, B. Filipovic, D. Tiosavljevic, V. Bojic. "Dementia Paralytica (neuro-syphilis): A Clinical Case Study." *World Journal of Biological Psychiatry* 4.3 (2003) 135–38.

Hanna, Joseph. "The Scope and Limits of Scientific Objectivity." *Philosophy of Science* 71.3 (2004) 339–61.

Hardin, Larry. "Perceptual Transparency." *Dialectica* 60.3 (2006) 341–45.

Hare, Robert. "The Wall Street Ten Percenters." *Without Conscience,* 20 May 2012. http://hare.org/comments/comment2.html.

Hare, Robert, and Paul Babiak. *Snakes in Suits: When Psychopaths Go to Work.* New York: Harper Business, 2007.

Harrison, G. W. "Neuroeconomics: A Rejoinder." *Economics and Philosophy* 24, Special Issue 03 (2008) 533–44. https://www.itd.bus.ucf.edu/cdn/economics/workingpapers/2008-02.pdf

Hawa, S. "Language as Freedom in Sartre's Philosophy." Paer given at 20th World Congress of Philosophy, Boston, 10–15 Aug 1998. http://www.bu.edu/wep/MainLite.

Hebb, D. O. *The Organization of Behavior: A Neuropsychological Theory.* New York: Taylor & Francis, 2002.

Heck, R. G. "Nonconceptual Content and the 'Space of Reasons.'" *The Philosophical Review* 109.4 (2000) 483–523.

Heidegger, M. *An Introduction to Metaphysics.* Translated by R. Manheim. New York: Doubleday, 1961.

Hendry, R. F. "Are Realism and Instrumentalism Methodologically Indifferent?" *Philosophy of Science* 68.3 (2000) 25–37.

Hesketh, Therese. "Abnormal Sex Ratios in Human Populations: Causes and Consequences." *Proceedings of the National Academy of Sciences,* 103.38 (2006) 13271–75. doi:10.1073/pnas.0602203103.

Hesse, Mary. "Is There an Independent Observation Language?" In *The Nature and Function of Scientific Theories,* edited by Robert Colodny, 36–77. Pittsburgh, PA: University of Pittsburgh Press, 1970.

———. "Laws and Theories." *The Encyclopedia of Philosophy,* Vol. 7, edited by Paul Edwards, 404–10. New York: Macmillan, 1967.

Hitti, Miranda. "The Health Perks of Marriage." *WebMD,* 15 Dec 2004. https://www.webmd.com/balance/news/20041215/health-perks-of-marriage.

Holton, G., H. Chang, and E. Jurkowitsz. "How a Scientific Discovery Is Made." *American Scientist—Sigma Xi Scientific Research Society* 84 (1996) 364–76.

Holveck, Eleanore. "The Birth of American Existentialism: Hazel E. Barnes, a Singular Universal." *Philosophy Today* 42 (1998) 7–16. http://www.questia.com/library/journal/1P3-42640566/the-birth-of-american-existentialism-hazel-e-barnes.

Horgan, John. "Is Lawrence Krauss a Physicist, or Just a Bad Philosopher?" 20 Nov 2015. http://blogs.scientificamerican.com/cross-check/is-lawrence-krauss-aphysicist—or-just-a-bad-philosopher/.

———. "Profile: Reluctant Revolutionary: Thomas S. Kuhn Unleashed 'Paradigm' on the World" *Scientific American*, 9 May 1991, 40–49.

———. "Was Philosopher Paul Feyerabend Really Science's 'Worst Enemy?'" *Scientific American*, 24 Oct 2016. https://blogs.scientificamerican.com/cross-check/was-philosopher-paul-feyerabend-really-science-s-worst-enemy/.

Hourani, George F. "Thrasymachus' Definition of Justice in Plato's Republic." *Phronesis* 7.2 (1962) 110–20. http://www.jstor.org/stble/ 4181704?seq=2.

Hoyningen-Huene, P. *Reconstructing Scientific Revolutions: Thomas S. Kuhn's Philosophy of Science*. Translated by Alexander T. Levine with a foreword by Thomas S. Kuhn. Chicago: University of Chicago Press, 1993. doclegend.com_paul-hoyningen-huene-reconstructing-scientific-revolutionspdf.

Hughes, John, M.D. "The Mozart Effect." *Journal of the Royal Society of Medicine* 94.6 (2001) 316–17.

Hull, Richard T. "Biography: Robert George Turnbull." The American Philosophical Association Centennial Series, 2013. https://www.pdcnet.org/pdc/bvdb.nsf/purchase?openform&fp=apapa&id=apapa_2013_0541_0543_277.

Hume, David. "Of the Idea of Necessary Connexion." *An Enquiry Concerning Human Understanding*, http://www.bartleby.com/37/3/9.html.

Hyde, Timothy. Review of Caitlin Smith Gilson, *The Metaphysical Presuppositions of Being-in-the-World: A Confrontation between St. Thomas Aquinas and Martin Heidegger* (New York: Continuum, 2010). *Notre Dame Philosophical Reviews*. http://ndpr.nd.edu/news/24496-the-metaphysical-presuppositions-of-being-in-the-world-a-confrontation-between-st-thomas-aquinas-and-martin-heidegger/.

Ingram, David. *The History of Continental Philosophy*. Vol. 5. Edited by David Ingram and Alan Schrift. London: Acumen, 2010.

Ivanova, Milena. "Pierre Duhem's Good Sense as a Guide to Theory Choice." *Studies in History and Philosophy of Science Part A* 41.1 (2010) 58–64.

Jacquette, Dale. "Subalteration & Existence Presuppositions in an Unconventionally Formalized Canonical Square of Opposition." *Logica Universalis* 10.2–3 (2016) 191–213.

Jaki, Stanley. *The Limits of a Limitless Science and Other Essays*. Wilmington, DE: Intercollegiate Studies Institute, 2000.

Jaroszyński, Piotr. "A Brief Overview of Lublin Thomism." http://www.piotrjaroszynski.pl/2014-01-30-14-36-01/english/for-reading/757-a-brief-overview-of-lublin-thomism.

Jarvie, Ian. "Popper's Philosophy and the Methodology of Social Science." In *The Cambridge Companion to Popper*, edited by Jeremy Shearmur and Geoffrey Stokes, 284–317. New York: Cambridge University Press, 2016.

Jellinek, M., M. Murphy, M. Little, M. Pagano, D. Comer, and K. Kelleher. "Use of the Pediatric Symptom Checklist to Screen for Psychosocial Problems in Pediatric Primary Care." *Archives of Pediatrics and Adolescent Medicine* 153.3 (1999) 254–60.

Jones, Nicholaos. "Don't Blame the Idealizations." *Journal for General Philosophy of Science* 44.1 (2013) 85–100.
Jones, Roger B. "Analytic Positivism." 7 Jan 2016. http://www.rbjones.com/rbjpub/philos/analypos.pdf.
Jorgensen, Larry M. "Seventeenth-Century Theories of Consciousness." *Stanford Encyclopedia of Philosophy*. 2014. http://plato.stanford.edu/entries/consciousness-17th/.
Kalb, Claudia. "Should You Have Your Baby Now?" *Newsweek* 88, 13 Aug 2001, 40.
Kall, Rob. "Chomsky Talks about Psychopaths and Sociopaths." *Op Ed News*, 15 Feb 2014. https://chomsky.info/20140215_2/.
Kant, Immanuel. *Critique of Pure Reason*. Translated by N. K. Smith. New York: Macmillan, 1965.
Kawalec, Pawel. "Understanding Science of the New Millennium." *Archives for the Philosophy of Science* (2005). http://philsci-archive.pitt.edu/archive/00002558.
Kelsky, Karen. "The Professor Is in: Let Us Never Speak of the Campus Strategic Plan Again." *The Chronicle of Higher Education*, 8 Apr 2014. http://chroniclevitae.com/news/430-the-professor-is-in.
Keshet, Ezra, and Florian Schwarz. "De Re/De Dicto." Sept 2014. http://florianschwarz.net/wp-content/uploads/papers/De_Re___De_Dicto.pdf.
Kidd, Ian. "Why Did Feyerabend Defend Astrology? Integrity, Virtue, and the Authority of Science." *Social Epistemology: A Journal of Knowledge, Culture and Policy* 30.4 (2016) 464–82. http://www.tandfonline.com/doi/abs/10.1080/02691728.2015.1031851?
Kiehl, Kent, and Morris Hoffman. "The Criminal Psychopath: History, Neuroscience, Treatment, and Economics." *Jurimetrics* 51 (2011) 355–97. https://www.ncbi.nlm.nih.gov/pmc/articles/ PMC4059069/.
Kind, Amy, and Peter Kungs. *Knowledge through Imagination*. Oxford: Oxford University Press, 2016.
Kirley, Kevin. "Father Henry Carr and Catholic Education in Canada." *The Free Library*, 1999. Catholic Insight, 31 July 2014. http://www.thefreelibrary.com/Father+Henry+Carr +and+Catholic+education+in+Canada-a076560118.
Klus, Helen. "The Limitations of Science." *The Star Garden*. 2016. http://www.thestargarden.co.uk/Should-we-trust-theoretical-science.html.
Kluth, F. J. "Hairstyles and Cosmetics in Ancient Greece." Paper presented to the Ohio Academy of Science, 2001. http://www.fjkluth.com/hair.
Knuuttila, Simo. "Medieval Modal Theories and Modal Logic." *Handbook of the History of Logic. Volume 2: Mediaeval and Renaissance Logic*, edied by Dov M. Gabbay and John Woods, 505–78. Amsterdam: Elsevier, 2008. http://home.uchicago.edu/~mendelsohn/Knuuttila.pdf.
Koertege, Noretta, and Daphne Patai. *Professing Feminism: Education and Indoctrination in Higher Education*. New York: Lexington, 2003.
Koons, Robert. "A New Look at the Cosmological Argument." *American Philosophical Quarterly* 34.2 (1997) 193–211.
Körner, Stephan. *Experience and Theory: An Essay on the Philosophy of Science*. London: Routledge & Kegan Paul, 1966.
Kowalski, Ludwik. "Julian Schwinger and Cold Fusion." D/Mathematical Sciences at Montclair State University, 8 Jan 2003. http://pages.csam.montclair.edu/~kowalski/cf/33schwinger.html.

Kreeft, Peter. "First Cause Argument." 2005. http://www.peterkreeft.com/topics/first-cause.
Kuhn, Thomas S. *The Essential Tension*. Chicago: University of Chicago Press, 1977.
Kurtz, Stanley. "Can We Make Boys and Girls Alike?" *City Journal* (Spring 2005). https://www.city-journal.org/html/can-we-make-boys-and-girls-alike-12866.html.
Kutrovátz, Gábor. "An Epistemological Cross-Section of Science Studies: In the Context of the Science Wars." PhD diss., Budapest: Budapest University of Technology and Economics, 2005.
Kvikstad A., et al. "Cancer Risk and Prognosis in Norway: Comparing Women in Their First Marriage with Women Who Never Married." *Journal of Epidemiology and Community Health* 50.1 (1996) 1826–27.
Lakatos, Imre. *The Methodology of Scientific Research Programmes: Philosophical Papers I*. Edited by J. Worrall and G. Guthrie. New York: Cambridge University Press, 1980.
Langbert, M. B. "Managing Psychopathic Employees." *Cornell HR Review*, 16 June 2010. http://www.cornellhrreview.org/managing-psychopathic-employees/.
Lashin, E. I., and Djamel Dou. "On the Correctness of Quantum Raychaudhri Equation and Its Implications." *Astro-Ph from Argelander-Institut fur Astronomie (AIFA)* 2016. https://www.researchgate.net/publication/303992808_On_the_Correctness_of_Quantum_Raychaudhuri_Equation_and_its_Implications.
Lauden, Larry. "A Confutation of Convergent Realism." *Philosophy of Science* 48.1 (1981) 19–45.
———. "Two Dogmas of Methodology." *Philosophy of Science* 43.4 (1976) 585–97.
Legg, Catherine. "Things Unreasonably Compulsory: A Peircean Challenge to a Humean Theory of Perception, Particularly with Respect to Perceiving Necessary Truths." *Cognitio*, 2014. http://www.commens.org/sites/default/files/biblio_attachments/things_unreasonably_compulsory_a_peircean_challenge_to_a_humean_theory_of_perception_particularly_with_respect_to_perceiving_necessary_truths.pdf.
Lehrman, Sally. "The Virtues of Promiscuity." Alternet. 21 July 2002. http://www.alternet.org/story/13648.
Levinson, Arlene. "A Century Awash in Blood–Spotlight Genocide." *The Associated Press*, 17 Sept 1995.
Levy, Neil. Review of Antoine Suuarez and Peter Adams, eds., *Is Science Compatible with Free Will? Exploring Free Will and in the Light of Quantum Physics and Neuroscience* (New York: Springer, 2013). http://ndpr.nd.edu/news/38756-is-science-compatible-with-free-will-exploring-free-will-and-consciousness-in-the-light-of-quantum-physics-and-neuroscience/.
Levy, Stuart, M.D. "Drugs Barely Keep Ahead of Bacteria." *Kentucky Enquirer* 338, 3 March 1995.
Liang, San. "Information Flow and Causality as Rigorous Notions *Ab Inition*." *Physical Review* E 94 (2016). https://doi.org/10.1103/PhysRevE.94.052201.
Luise, Vincent de, M.D. "Mozart's Effect on Us: A Twenty-Five Year Meta-Analysis of the Mozart Effect." http://amusicalvision.blogspot.com/2014/06/mozarts-effect-on-us-twenty-year-meta.html.
MacFarquhar, Larissa. "Two Heads: A Marriage Devoted to the Mind-Body Problem." *The New Yorker*, 12 Feb 2007. http://www.newyorker.com/magazine/2007/02/12/two-heads.

———. "Why Interpret Quantum Physics?" *Open Journal of Philosophy* 6 (2016) 86–102. http://www.scirp.org/journal/ojpp.
MacKinnon, Edward. "Introduction." In *The Problem of Scientific Realism*, edited by Edward MacKinnon, 1–71. New York: Appleton-Century-Crofts, 1972.
———. "The Truth of Scientific Claims." *Philosophy of Science* 49.3 (1982) 437–62.
Magee, Joseph M. "Aquinas and the Freedom of the Will." Aquinas Online, 2015. http://www.aquinasonline.com/Topics/freewill.html.
Maisey, D. S., et al. "Characteristics of Male Attractiveness for Women." *The Lancet: International Journal of Medical Science*, 353.9163 (1999) 1500.
Malcolm, Norman. *Ludwig Wittgenstein: A Memoir*. New York: Oxford University Press, 1984.
Maller, Mark. "Problems with Reification." PhilPapers, 8 Aug 2013. http://philpapers.org/post/7859.
Marcus, Ruth Barcan. *Modalities: Philosophical Essays*. New York: Oxford University Press, 1993.
Martellucci, Sergio et al., eds. *COLD FUSION—The History of Research in Italy*. Rome: ENEA, 2011. http://www.enea.it/en/publications/volume-pdf/Cold_Fusion_Italy.pdf.
Massarenti, Armando (an interview with). "Constructivism." Philosophy to Go: Where Science Meets Philosophy, 2011. http://www.philosophytogo.org/wordpress/?p=2283.
Massimi, Michela. "Non-Defensible Middle Ground for Experimental Realism: Why We Are Justified to Believe in Colored Quarks." *Philosophy of Science* 71.1 (2004) 36–60.
Mastin, Luke. "Ethical Non-Naturalism." Philosophy Basics, 2008. http://www.philosophybasics.com/branch_ethical_nonnaturalism.html.
Mayer, Jane. *Dark Money*. New York: Doubleday, 2016.
Mayo, Deborah. "Peircean Induction and the Error-Correcting Thesis (Part I)." *Transactions of the Charles S. Peirce Society* 41.2 (2005) 299–319. https://errorstatistics.com/2016/09/10/peircean-induction-and-the-error-correcting-thesis-part-i-3/.
McClamrock, Ron. "Final Lecture on Sartre." SUNY, Albany, Spring 1988. http://www.albany.edu/~ron/papers/sartre.html.
McPherson, M. "Needed: A Nobel Prize for the Giants of Social Science." *The Chronicle of Higher Education*, 30 Jan 1998.
Miller, David. "Qualitative Theory of Verisimilitude." *British Journal for the Philosophy of Science* 25 (1974) 178–88.
Modesti, P. A., et al. "Daily Sessions of Music Learning in Mild Hypertension Can Reduce 24-Hour Ambulatory Blood Pressure after One Month." Paper presented to the American Society of Hypertension, 14–17 May 2008 in New Orleans. http://www.mindcull.com.
Moody, Ernest A. *Studies in Medieval Philosophy, Science, and Logic*. Berkeley: University of California Press, 1975.
Mudur, Ganapati. "Indian Medical Authorities Act on Antenatal Sex Selection." *British Medical Journal* 319.14 (1999). http://www.bmj.com/cgi/content/full/319/7207/401.
Murti, T. R. V. *The Central Thought of Buddhism*. 2nd ed. London: Allen & Unwin, 1974.
Nahmias, Eddy. "Did My Brain Make Me Do It? Free Will and Neuroscience." Symposium: Does Neuroscience Have Normative Implications? 15–16 April

2016 at Illinois Institute of Technology, Chicago, abstract. http://ethics.iit.edu/neuroscience_normativeimplications#Nahmias.
NASA. "Expanding Universe Shapes." 2007. http://map.gsfc.gov/universe/bb_concepts.
Newton-Smith, W. H. *The Rationality of Science*. London: Taylor & Francis e-Library, 2003.
Niiniluoto, Ilkka. "Scientific Progress as Increasing Verisimilitude." *Studies in History & Philosophy of Science* 46 (2014) 73–77. http://www.sciencedirect.com/science/article/pii/S0039368114000144.
Norris, Christopher. "Hilary Putnam on Realism, Truth & Reason." *Philosophy Now* 49 (2016). https://philosophynow.org/issues/49/Hilary_Putnam_on_Realism_Truth_and_Reason.
Novak, Patricia (clinical ed.). *Mosby's Medical, Nursing and Allied Health Dictionary*. Oxford: Elsevier Science, 2002.
Oddie, Graham. "Truth, Verification, Verisimilitude, and Evidence: Philosophical Aspects." *International Encyclopedia of Social and Behavioral Sciences* 11 (2001) 15932–37. http://dx.doi.org/10.1016/B0-08-043076-7/01014-7.
Panné, Jean-Louis, et al. *The Black Book of Communism: Crimes, Terror, Repression*. Cambridge: Harvard University Press, 1999.
Parsons, Kathryn Payne. "Nietzsche and Moral Change." In *Nietzsche*, edited by Robert Solomon, 169–93. New York: Anchor, 1973.
Paul, A. M., J. D. Sommer, and R. T. Harris. "Memorial Statement for Raymond E. Olson." Miami University Faculty Memorial Statements, 9 April 1969. http://digital.lib.miamioh.edu/cdm/ref/collection/facmem/id/266.
Penfield, Wilder. *Mystery of the Mind: A Critical Study of Consciousness and the Human Brain*. Princeton, NJ: Princeton University Press, 1978.
Peters, Michael A., ed. *Heidegger, Education, and Modernity*. Lanham, MD: Rowman & Littlefield, 2002.
Petrenko, V. W., and R. W. Whitworth. *Physics of Ice*. New York: Oxford University Press, 2002.
Pietsch, Wolgang. "Hidden Underdetermination: A Case Study in Classical Electrodynamics." *International Studies in the Philosophy of Science* 26.2 (2012) 125–51.
Plato. Meno. Translated by W. K. C. Guthrie. In *Plato: The Collected Dialogues*, edited by Edith Hamilton and H. Cairnes. Princeton, NJ: Princeton University Press, 1971.
Popper, Karl. "Quantum Theory and the Schism in Physics." From *Postscript to the Logic of Scientific Discovery*, edited by W. W. Bartley, 97–211. Totowa, NJ: Rowman and Littlefield, 1982.
Popper, Karl, and David Miller. "A Proof of the Impossibility of Inductive Probability." *Nature* 302 (1983) 667–68. http://doi.10.1038/302687a0.
Preston, John. *Conjectures and Refutations: The Growth of Scientific Knowledge*. London: Routledge & Kegan Paul, 1963.
———. *The Logic of Scientific Discovery*. London: Hutchinson, 1968.
———. "Paul Feyerabend." *Stanford Encyclopedia of Philosophy*. 2016. https://plato.stanford.edu/entries/feyerabend/.
Puligandla, R. "Thoughts on Studying Consciousness." *Metanexus*. 2003. www.users.global net.co.uk.
Putnam, Hilary. "Philosophers and Human Understanding." *Scientific Explanation*, edited by A. Heath, 99–120. Oxford: Clarendon, 1981.

———. *Philosophy in an Age of Science*. Edited by M. De Caro and D. Macarthur. Cambridge: Harvard University Press, 2012.

———. "Problems with the Observational/Theoretical Distinction." *Scientific Inquiry*, edited by Robert Klee, 25–29. New York: Oxford University Press, 1999.

———. "What Theories Are Not." In *Logic, Methodology, and the Philosophy of Science*, edited by E. Nale, P. Suppes, and A. Tarski, 240–51. Berkeley: Stanford University Press, 1963.

Rabinowitz, Mario. "In Memory of Julian Schwinger." *Transactions of Fusion Technology* 26 (1994) ix–x. http://arxiv.org/abs/physics/0303078v1.

Ramberg, Bjørn. "Richard Rorty (Against Epistemology)." In *Stanford Encyclopedia of Philosophy*, 2011. http://plato.stanford.edu/entries/rorty/#2.

Ratzinger, Joseph, and the Interdicasterial Commission. *Catechism of the Catholic Church*, 1994. http://www.vatican.va/archive/ENG0015/_P7Z.HTM.

Rawlings, Hunter R. "Public Colleges Face Major Threat from Some Trustees." *The Chronicle of Higher Education*, Nov 2014. http://chronicle.com/article/Video-Public-Colleges-Face/150097/.

Redpath, Peter A. "An Abbreviated Biography of Étienne Gilson's Intellectual Life." Adler-Aquinas Institute. 2013. http://www.adleraquinasinstitute.org/etienne-gilson-society/biography-of-etienne-gilsons-intellectual-life/.

———. "Globalization, Nationalism, and the Present US Immigration Troubles." *Studia Elckie* 14 (2012) 137–46.

———. *A Not-So-Elementary Christian Metaphysics*. Manitou Springs, CO: Socratic, 2012.

———. "Understanding the Current Revolution in Western Higher Education." In *Art and Realism (Sztuka i realism): Commemorative Book, Jubilee Birthday and Scientific Work of Professor Henry Kieresia at KUL*, edited by Fr. T. Duma, A. Maryniarczyk SDB, and P. Sulenta, 703–20. Lublin: Polish Society of St. Thomas Aquinas and the Faculty of Philosophy—Catholic University of Lublin, 2014.

Reiss, Julian. "Epistemic Virtues and Concept Formation in Economics." PhD diss., London School of Economics and Political Science, University of London, 2002. http://etheses.lse.ac.uk/1646/1/U162150.pdf.

Roberts, T., S. Schleif, and J. M. Dlugosz, eds. "What Is the Experimental Basis of Special Relativity?" *Usenet Physics FAQ*, 17 March 2014. University of California, Riverside. http://wwwdesy.de/user/projects/Physics/Relativity/SR/experiments.html.

Rohrlich, Fritz. "Cognitive Scientific Realism." *Philosophy of Science* 68.2 (2001) 185–202.

———. "Realism Despite Cognitive Antireductionism." *International Studies in the Philosophy of Science* 18.1 (2004) 73–88.

———, "Scientific Realism: A Challenge to Physicists." *Foundations of Physics* 26.443 (1996) 443–51. http://link.springer.com/article/10.1007/BF02071214.

———. "The Theory of the Electron." Thirty-first Joseph Henry Lecture, read before the Society 11 May 1962. http://www.philsoc.org/1962Spring/1526transcript.html.

Rohrlich, Fritz, and Larry Hardin. "Established Theories." *Philosophy of Science* 50.4 (1983) 603–16.

Roney, J. R., et al. "Reading Men's Faces: Women's Mate Attractiveness Judgments Track Men's Testosterone and Interest in Infants." *Proceedings of the Royal*

Society B: Biological Sciences, 9 May 2006, #4, Discussion 12. http://rspb.royalsocietypublishing.org/content/273/1598/2169.full.pdf+html.
Ross, Kelly L. "The Erotic as an Aesthetic Category." Friesian.com, 17 July 2014. http://www.friesian.com/erotic.htm.
Ross, Steven. Review of "Seeing Things As They Are: A Theory of Perception." *Essays in Philosophy* 17.1 (2016). http://dx.doi.org/10.7710/152605691550.
Roth, Wolff-Michael, and Alfredo Bautista. "Transcriptions, Mathematical Cognition, and Epistemology." *The Montana Mathematics Enthusiast* 8.1–2 (2011) 51–76.
Rothwell, Jed. *Cold Fusion and the Future*. 4th ed. LENR-CANR.org. http://lenr-canr.org/wordpress/.
Russell, Bertrand. *The Autobiography of Bertrand Russell*. Boston: Little, Brown, & Co., 1967.
———. *Our Knowledge of the External World*. London: Allen & Unwin, 1914.
Salmon, M. *Introduction to Logic & Critical Thinking*. New York: HBJ, 1989.
Sargent, R. M. "Baconian Experimentalism." *Philosophy of Science* 68 (2001) 311–18.
Sartre, Jean-Paul. *Being and Nothingness*. Translated and with an introduction by Hazel Barnes. New York: Philosophical Library, 1956.
———. *Existentialism and Human Emotions*. Citadel-Reissue ed. New York: Philosophical Library, 2000.
———. *Existentialism Is a Humanism*. Translated by Carol Macomber. New Haven: Yale University Press, 2007.
———. *The Imagination*. Translated by Kenneth Williford and David Rudrauf. New York: Routledge, 2012.
———. *The Transcendence of the Ego: An Existentialist Theory of Consciousness*. New York: Hill and Wang, 1991.
Schick, Finnegan. "Up Close: Is Yale Becoming too Corporate?" *Yale News*, 14 April 2016. http://features.yaledailynews.com/blog/2016/04/14/up-close-is-yale-too-corporate/.
Schlipp, P. A., ed. *The Philosophy of Karl Popper*, Books I and II. La Salle, IL: Open Court, 1974.
Schwandt, Thomas A. "Theory-Observation Distinction." *Sage Dictionary of Qualitative Inquiry*, 3rd ed., 2007. http://dx.doi.org/10.4135/9781412986281.
Schramm, David. "Counting the Cost if Divorce." *The Natural Family*. 2009. http://familyinamerica.org/journals/fall-2009/counting-cost-divorce-what-those-who-know-better-rarely-acknowledge/.
Scorolli, C., S. Ghirlanda, M. Enquist, S. Zattoni, and E. A. Jannini. "Relative Prevalence of Different Fetishes." *International Journal of Impotence Research* 19.4 (2007) 432–37. doi:10.1038/sj.ijir.3901547.
Scottish Qualifications Authority. *2016 Religious and Philosophical Studies*. https://www.sqa.org.uk/pastpapers/papers/instructions/2016/mi_NAH_Religious-Moral-and-Philosophical-Studies_all_2016.pdf.
Secretariat of Pro-Life Activities. U.S. Conference of Catholic Bishops. 2011. http://www.usccb.org/about/pro-life-activities/respect-life-program/2011/upload/life-matters-love-and-marriage.pdf.
Senthilingam, Meera. "5 Things You Need to Know about Antimicrobial Resistance." 2016. http://www.cnn.com/2016/09/21/health/what-is-antimicrobial-resistance-amr/.

Shalkowski, Scott A. "The Ontological Ground of the Alethic Modality." *The Philosophical Review* 103.4 (1994) 669–88.
Shan, Yafeng. "The Structure of Scientific Revolutions." Durham University. https://www.dur.ac.uk/ias/events/events_listings/?eventno=34858.
Shan, Yafeng, et al. "Scientific Realism and the Challenge from the History of Science." Paper given at conference, Indianapolis, 19–21 Feb 2016. http://community.dur.ac.uk/evaluating.realism/people.html.
Shariff, A. F., and J. W. Schooler. "His Brain Made Him Do It: Encouraging a Mechanistic Worldview Reduces Punishment." 2011. http://www.wjh.harvard.edu/~jgreene/.
Shuttleworth, Martyn. "Cathode Ray Experiment: The Electric Experiment by J. J. Thomson." http://explorable.com/cathode-ray-experiment.
Singh, A. "Regulation of Human Sexual Behavior, Sex Revolution and Emergence of AIDS." *Bulletin Ind. Institute of the History of Medicine* 27 (1997) 63–74.
Slavov, Matias. "Empiricism and Relationism Intertwined: Hume and Einstein's Special Theory of Relativity." *Theoria* 31.2 (2016) 247–63. http://www.ehu.eus/ojs/;index.php/THEORIA/article/viewFile/14846/14450.
Smith, A. D. *The Problem of Perception*. Cambridge: Harvard University Press, 2004.
Smith, D. W. "Phenomenology." *Stanford Encyclopedia of Philosophy*. 2013. http://plato.stanford.edu/entries/phenomenology/.
Smith, Howard. *Let There be Light: Modern Cosmology and Kabbalah*. Novato, CA: New World Library, 2006.
Smith, Quentin. "Can Everything Come to Be without a Cause?" *Dialogue: Canadian Philosophical Review* 33.2 (1994) 313–23. https://infidels.org/library/modern/quentin_smith/cause.html.
Smolchenko, Anna. "Putin Dismisses Concerns as Officials Sound Alarm Over Economy." AFP (*Agence France-Presse*) News, 3 Sept 2014.
Sneller, D. H. "Synchronicity or Coincidence: The Limits of Causality." University of Leiden. 2016/2017. https://studiegids.leidenuniv.nl/courses/show/64765/synchronicity-or-coincidence-the-limits-of-causality.
Sokolowski, Msgr. Robert. "Husserl on First Philosophy." In *Philosophy, Phenomenology, Sciences: Essays in Commemoration of Edmund Husserl*, edited by Carlo Ierna, Hanne Jacobs, and Filip Mattens. *Phaenomenologica* 200 (2010) 3–23.
Stanford, P. K. "Refusing the Devil's Bargain: What Kind of Underdetermination Should We Take Seriously." *Philosophy of Science* 68.3 Supplement (2001) S1–S12.
———. "Scientific Realism, the Atomic Theory, and the Catch-All Hypothesis: Can We Test Fundamental Theories Against All Serious Alternatives?" *British Journal for the Philosophy of Science* 60.2 (2009) 253–69.
Stenger, Victor J. "Free Will Is an Illusion." *Huffington Post*, 1 June 2012. http://www.huffingtonpost.com/victor-stenger/free-will-is-an-illusion_b_1562533.html.
Stiftung, Carl F. von Siemens. "The Form of Our Life with Language." Conference at München Germany May 23, 2016–May 25, 2016. http://philevents.org/event/show/22118.
Stone, Cassie. "The Face of Chaos." *Free Inquiry* 13 (1993) 13–14.
Stromberg, Joseph. "The Neuroscientist Who Discovered He Was a Psychopath" (2013) http://www.smithsonianmag.com/science-nature/the-neuroscientist-who-discovered-he-was-a-psychopath-180947814/.
Suppe, Frederick. "Afterword." *The Structure of Scientific Theories*, 2nd ed., edited by Frederick Suppe, 716–28. Chicago: University of Illinois Press, 1979.

———. "Criticism of the Received View." In *The Structure of Scientific Theories*, 2nd ed., edited by Frederick Suppe, 62–118. Chicago: University of Illinois Press, 1979.

———. "Introduction to the Structure of Scientific Theories." 2014. http//:www.soaziglebihan.org/docs/PhilSci/050312-Suppe1.pdf.

Svozil, Karl. "Feyerabend and Physics." Institut für Theoretische Physik, Technische Universität Wien, 2004. http://arxiv-org/abs/physics/0406079.

Taylor, Mark. "Get Politics Out of the Common Core." *Chronicle of Higher Education* 60.42 (2014). http://chronicle.com/blogs/conversation/2014/07/28/get-politics-out-of-the-common-core/.

Tichy, Paul. "On Popper's Definition of Verisimilitude." *British Journal for the Philosophy of Science* 25 (1974) 155–60.

Toon, Adam. "The Ontology of Theoretical Modelling: Models as Make-Believe." *Synthese* 172.2 (2010) 301–15. https://ore.exeter.ac. uk/repository/bitstream/handle/10871/13842/.

Trundle, Robert C. "America's Religion and Religion in America: A Philosophic Profile." *Journal for the Study of Religions and Ideologies* 11.33 (2012) 3–20.

———. *Ancient Greek Philosophy*. Avebury Series in Philosophy. Farnham, UK: Ashgate, 1994.

———. "Aristotle *Versus* Van Til and Łukasiewicz on Contradiction: Are Contradictions Irrational in Science & Theology?" *Logos & Episteme: International Journal of Epistemology* 3.2 (2012) 323–44.

———. *Camus' Answer: "No" to the Western Pharisees Who Impose Reason on Reality.* Eastbourne, UK: Sussex University Press, 2002.

———. "De Interpretatione IX: [Aristotle's] Problem of Future or Infinite Past Truth?" *The Modern Schoolman: Quarterly Journal of Philosophy* 57 (1981) 49–55.

———. "An Existential-Phenomenological Approach to Scientific Realism." *Explorations in Knowledge* IX (1992) 38–65.

———. *From Physics to Politics: The Metaphysical Foundations of Modern Philosophy*. Foreword by Peter Redpath. 2nd ed. Piscataway, NJ: Transaction, 2002. 2nd ed. London: Routledge, 2017.

———. *Medieval Modal Logic and Science*, Forewords by D. Lamb and R. Ramirez. Lanham, MD: Rowman & Littlefield, 1998.

———. "Paradoxes of Human Nature: Their Ignored Implication for Ethics, Politics and Political Science." *Ethics & Politics / Etica & Politica* 9.1 (2007) 181–86.

———. "Physics and Phenomenology." *New Horizons in the Philosophy of Science*, edited by David Lamb, 66–86. Farnham, UK: Ashgate, 1992.

———. "Quantum Fluctuation, Self-Organizing Biological Systems and Human Freedom." *Idealistic Studies: An International Philosophical Journal* 24.3 (1994) 269–81.

———. "Sartre on Being: An Updated Ontology for Anglo-American Epistemology." *Method & Science: Journal for Empirical Study of the Foundations of Science* 24.3 (1991) 135–62.

———. "Thomas' 2nd Way: A Defense by Modal Scientific Reasoning." *Logique et Analyse: The Belgium National Centre for Research in Logic* 37.146 (1994) 145–68.

———. "St. Augustine's Epistemology: Ignored Aristotelian Themes and Their Intriguing Implications." *Laval Théologique et Philosophique* 50.1 (1994) 187–205.

———. "St. Thomas' Modal Logic: Did Wittgenstein and Heidegger Embrace It?" *Idealistic Studies: International Philosophical Journal* 26 (1996) 79–99.

———. *A Theology of Science: From Science to Ethics to an Ethical Politics*. With a foreword by Peter Redpath, 2nd ed. Boca Raton: BrownWalker, 2009.

———. "A Thomistic Integration of Truth vs. a Truthlessness of Today's Science, Ethics & Politics." *Art and Realism (Sztuka i realism): Commemorative Book, Jubilee Birthday and Scientific Work of Professor Henry Kieresia at KUL*, edited by Fr. T. Duma, A. Maryniarczyk SDB, and P. Sulenta, 721–38. Lublin: Polish Society of St. Thomas Aquinas and the Faculty of Philosophy—Catholic University of Lublin, 2014.

———. "Value and Scientific Theory." *The Modern Schoolman: Quarterly Journal of Philosophy* 60 (1983) 85–100.

———. "Women's Fashion: Function of Sex or Social Construction?" *Cultura: International Journal of Philosophy of Culture and Axiology* 6.2 (2009) 1–21.

Trundle, Robert C., and Michael Vossmeyer, M.D. "Sex Revolution and Psychosocial Disorder: A Historical Perspective on the Delusion of Medical Neutrality." *Bulletin Ind. Institute of the History of Medicine* 33.2 (2003) 129–48.

Tzortzis, Hamza Andreas. "Has Evolution Been Misunderstood? Revelation, Science and Certainty." 2013. http://www.hamzatzortzis.com/essays-articles/philosophy-theology/has-evolution-been-misunderstood-revelation-science-and-certainty.

UC Boulder, Chancellor. "Hazel Barnes Prize." *From the Chancellor*. 2017. http://www.colorado.edu/chancellor/hazel-barnes-prize.

Vacariu, Gabriel. *More Troubles with Cognitive Neuroscience: Einstein's Theory of Relativity and the Hyperverse*. Bucharest: Editura Universitatii din Bucuresti, 2014. Introduction: http://www.scribd.com/doc/130421361/Gabriel-Vacariu-2012-Cognitive-neuroscience-versus-epistemologically-different-worlds.

Van Fraassen, Bas C. *The Scientific Image*. Oxford: Clarendon, 1980.

Velasquez, Manuel, Claire Andre, Thomas Shanks, S.J., and Michael J. Meyer. "Ethical Relativism." Markkula Center for Applied Ethics. 1992. https://www.scu.edu/ethics/ethics-resources/ethical-decision-making/ ethical-relativism/.

Venosa, Ali. "The Environmental and Biological Factors That Contribute to Sexual Orientation and Behavior." *Medical Daily*. 2016. http://www .medicaldaily.com/sexual-orientation-bisexual-biological-environmental-factors-383541.

Vickers, Peter. "Towards a Realistic Success-to-Truth Inference for Scientific Realism." *Synthese*. 2016. doi.10.1007/s11229-016-1150-9.

Voight, Kevin. "Bad Bosses: The Psycho-path to Success." CNN. 19 Jan 2012. http://edition.cnn.com/2012/01/19/business/psychopath-boss/index.html.

Vospernik, Miklavž. "Measurement and the Verificationist Theory/Observation Distinction." *Acta Analytica* 19.33 (2004) 95–117. doi.10.1007/s12136-004-1015-6. https://www.researchgate.net/publication/248139264_Measurement_and_the_verificationist _theoryobservation_distinction.

Vrahimis, Andreas. "'Was There a Sun before Men Existed?' A. J. Ayer and French Philosophy in the Fifties." *Journal of the History of Analytical Philosophy 1.9 (2013)*. https://jhaponline.org/jhap/article/view/12/11.

Walsh, William H. "True and False in Metaphysics." *Cross Currents* 11.3 (1961) 269–82.

Waltham, David. "Alone in the Cosmos." *The Chronicle of Higher Education*, 60.30 (2014). http://chronicle.com/article/Alone-in-the-Cosmos/145677/.

Watts, Anthony. "Physicists Send Letter to Senate—Cite 160 Scientists Protest Regarding APS Climate Position." 2009. https://wattsupwiththat.com/2009/11/02/160-physicists-send-letter-to-senate-regarding-aps-climate-position/.

Weigel, Moira. "Was She a Feminist? The Complicated Legacy of Helen Gurley Brown." *New York Times*, 14 July 2016. http://www.nytimes.com/2016/07/17/books/review/helen-gurley-brown-biographies-enter-helen-and-not-pretty-enough.html?
Waite, Linda, and Maggie Gallagher. *The Case for Marriage: Why Married People Are Happier, Healthier, and Better Off Financially*. New York: Doubleday, 2000.
Wallace, William. *Philosophy of Science and Philosophy of Nature in Synthesis*. Washington, DC: Catholic University of America Press, 1996.
Walsh, William H. *Metaphysics: An Exposition and Defense of a Controversial Branch of Philosophy* Farnham,UK: Ashgate, 1991.
Waltham, David. "Alone in the Cosmos." *The Chronicle of Higher Education* 60.30 (2014). http://chronicle. com/article/Alone-in-the Cosmos/ 145677/.
Watts, Anthony. "Physicists Send Letter to Senate—Cite 160 Scientists Protest Regarding APS Climate Position." 2009. https://wattsupwiththat.com/2009/11/02/160-physicists-send-letter-to-senate-regarding-aps-climate-position/.
Wilkins, John S. "Metaphysical Determinism." http://evolvingthoughts.net/2012/05/metaphysical-determinism/.
Williams, Liz. "Karl Popper, The Enemy of Certainty, Part 4: Kuhn and Feyerabend." *The Guardian*, 1 Oct 2012. https://www.theguardian.com/commentisfree/belief/2012/oct/01/karl-popper-lakatos-kuhn-feyerabend.
Wittgenstein, Ludwig. *The Blue and Brown Books*. Oxford: Blackwell, 1960.
———. *On Certainty*. Edited by G. E. M. Anscombe and G. H. von Wright. Translated by Denis Paul and G. E. M. Anscombe. New York: Harper, 1986.
———. "On Heidegger on Being and Dread." 30 Dec 1929 at Schlick's. In *Heidegger and Modern Philosophy*, edited by Michael Murray, 80–83. New Haven: Yale University Press, 1978.
Wolchover, Natalie. "Have We Been Interpreting Quantum Mechanics Wrong This Whole Time?" https://www.wired.com/2014/06/the-new-quantum-reality/.
Wolf, M. P. "Philosophy of Language." http://www.iep.utm.edu/lang-phi/#SH3b, 2009.
Worrall, John. "Scientific Realism and Scientific Change." *The Philosophical Quarterly* 32.128 (1982) 201–31.
Yavorsky, B. M., and Yu Seleznev. *Physics: A Refresher Course*. Translated by G. Leib. Moscow: MIR, 1979.
Young, Arthur. "The Quantum of Action." *Foundations of Science*. 1984. http://www.arthuryoung.com/foundexc.html.
Youssef, Saul. "Is Quantum Mechanics an Exotic Probability Theory?" *Fundamental Problems in Quantum Theory*, edited by D. M. Greenberger and A. Zeilinger, 904–5. New York: Annals of the New York Academy of Sciences, 1995.

Name and Subject Index

a priori vs. *a posteriori* reasoning, 4 *See also* contradiction / paradox
American healthcare, 180
anti-realism, 6–7, 10–11, 13, 89, 130, 134, 142
Aquinas, St. Thomas, *See* Thomas, St.
analytic philosophy, 2, 6n11, 21, 30–31, 56–58, 64, 130, 158
Anglo-American philosophers, 2, 21, 23, 53–54, 65, 98
Anglo-American positivist, analytic, and feminist traditions, 22
Aristotle / Aristotelian, xi, 7, 30, 47–48, 75–76, 81, 92n39, 114–15, 118, 125, 127, 130–32, 135, 164, 168, 175, 178, 180, 184–85, 206, 209
    Aristotelian-Thomism, 175
    consciousness, 115
    direct realism, 115
Asma, S. T., 118–19
atheism, 36, 40, 64
atomism, 34
Augustine, St., 4–5, 64, 66, 84, 99–100
Ayer, A. J., 21–23

Barnes, Hazel E., 17–21, 41–42, 53, 109
    reductionist fallacy, 41–42
    Simone de Beauvoir, 20
    UC Boulder, 20–21
Baumeister, Roy, 43

Beauvoir, Simone de, 20
Beauvoir scholars, 20
Big Bang Theory (singularity), 4–5, 154, 176, 188–89, 211
    Aristotle, 5
    Augustine, St., 4–5
    quantum-corrected Raychaudhuri equation, 211
    Scripture, 5
Bokulick, Alisa, 135
Bokulick, Peter, 100
Brown, Curtis, 82–83
Brown, Helen Gurley, 116
Buckley, William F., 180

Camus, Albert, 19, 167n59
Cartwright, Nancy, 8–9, 11, 101, 131, 136
Caston, Victor, 115
causal determinism, 36, 40, 42–43, 93
causal principle, xv–xvi, 14, 16–17, 48–49, 73–74, 92n39, 165–68, 182, 188–89
    and regularities, 48
    as a modal conditional, 17, 170–73
    as a truthless *synthetic-a priori* judgment (per Kant), 14, 49, 166
    implication of first cause, 173–76
    Kant's view, 48–49
causality (*aitia*), 185
Chomsky, Noam, 180–81

Churchland, Paul, 36, 40–41
Ckakravartty, Anjan, 88–89
Clark, S.J., Joseph, 178
cognitive science, 34, 42–43, 155
cold fusion, 149–54
Compton, John, 28, 30, 54–55, 60–61, 69, 71–73, 75, 161
consciousness, observational, ix, xi, xv, 1, 4, 6n11, 14–15, 17–19, 24, 30–31, 44, 49–50, 54–55, 61–62, 69, 76, 101, 155, 157, 167
    as a pure translucency, 50
    analogue of analytic philosophy (F. I. Dretske and non-epistemic seeingn), 30–31
    conceptual consciousness, 17
    conceptualizations, 60, 67,157
    consciousness as *no thing* (*néant* or *nothingness*), 19
    consciousness of aspects of reality, 54–58, 61–62, 69
    consciousness of *things* (*in*) *themselves*, 1, 167
    consciousness vs. reality, xi
    direct and indirect consciousness, 24, 74, 101
    hard problem of, 44
    has a *theory-independent non-conceptual touchstone* with physical reality, 155
    indirect consciousness as a self-consciousness), 18, 24, 30, 74, 101–2
    Jean-Paul Sartre, ix
    no structure of consciousness, 55
    non-conceptual consciousness, xv–xvi, 1, 4, 6n11, 15, 54, 69, 74
    not reducible to empirical phenomenon, 47
    self-consciousness and creativity / imagination, 65–66, 76
contradiction (paradox), 3–4, 7, 9, 25–26, 26n22, 52n88, 104, 133, 162–63
a priori vs. *a posteriori*, 4

existentialism, 25
internal inconsistencies of theories, 162
our limitedly being both free and not free determined), 25–26
per Jean-Paul Sartre, 52n88
realism, 3–4, 7, 9
Copi, Irving, 96–97, 162–63
Coyne, S.J., Fr. George, 4–5
Craig, William Lang, 37

Dennett, Daniel, 121–22
Descartes, René (and Cartesian issues), 32–34, 50, 66, 68, 129
deterministic materialism, 37, 39–40, 42–43, 141–42
Dretske, Fred I., 30, 51, 56–58, 64, 97–98, 103–4, 130

Ebbesen, Sten, 176
Edelman, Gerald, 18, 42
Einstein, Albert, 6–7, 47, 76, 84, 104–5
epistemology, 2–3, 5, 14–15, 111, 116–17, 120
    as observationally grounded, 15
Estany, Anna, 88
ethics, general issues, 27, 39, 44–45
existential phenomenology, ix–xi, xv, 1, 21, 18–24, 23–24, 33, 40, 49–51, 56–57, 64, 70, 81, 159–60
    analytic philosophy, 21, 56–57
    angst, 21
    describes Being itself, 51–52
    difference from essentialism, 167, 168
    difference from metaphysics, 51
    existentialism, 18–24
    free will x–xi, 40
    Logical Positivism, 21
    rejecting Kant's *a priori* structure of mind, 49
    Sartre's basic analysis, xv, 23–24

existentialism, 18–24, 184–85
  Thomistic, 184–85
  vs. existential phenomenology, 23

fallacy of reductionism, 34, 39–40, 156
Fallon, James, 40–41
falsification of theories, 16, 71, 107, 111, 117
feminism / feminists, bio-denying, 20n3, 20–21, 62–63, 116, 122–23, 205–6
Feyerabend, Paul, ix, 7, 10, 13, 65, 108, 123–23n48, 127–31, 134, 139–42, 157–60
Feyerabend and his heirs, 157
first cause, 16–17, 165, 169, 171–80, 182–90, 192–93, 204, 209–11
  as a supreme norm, 16, 52
  as God, 171
  creationism and evolution, 176–77
  ethics, art and politics, 17
  nature's God, 210
  proof of, 182, 185–88
  proof rooted in a consciousness of reality, 17
  St. Thomas, 17, 171
  strictly implied by causal principle, 169, 171, 173–176
free will / free choice of will x–xi, 15, 23–27, 35–36, 38–40, 42–43, 66–67, 77–79, 126–27, 168–70
  acting as if we have free will (per Kant), 27, 40
  moral responsibility, 43
  Sartre on absolute freedom, 25
  as a *noumenon* per Kant, 15, 168–70
  as an illusion, 36
  as mere possibility per Kant, 15
  based on existential phenomenology, x–xi, 23–24, 40
  denial of, 38, 40
  our being free and not free (determined), 25–26, 77–79, 94
  not known logically, 27
  rooted in our phenomenological conscousness, x–xi, 15, 24, 26, 66–67

Galilei, Galileo, 75–76
Geach, Peter, 177–78, 210
Giancoli, Douglas, 75–76
Gibson, Arthur, 177–78
Gilson Étienne, xi, xiv, xvii, 26–27, 37–38, 46, 127, 161–62, 166–67, 185n57, 212
Glass, Lillian, 40
Glasersfeld, Ernst von, 131
Green, Jeffrey, 180
Greene Joshua, 39–41, 44
Grover, Maxwell, 99

Hack, Susan, 109, 142
Hacking, Ian, 8–9, 13
Hardin, Larry, 13, 68–69
Hare, Robert, 38n58, 39
Heidegger, Martin, 21–22
Hume, David, 15, 28, 31, 48–50, 60, 65, 97, 104–5, 108, 120, 128–29, 158
  anti-induction, 48–49, 108
  Paul Feyerabend, 128
  radical empiricism, 120
  sensorial sentences, 128
  sensations and truth, 129
  skepticism, 50
Husserl, Edmund, 21, 30, 50, 97

Idealism, 26
induction, optimistic, 11–13, 71–72, 110–11, 147, 160, 189n62, 193
induction, pessimistic, 11–13, 71–72, 110–11, 147, 160, 189n62, 193
Ingram, David, 2–3
instrumentalism, 6, 134
inverse-probability thesis, 143–45

236   NAME AND SUBJECT INDEX

Jaki, Stanley, 75
Jaroszyński, Piotr, 167
Jorgensen, L. M., 33

Kant, Immanuel, xi, 14–15, 17, 26–31, 40, 48–51, 55, 64, 73–75, 93–94, 105, 114–15, 127
  acting as if we have free will, 27
  categories of mind, 15, 28, 48, 51, 119, 159
  Ding an sich, 48
  ethics presupposing free will, 127
  Étienne Gilson's criticism of, 26
  free will as a *noumenon*, 15, 64, 127
  idealism, 49
  Kant's un-Solomonic compromise, 94
  mediating between rationalism and empiricism, 49, 50, 94
  metaphysical judgments, 93
  practical reason, 27
  practical vs. theoretical reasoning, 114–15
  situating the *a priori* in our mind, 49
  structure of mind, 17, 50
  (worst of both worlds as a mediation), 55
  suggests *pragmatisch*, 14
  transcendental (Kantian) Thomism, 29
Kantian-positivist-analytic tradition, 2
Kawalec, Pawel, 3–4
K-K Thesis (how do we *Know* we *Know*?), xviii, 14, 70–71, 74, 166, 168
Kelsky, Karen , 175
Keshet, Ezra , 137
Kierkegaard, Søren, 22n13, 178–79
  Protestantism, 178–79
Kind, Amy, 155
Koertege, Noretta, 63
Körner, Stephen, 69n16, 93, 157
Krauss, Lawrence, 37

Kuhn, Thomas, ix, 7, 10, 13, 60–61, 65, 108, 115–18, 127–28, 135, 142, 205–6
Kung, Peter, 155
Kurtz, Stanley, 63
Kutrovátz, Gábor, 60–61

Laing, M. D., Ronald D. 25
Lakatos, Imre, 206
Laudan, Larry, ix, 10–13
Legg, Catherine, 158
Lewis, C. I., 177–78
logic, modal, xv, 13–16, 61, 69–71, 96, 171
  analytic philosophy, 150
  and Ludwig Wittgenstein, xv, 148–49
  de dicto and *de re*, 137–38
  epistemic impossibility, 17, 71, 137
  epistemic vs. alethic, 96–97
  explanation of, 96, 148–49
  skepticism based on Hume, 158
  modal reasoning to true theories, 16–17, 61, 69–70
  necessity, 138, 171
  predictions strictly implying theories, 69–70
  physical impossibility, 97
  strict implication, 61, 69–70, 96–97
logic, truth-functional, xv, 8, 16, 110, 133, 144, 148
  inapplicable to first-cause proof, 176–78
  Karl Poppers's falsification, 16, 110, 144
logical positivism, 2–3, 6, 21, 34, 81–83, 116
  meaninglessness, 2
  Wittgenstein, 2–3
  ethics reduced to psychology, 34
  verification principle, 2–3

Mackinnon, Edward, 29–30
Marcus, Ruth Barcan, 44–45, 167–68

Marenbon, John, 210
Marx, Karl (Marxism), 65, 122, 204–6
materialism, scientific, 44
Mayo, Deborah, 108
McClamrock, Ron, 33
Merleau-Ponty, Maurice, 21
metaphysics, 2–3, 14, 49, 51, 73–74, 85, 92–94, 98, 124, 166
   as a truthless *a priori-synthetic-*judgment, 14, 73–74
   vacuous realism, 116
Mill, John Stuart, 124
Moody, Ernest A., 47–48, 178, 210
Moore, G. E., 67–68

natural theology, *See* theology, natural
naturalistic ethics, 16–17, 181–82, 206
naturalistic fallacy, xvi, 16n32, 182, 189–93
nature, our psycho-biological, xvi, 16–17, 43, 62–63, 176, 180, 182, 194–203, 207
   criticism of, 207
   fulfilled by art, music, and politics, 199–203
   fulfilled by the family, 194–199
neuro-thugs, 39
neuroscience as itself a phenomenon, 40
neuroscience philosophy, 36, 38–39, 45–47, 79
neuro-economics, 39
Newton, Sir Isaac, 6–7
Newton-Smith, W. H., ix, 6n11, 15, 71, 80, 84, 90–91n38, 92, 95, 98, 101, 103, 132–33, 137–38, 140–41n19, 145, 147, 154–55, 157–63, 189n62,
Nietzsche, Wilhelm, 117n31, 117–18, 122

O-reports, 91–95
observation, objective / invariant, 6–7, 15, 80

observation, concept-free, *See* consciousness, observational
observation, theory-dependent, 6, 13–15, 81, 116, 118
observation, theory-laden, 14–15, 80, 131–32
   a phenomenological account, 131–32
observation-laden theoretical terms, 89–90, 99, 131–32, 164
Observation-laden theories, 100, 164
observation terms, 83–85
observation-theoretical distinction, 6–7, 82, 84, 98
Olson, Raymond, 19, 19n2

Panné, Jean-Louis, 205
"Paradoxes of Human Nature," the article, 26, 26n22
Parsons, Kathryn Payne, 205–6
Patai, Daphne, 63
Penfield, Wilder, 35
Plato, 37, 50
Poincaré, Henri, 12, 86
politics, xvi, xix, 1, 5, 7, 8, 16–17, 62–64, 81, 116, 120–21, 123, 149, 159, 165–67, 169, 175, 180–84, 192, 194, 196–97, 199, 205, 212
   Anarcho-Totalitarianism, 180
   as the *institutionalization of ethics*, 165–66
   democracies (so-called), 180–81
   economic liberty, 212
   evidence-based (certifiably healthful)
   Étienne Gilson, 212
   political policies, 212
   ideologies, 196, 199, 205
   oligarchies, 180–81
   political correctness, 62–64, 116, 175, 194
   polities, 180
   psychopathic / sociopathic society, 180–81
   "Wall Street" regulating Congress, 181–82

238   NAME AND SUBJECT INDEX

Popper, Sir Karl, ix, 7, 16, 71, 80, 115–16, 104–23, 131, 134–35, 140, 142–49, 157–60, 163–64, 193, 206
   falsification thesis, 16, 71, 107, 111, 113, 119, 164
   Paul Feyerabend and Thomas Kuhn, 122
   his pseudo "critical rationalism", 109
   his relativism, 115, 121n39
   Hume, 112, 158
   influence on Feyerabend and Kuhn, 121–23, 134–35
   Inverse-probability thesis, 108, 120, 145
   self-avowed realism, 134–35
   theory-dependence, 113–14, 135
post-modern social constructionism, 116, 130, 134
pragmatism, 6, 14, 27, 81, 90, 104, 130
   anti-realism, 130
   as Kant's *pragmatisch* to deal with a truthless metaphysics 14
   acting as if we have free will (per Kant), 27
psychiatry, 25, 40–41
psychology, 43
psychopaths / psychopathy, 38–41, 180–81
   causal language, 40
   emotional empathy, 40–41
   free will (denial), 38, 40–41
   mind equals brain, 40
   moral idiot, 38, 181
   psychopathic / sociopathic society, 180–81
   rationalizing their behavior, 40
   traits, 38, 40
Ptolemaic and Copernican astronomy, 4, 11, 26, 48
Putnam, Hilary, ix, 2, 86–87

Raftopoulos, Athan, 31

Rahner, Karl, 29
Rand, Ayn, 181
realism, xi, xvi, xvii, 1–2, 4, 5, 8–16, 31, 33, 115, 127, 134, 136
   direct, 31, 33, 115
   perceptual, 115
   source in Sartre, 18
   strong / robust, 1, 9, 134
   Thomas, St., xi
   Thomistic, xvii
   weak, 1, 8–11, 136
realism, scientific, 2, 4, 11–13, 15–16, 18, 51, 60, 115, 134, 136
   argument for, 11–12
   mature theories, 134
   source in Sartre, 18
   strong / robust, 2, 4, 15, 134
   truth via strict implication, 134
   weak, 16, 136
reality, xv, 1, 4, 14–15, 28, 51, 54, 56–58, 71–73, 102, 139, 167
   aspects of reality, 53–58, 71–73
   Being-in-itself, 51, 167
   composed of *things* (*in*) *themselves*, 1, 4, 14–15, 28, 102
   conceptually conscious of its independence, 71
   its *thereness*, 55
   reality *in itself*, 139
relativism, cultural, 102–3
relativism, epistemic, 15, 60–68, 80, 116–18, 130, 135
   political correctness, 62–64
Redpath, Peter A., ix–xvi, 175, 204
Rohrlich, Fritz, 11–13, 68–69, 132, 134, 141
Russell, Bertrand, 23–24, 122, 177–78, 210

Sartre, Jean-Paul, ix, xv–xvi, 1–1n1, 18–25, 28–33, 41–42, 46, 51–56, 64, 66, 74, 115, 122, 124–26, 128–31, 159
   basic phenomenological analysis, 1, 23–24
   death of, 20

Eastern European foes, 21
existence precedes essence, 122
exploited by new-left students, 124
phenomenological realism, 131
scientific realism, 23
sensations and truth, 129
Simone de Beauvoir, 20
skepticism, 159
schemas on interrelation of science, theology, ethics, art, and politics, 179–84
Schwarz, Florian, 137
science, history and philosophy of, 13–14, 75–76, 134
   as history of epistemology 13–14
science, modern, xv, 4, 5, 7–8, 11–14, 16–17, 69–70, 75, 94, 134, 148–58, 164
   de Broglie equation, 163
   domains, 164
   duplication, 150–54
   internal inconsistencies of theories, 158
   mature theories being true, 17, 75, 134, 164
   methodology, 148–50
   modal reasoning to true theories, 16, 17, 69–70
   novelty and new research, 154–58
   paradigm knowledge-yielding enterprise, 5, 7–8, 16, 168
   predictions strictly implying theories, 69–70
   realism via mature theories, 11–14
   restricting "truth" to valid domains, 11, 14, 71
   science informing ethics, art and politics 16, 164
   success strictly implies truth, 135
   truth involves free will and causal determinism, 77–79, 94
   truth via strict implication, 134
   truth restricted to domains, 164

scientism, 37, 64
Searle, John, 31
seeinge, epistemic, 31, 58–59, 103–4
seeingn, non-epistemic, 31, 56–58, 103–4, 130
Shalkowski, Scott, 138
Sidgwick, Nevil, 11
Smith, D. W., 125
Smith, Howard, 27
Sokolowski, Rev. Msgr. Robert, 29–30, 34
sophism, 34, 117–18, 141
Sovizol, Karl, 129
Stenger, Victor, 36–37, 40
supernatural theology, *See* theology, supernatural
Suppe, Frederick, ix, 22, 16n32, 87–88, 116, 123–23n47, 135, 166, 168n9
synthetic-a priori / a priori-synthetic judgment, 49, 73–74, 93n40, 105, 116
   See also metaphysics

theology, natural, xvi, 176, 180
theology, supernatural, xvi, 4–5, 176–79
theoretical terms, 83–84
theory-dependent observation, 3–4, 60, 93
thermodynamics, laws of, 150
things (in) themselves, 1, 4, 14–15, 28–29, 33, 59, 67
   thing itself and its conceptualization, 59, 67 *See also* reality
Thomas, St., ix–xv, 17, 37, 46, 48, 70–71, 75, 81, 115, 124–27, 130, 137, 170–71, 173–74, 176–78, 206, 209, 211
   consciousness, xi, 115
   free will, xi
   Peter Geach on, 177–78
   ground zero for realism, 115
Thomism / Thomists, ix, xi, xv, xvii, 29, 29n27, 101, 128, 167, 175–76, 179

Thomistic phenomenology of Edith Stein, 128
Thomson, J. J., 101, 136, 140–41, 164
Toon, Adam, 83
Trump, Donald, 38–39
Turnbull, Robert, 21–22

Under-determination-of Theory-by-Data (UTD) Thesis 3–4, 7–10, 41–42, 51, 54–55, 79, 85–86, 89, 132–33
and *things (in) themselves*, 4
compatible with realism, 133

Vacariu, Gabriel, 36
Van Fraassen, Bas C., 8
verification principle (conservative and liberal views), 2, 34, 82
verisimilitude (increasing truth likeness), xviii–xix, 5, 115, 119, 135, 142–43, 146, 160, 163–64, 211–12

Wang, Stephan, ix–x, 125–26
Watzlawic, Paul, 131
Williams, Liz, 122–23
Wittgenstein, Ludwig, xv, xviii, 2–3, 22n13, 22–23, 56, 67–68, 85–86, 102, 102n61, 144n24, 144–45, 148n34, 148n35, 148–49, 172–73, 182
Young, Arthur, 156
Youssef, Saul, 163n85

www.ingramcontent.com/pod-product-compliance
Lightning Source LLC
Chambersburg PA
CBHW050438240426
43661CB00055B/2428